WILDFIRE LOOSE:
THE WEEK MAINE BURNED

Wildfire Loose
The Week Maine Burned

Joyce Butler

Camden, Maine

Also by Joyce Butler:
Pages from a Journal
Kennebunkport Scrapbook, Volume I and II
A Kennebunkport Album
The Duchess Who Lived in the Mansion (Juvenile)

Contributor:
Agreeable Situations: Society, Commerce, and Art in Southern Maine, 1790–1830
Maine in the Early Republic: From Revolution to Statehood
A Passionate Intensity: The Life and Work of Dorothy Healy
Maine: The Pine Tree State from Prehistory to the Present
Sketch of an Old River

Published by Down East Books
A wholly owned subsidiary of The Rowman & Littlefield Publishing Group, Inc.
4501 Forbes Boulevard, Suite 200, Lanham, Maryland 20706
www.rowman.com

16 Carlisle Street, London W1D 3BT, United Kingdom

Distributed by NATIONAL BOOK NETWORK

The 2014 edition of *Wildfire Loose* is an unabridged republication of the third edition published in Camden, Maine, in 1997 by Down East Books.

British Library Cataloguing in Publication Information Available

Library of Congress Cataloging-in-Publication Data

The third edition of this book was previously catalogued by the Library of Congress as follows:

Butler, Joyce.
  Wildfire loose : the week Maine burned / Joyce Butler. — Third edition.
    xxi, 278 p. : ill., maps ; 23 cm.
  "New 50th anniversary edition"—Cover.
  Includes bibliographical references (p. 255–261) and index.
  1. Wildfires—Maine—History. 2. Forest fires—Maine—History. 3. Great Fire, Maine,1947. I. Title.
  SD421.32.M2 B87 1997
  97065236

ISBN 978-1-60893-296-2 (pbk. : alk. paper)—ISBN 978-1-60893-270-2 (electronic)

∞™ The paper used in this publication meets the minimum requirements of American National Standard for Information Sciences—Permanence of Paper for Printed Library Materials, ANSI/NISO Z39.48-1992.

Printed in the United States of America

This book is for those who will
read it and remember.

Contents

Acknowledgments ix
Introduction to the 50th Anniversary Edition xiii
Prologue: A Very Wet Spring xvii
I "Lord, I wish it would rain." 1
II The Race of Terror 1
III "I thought it was the end of the world." 17
IV The Common Enemy 35
V Down Millionaires' Row 49
VI "We knew we were doomed." 77
VII The Day of the Big Wind 85
VIII "We thought we were going to be comfortable." 139
IX "All safe. Home gone." 159
X "Rumor has a thousand tongues." 173
XI The Battle of the Bulldozers 187
XII Rain, Beautiful Rain 209
XIII "I wouldn't want to see it repeat." 229
Epilogue: The '47 Fire 241
Appendix A: Glossary of Firefighting Terms 251
Appendix B: Damage Estimates from the 1947 Fires 253
Bibliography 255
Index 263

About the Author 277

Photographs following page 100

Maps following page xxi

Acknowledgments

The 1947 forest fires touched the lives of Maine people, even those who were not directly involved.

I was a schoolgirl living in Portland in 1947. My involvement with the fires was minor, and yet they made a strong impression on me. My older brother went off to serve as a firefighter. I remember he would be gone two or three days at a time and would come home— once in the middle of the night—black with soot, exhausted, to fall into bed to sleep for a few hours before going out again. At school in home economics class we made sandwiches for the firefighters, and I remember the day the Maine State Pier in Portland caught fire. I stood on the lawn in front of my house that morning. There were no cars going by on the road, the air was veiled with smoke, and I felt a strange sense of doom. "Doom" is not too strong a word. Everyone had been talking about the fires that were burning all over the state, and I thought, "Now there is a fire in Portland. Maybe the whole city will burn." It seemed possible to me that the fires would spread and spread until the whole state of Maine was burning. Others have told me that they had the same thoughts.

Many have told me how they went out on their lawns at night to see the red glow in the sky over some distant town, and how incredible it seemed that houses—whole villages—were burning. Those who lived in the houses and the villages have told me that what was happening seemed unreal. "It was like a bad dream," they have said.

What happened in the fall of 1947 is an important part of Maine's history. For that reason, when I was asked to write this book, I accepted readily. It was, I believed, a story that should be preserved for future generations. It was important to gather the facts before it was too late.

When I began my research I found that it was already almost too late. Many of the key men who fought the fires, and knew how they traveled and were stopped, were dead. Reports that were written after the fires had either not been preserved or were buried in poorly stored back files. Most of the excellent pictures that were taken at the time had disappeared. I found that published accounts of the fires needed to be carefully checked for misinformation: fact was often mixed with exaggeration and rumor.

I also discovered that although the fires are remembered vividly by many people, a careful, day-by-day accounting of just what happened cannot depend on thirty-year-old memories, and that, as one man said to me, "The '47 fire is like politics and religion—nobody's got the same story." For this reason, newspaper accounts have been vitally important in the writing of this book. Luckily, the key newspapers that followed the fires—the *Portland Press Herald* and *Sunday Telegram,* the *Biddeford Daily Journal,* and the *Bangor Daily News*—have been preserved on microfilm. If this were not the case, this book could not have been written, for only by reading them could I learn the chronology of the fires. I cannot express too strongly my debt to this source of information.

I also wish to acknowledge my debt to the reporters from these newspapers, and others, who visited each fire area. Their eye for details and their sensitivity in interviewing people on the scene is largely responsible for any sense of immediacy this book has.

I also wish to express my deep appreciation to the people who were willing to share with me, and allow me to tell, their very personal stories. They have made it possible for me to bring the effect of the fires down to a human level, to show what the fires meant in terms of people's lives. I have been impressed with their storytelling ability, and I believe the reader will be moved, as I was, by the drama, poetry, humor, and philosophy in the accounts of Christine Rowell, Dorothy Stanley, Esther Boynton, John Kelley, Arthur Roberts, Cliff Seavey, Mabel Emery, Frank Handlen, Allen Salisbury, Bessie Ricker, and others. These people epitomize, I believe, the strength, common sense, good humor, morality, and sensitivity of people who have been nurtured by strong traditions. Such people are not unique to Maine, but it does seem that many of them have their roots here.

There are others who deserve special thanks. This book would have been seriously flawed without the generous assistance and important insights provided to me by Austin H. Wilkins, former Maine forest commissioner. He more than any other person is responsible for preserving and interpreting the history of the fires.

I am indebted to J. Malcolm Barter, senior editor of *Down East* magazine, not only for sharing with me his experience as a reporter covering the fires, but for providing me with valuable leads and assistance.

State Fire Inspector Lawrence Dolby helped me to understand the nature of fire, and Monte Glovinsky, fire weather meteorologist for the National Weather Service, provided me with information about meteorological conditions on October 23, 1947—the Day of the Big Wind.

I wish to thank Donald Rowell for allowing me to quote extensively from his mother's moving account of her experiences at Bar Harbor during the fire, and Marjorie Ellis for providing me with material from Kenneth Roberts's diary, and letters she herself wrote about the Kennebunkport fire.

My thanks are due also to all the postmasters who passed my letters of inquiry on to people in their towns who were there in 1947, and to the people who answered the letters. I am especially indebted to Irene Randall; Isabelle Forbis; Fritz Carter, manager of the Malvern Hotel at Bar Harbor; and Captain William Berry of the Maine Sea Coast Missionary Society's ship, *Sunbeam,* who wrote to me in detail about events in 1947.

My thanks to all those who ferreted out from back files reports that were written following the fires, particularly Douglas Stark and his staff at the Maine Forest Service's Entomology Laboratory at Augusta, in whose care the Forest Service's records for 1947 had been left, and Robert Foye of the state's Department of Inland Fisheries and Game.

A special kind of personal thank-you is due to Joan Verrill and Dorothy Butler, whose enthusiasm and moral support carried me from beginning to end of this endeavor; to Leslie, Stephanie, and James for patience and understanding; and to G. R. B. because. Last, and perhaps most important of all, I wish to thank Zoe and Oliver Durrell, who asked for the book in the first place.

Joyce Butler
Rosemary House
Kennebunk, Maine
April, 1978

Introduction to the 50th Anniversary Edition

John Smith came out of the army in 1946 and went home to Limington. He was twenty-one and ready to get on with his life. He got a job and set about courting his wife-to-be, Josephine Ham of Hollis. During the dry summer months of 1947 he volunteered to fight a forest fire in Limington's Blake's Mill neighborhood. He remembers how the fire consumed two feet of duff and burned deep into the ground so that it had to be dug out. In October when the worst forest fires in Maine's history erupted in southern Maine, John Smith was on the front lines.

Today, a veteran volunteer firefighter, he is amazed when he looks back to 1947, remembering the scope of the fires and the firefighters' confusion, hard work, and inadequate equipment. Smith fought the fires in the Waterboros. He remembers how someone—often no one they knew, but someone who was assuming command—would come to a crew of men on a fire line and say, " 'We've got to get out of here.' They'd load you into somebody's truck, and you'd go somewhere else." Smith was in North Waterboro when the board yard at Johnson's Mill went up in flames. "It was just like an explosion." Pieces of pine boards "all afire, flew into the air." Smith was there to see the fire that caused so much damage in the Waterboros sweep on to the Saco River, "rolling across the top of the trees. You figured everything was going to burn. That fire—they claimed it traveled eight to ten miles in twenty minutes."

Smith remembers how at night, when the wind died down and the smoke settled to the ground so that you couldn't see or breathe, firefighting crews stopped their work. The fire was not moving, it seemed less threatening; it was, they thought, a good chance to take a rest, get a meal, go home to see how the family was. That was a mistake, a missed opportunity. In 1953 when serious forest fires burned in York County, firefighters knew that nightfall was the time to really dig in and do some meaningful firefighting. They had learned one of the lessons of 1947.

Tom Parent, state supervisor for forest fire control with the Maine Forest Service, points out that many important lessons were learned from 1947. Firefighters are now trained to national standards, equipment is standardized, detection has been modernized (aircraft have replaced spotting towers), and clear lines of command to be followed during fire emergencies have been established. The Northeastern Forest Fire Protection Compact, which was organized as a result of Maine's forest fire disaster and became law in 1949, began with a membership of five New England states and New York. It now includes the six New England states and New York, three Canadian provinces, and the U.S. Forestry Service. The Compact is part of a national mobilization system. The Maine Forest Service understands the threat of wildfire and believes it is prepared to meet that threat.

It is the general public that needs to be made aware of the danger of forest fires. In the fifty years since Maine's disaster, better detection systems and improved training and equipment have reduced the reach of Maine's forest fires. In the 1960s single fires burned tens of thousands of acres. In the 1970s their scope was in the four-thousand-acre range. Since the 1980s fires have been contained to a thousand acres or less. This record has given Maine people a complacency they shouldn't have. Although 94 percent of fires occurring in Maine in any given year are reported by the public, many do not understand the ferocity of wildfire running loose, burning everything in its path, and the difficulty of stopping it, even with good equipment. Many people who live in Maine today were not here in 1947 to hear the freight-train-roar of a forest fire, to see flames rolling across the tops of trees like waves breaking on the sand, traveling ten miles in twenty minutes.

Educating the public to the destructive potential of forest fires is a high priority for the Maine Forest Service's Department of Conservation. In 1987, the fortieth anniversary of the fires, the Forest Service erected billboard-style signs in the seventeen towns that suffered the most severe damage. The maps and text on those signs paint a grim picture of what was lost, and, hopefully, alert those who stop to read them to the need to be vigilant so it won't happen again. Forest Service officials tell me that *Wildfire Loose: The Week Maine Burned* is also an important tool for getting their fire prevention message out to the public. Educators on all grade levels tell me it is a perennial favorite for book reports. That means a new generation is learning about the dangers of wildfire. I am pleased that the book is useful in such an important way.

This new edition of *Wildfire Loose* gives me an opportunity to thank those who have contacted me since 1979, to correct mistakes made in the first edition, and to provide new information about Maine's disastrous trial by fire. In 1980 I learned that Jane Obermeyer of Kennebunk was the sister of Helen Cormier, the teenage girl who lost her life during Bar Harbor's ordeal. Jane shared with me her knowledge of that sad day in 1947. In 1981 Cyrus Hamlin, also of Kennebunk, provided me with a detailed account of his experiences on Mount Desert Island in 1947. Marjorie Kenney Lewis of Springvale contacted me in 1987 to tell me about a group of Sanford firefighters who passed their firefighting time in the woods singing in harmony. Their singing gave them such pleasure and sounded so well rising over those smoke-shrouded woods and fields that they continued singing together after the fires and formed a choir called The Merrymen. Letitia M. Church of Birch Harbor wrote to me in 1988 about the ordeal of her grandmother, Maud Cote, at Goose Rocks Beach. Mrs. Cote was housekeeper for Lawrence Ireland, and "during that awful day when his house burned, stood in the water with her sister, Theresa Foster, who was in her eighties and nearly blind, and watched Mr. Ireland's house go up in flames with a new vehicle in the garage because neither of the ladies could drive." In 1989 A. H. Drummond, Jr., set me straight on the automobile accident that claimed the lives of two college classmates and injured him and another. Leland H. Gile, Jr., wrote from Las Cruces, New Mexico, in 1990 to describe the fire at Ross Corner in Waterboro. In 1991 Deborah Parks sent me photographs of Brownfield buildings that "went"— were burned—when that small town was swept by the Fryeburg fire. To these and others who contacted me, my thanks.

It would be a mistake to think that what happened in Maine in 1947 pales beside the western wildfires we have seen in recent years on television news programs. Maine's disaster still ranks at the top of the national scale. While vast areas of forest and valuable real estate have been lost in western states, it is important to remember that within the 200,000 acres that burned in Maine were seventeen communities, nine of which were leveled.

Could it happen again? Even those who answer that it is unlikely would agree with Lloyd Davis, who told me in 1977, "You take any time that Nature goes on a rampage . . . a human being is almost a useless thing." How often Mother Nature has shown us that "what's past is prologue."

Joyce Butler
Rosemary House
Kennebunk, Maine
October 1996

Prologue: A Very Wet Spring

The year 1947 is remembered as a time of drought in Maine. But those who remember well, those who have reason to recall the weather of April, May, and June, remember that it rained and rained and rained. The winter had been mild with a normal snowfall, but above average temperatures in all parts of the state. An unseasonable warm spell at the beginning of March promised an early spring, but although temperatures climbed into the high eighties, melting the snow from fields and woods, the weather turned cold again, and wet. Day after day it rained; if not a downpour, a drizzle.

Maine winters are long, even the mild ones. The precious phenomenon of spring is always eagerly awaited, but in 1947 this was especially true. World War II had ended on August 15, 1945, but the gloom of war lingered. The Nuremberg trials had begun, the horrors of Hiroshima were coming to light, newspapers were filled with stories of the plight of displaced persons in Europe, and war in Palestine seemed imminent. Servicemen and -women were coming home, and they, even more than those who had manned the home front, were looking forward to the joys of spring and the pleasures of summer. But it rained and stayed cold well into June. The weather was a disappointment and a frustration.

To farmers it was more than that. It was a serious handicap. The ground was so wet that spring planting was delayed, and seed, once planted, was slow to sprout.

Only Maine's forest wardens must have welcomed the rain. To them the early melting of the snow had been an ominous sign, for forest fire danger is heightened when the snow disappears early from the woods.

Maine, which is 90 percent forested, has to be concerned with forest fires. Until 1947 her record for a low incidence of fires was one of the best of the eastern states.[1] The worst fire in Maine's history had been the so-called Miramichi Fire in 1825 when more than 800,000 acres and the homes of settlers in the Piscataquis River valley (who had caused the fire when they attempted to clear land by burning it over) had burned.[2] There had been bad fires since then, but Maine's record was good. Officials wanted to keep it that way.

In April Maine's Forest Commissioner Raymond Rendall and a group of legislators—members of the state's Land and Forest Preservation Commission took an unprecedented 350-mile flight over Maine's Forestry District to ascertain the need there for improved fire and insect control. The District, ten million acres of forest in northern Maine, unbroken except for potato farmlands on its eastern border, was the only part of the state where forest fire control, although funded by private landowners and federal grants, was the responsibility of the Maine Forest Service. The District had been created in 1909, by what had been widely acclaimed as model legislation, in response to a series of bad fires the year before and in 1903.

Fire control in Maine's other six to seven million acres of forests was the responsibility of the 450 municipalities in the southern, central, and eastern parts of the state within whose borders they lay.[3] The organized territory was divided into six fire control administrative districts, each with a trained state warden answerable to a Forest Service supervisor. Although the state also maintained lookout towers, made available extra firefighting equipment from centrally located storehouses, and helped to pay the cost of suppressing forest fires, it functioned as a cooperating agency only. Acting with the authority of legislation passed in 1891, the towns and cities took care of their own forest fires, calling on the state only when the severity of a fire seemed to warrant it. Although relationships usually were good between local officials and their district warden, the warden had no real authority.

At the end of their April inspection trip, Commissioner Rendall and the legislators concluded that much needed to be done in the District to improve forest fire control. Ironically, when fire disaster came to Maine's woods, it did not strike the District.

But during the summer of 1947, Maine people were not thinking about forest fires. By the end of June the rainy weather had ended. The sun came out, and temperatures rose. Cottagers all over the state—at Kennebunk Pond, Highland Lake, Goose Rocks Beach, Fortunes Rocks, Bar Harbor—looked forward to the pleasures of swimming, boating, and long, lazy days. In later years Christine Rowell was to remember the precious days of early summer she spent in 1947 at Barberry Ledge ("my dear place") at Bar Harbor. If spring had been lost, summer had been gained.

The business of summer went forward. Crops responded to the good weather, and the truck gardeners of York County, the potato farmers of Aroostook, and the blueberry growers of Washington County looked forward to a good harvest. Sporting camp owners hosted fishermen and made plans for the fall hunting season. Although ammunition was scarce, hunters from all over the country were making reservations for the deer season.

In York County, as in other parts of the state, lumbermen responded to the postwar building boom. Dozens of portable and stationary sawmills were operating, cutting in the woods, getting out the lumber that was in demand for new houses, many of them being built by young couples who had waited for the war to end to make a permanent home. If Sunday drivers—for the custom of the Sunday afternoon ride was reviving now that gasoline was more readily available—regretted the unsightly piles of slash and the shacks of the workers who followed the mills, they could not regret the prosperity the industry was bringing to rural villages like South Waterboro and Newfield.

Actually it was a continuing prosperity. During the war years lumbermen had responded to the wartime need for wood. Before that the blowdowns and uprooted trees left by the hurricane of 1938 had actually revived the lumber industry in York County, and lumbermen are quoted as having said, "It is an ill wind that blows nobody good."[4]

In Brownfield, in Oxford County, Guy Boynton went into his woods in the summer of 1947 to find trees to be cut in the fall to make new sills for the hundred-year-old farmhouse where he and his wife, Esther, lived. The Boyntons had been burned out of an earlier home in 1930 and had lost timber during the 1938 hurricane, but they had worked hard and saved, and at last they could see their way clear to making some improvements on their home. Finding trees that were tall enough and large enough to replace the big, old sills had not been easy, but before the summer was over they had been found and marked.

The Boyntons' farm was a subsistence farm, and the storing up of food was an important part of Esther's work. Canning, pickling, and preserving were easier in 1947 than they had been for years, for it was the first summer since the war started that sugar was not rationed.

Esther canned everything she could from the garden. In fact, she canned everything she could get her hands on. A friend brought her a peck of plums, and she bought peaches. She made jelly. She made jam. All the gleaming jars were carried to the cellar, "clear to the other end of the house," Esther remembers, adding, "I used to plan how much and what I was going down cellar for, because I didn't intend to travel, especially in the wintertime." By the end of the summer, squash, potatoes—everything—was in the cellar: it was full.

The corn house was full too, with corn that would be ground during the winter for the pair of oxen and the cow in the barn. In a pen in the backyard were a couple of hogs. There would be salt pork to put in the cellar too.

It had been a good summer. The lyrics of the song "Zip-a-dee-do-dah" from the new Walt Disney movie, *Song of the South,* had seemed appropriate on so many days. There was "plenty of sunshine." There were so many "wonderful" days. Jackie Robinson was in the news, the first Black man to play professional baseball, and fans were looking forward to the World Series. At East Livermore the Methodists had celebrated the hundredth anniversary of their campground. The turnpike into Maine was nearing completion, and although Maine's first war dead were due to arrive home in the autumn, people were looking forward to Indian summer, to those beautiful blue and gold days that come before winter sets in.

But it was dry. Almost no rain had fallen in the southern half of the state since June 25. The District, although wetter, still was having a below average rainfall. Here and there farmers were hauling water because their wells had gone dry. In Waterboro Liz Gould noticed that leaves which fell on the surface of the pasture brook just sat there: there was no run of water to carry them away. The warden at the Pleasant Mountain lookout tower in Denmark near Fryeburg watched for smoke, and sometimes, thinking he had seen a fire, and sending someone to check, would learn that what he had seen through the haze was the sunlight glancing off a tin roof.

At Goose Rocks Beach students at Eliot O'Hara's watercolor school, whose study of landscape painting took them into the woods and fields, were warned if they smoked to put matches in their water jugs and cigarettes in their paint boxes. By the end of August, Marjorie and Warren Walker of Clark's Mills were anxious about the dry conditions, but although they worried about forest fires, they assumed the local volunteer fire companies, of which there were three within five miles of their house, would take care of them as they always had.

But for the most part, in early September Maine people were not giving much thought to the lack of rain. Out-of-staters who owned cottages at Maine's beaches and lakes were closing them for the winter, and did not plan to visit them again until spring. Only a few lucky ones like Dot and Fred Smith of Goose Rocks Beach could stay on to enjoy what good weather September might bring.

Most Maine natives were not concerned with the dry conditions either. Soon the rains of autumn would begin. Parched, brown lawns would turn green again; dangerously low wells would fill up; and the danger of fire in the woods would lessen. There would be some forest fires—autumn was the forest fire season in Maine. Rain would be welcome, and not just because it was needed. Day after day of sunshine had become tiresome. New Englanders are used to a change in the weather.

But it did not rain. Maine, indeed all of New England, enjoyed one of the most glorious Indian summers in living memory. In November a reporter for *Time* magazine looked back and described it:

> Day after day, week after week, a warm haze hung over the states of the Northeastern United States. Maple and sumac painted the hills and shed bright, crackling drifts of leaves. Offshore, the sea was blue. Streams ran gently . . . and at dusk the smell of dust and wood smoke perfumed the air. No rain clouds obscured sun or bright autumn moon.[5]

The total rainfall for September in Portland was 1.73 inches, about half the normal measure. In August only .27 inches had fallen. Maine was well into its severest drought in thirty years.

NOTES

1. A. G. Hall, "Four Flaming Days," *American Forests,* December 1947.
2. This fire was mistakenly called the Miramichi Fire in confusion with the real Miramichi Fire that occurred on the same day in the Province of New Brunswick, Canada, two hundred miles away.
3. Maine's organized territory is divided into cities, towns, and plantations, each with its own unit of government. The unorganized territory, which includes the Forestry District, is made up of townships and ranges. Because their populations are small and scattered, they are governed by the state.
4. Elizabeth Ring, "Catastrophe Again Changes the Economy of the Ossipee Towns," *Portland Sunday Telegram,* November 2, 1947.
5. "Disaster: A Lovely Time of Year," *Time,* November 3, 1947. Reprinted by permission from *Time,* The Weekly News Magazine; Copyright Time Inc., 1947.

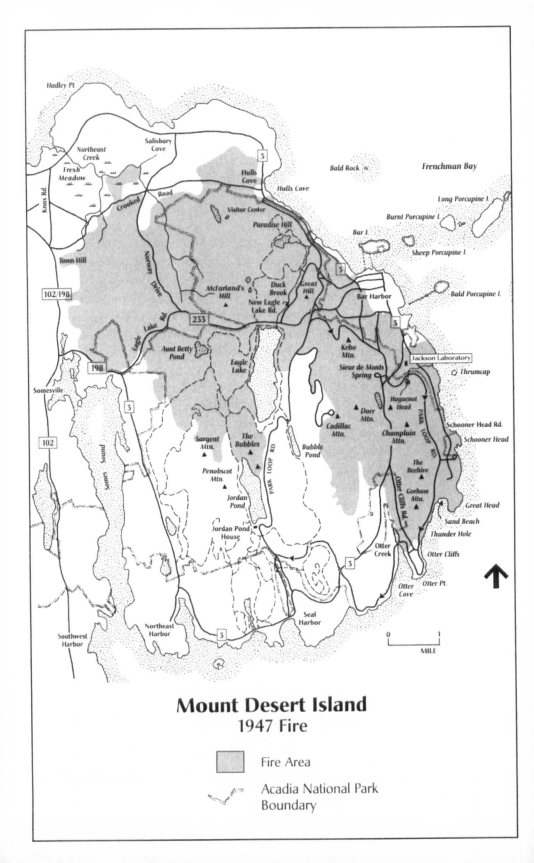

Mount Desert Island
1947 Fire

Fire Area

Acadia National Park
Boundary

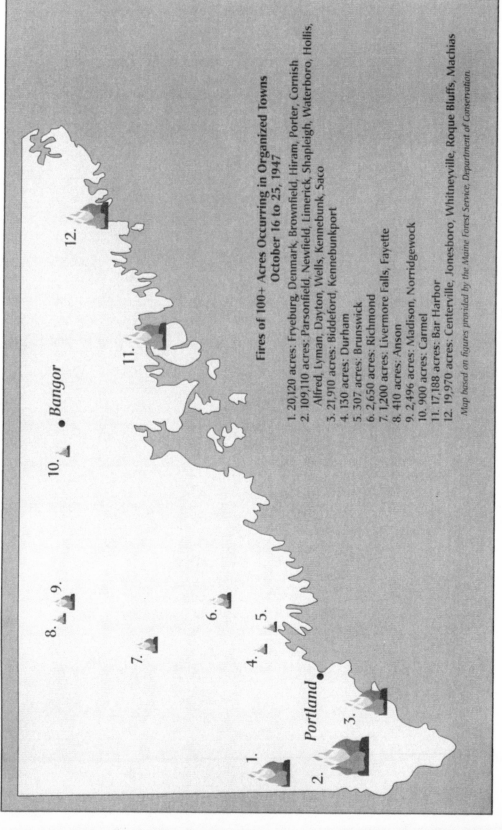

Fires of 100+ Acres Occurring in Organized Towns
October 16 to 25, 1947

1. 20,120 acres: Fryeburg, Denmark, Brownfield, Hiram, Porter, Cornish
2. 109,110 acres: Parsonfield, Newfield, Limerick, Shapleigh, Waterboro, Hollis,
   Alfred, Lyman, Dayton, Wells, Kennebunk, Saco
3. 21,910 acres: Biddeford, Kennebunkport
4. 130 acres: Durham
5. 307 acres: Brunswick
6. 2,650 acres: Richmond
7. 1,200 acres: Livermore Falls, Fayette
8. 410 acres: Anson
9. 2,496 acres: Madison, Norridgewock
10. 900 acres: Carmel
11. 17,188 acres: Bar Harbor
12. 19,970 acres: Centerville, Jonesboro, Whitneyville, Roque Bluffs, Machias

Map based on figures provided by the Maine Forest Service, Department of Conservation.

Chapter I:
"Lord, I wish it would rain."

The World Series, between the New York Yankees and the Brooklyn Dodgers, began on September 30. The *Portland Press Herald*'s headline on October 1 was "Yanks Capture Opener, 5–3." Other front-page news was the escalating Cold War, and the possibility that food might have to be rationed again in order to feed the starving people of Europe. The Freedom Train, a special train that was touring the country carrying a hundred priceless documents—among them the Bill of Rights and the Declaration of Independence—was coming to Maine at the end of the month. Readers were advised that record low temperatures were on the way. Bangor had already had a killing frost.

On the first page of the sports section the headline was "Maine's Hunting Season Opens Today." The bird hunting season had begun at dawn. The deer season would begin on October 21 in the six northern counties and on November 1 in the rest of the state. Officials reported good prospects for the hundred thousand sportsmen who were expected to hunt in Maine's woods before the 1947 season ended.

On opening day hunters looking for pheasant, partridge, and woodcock found the bird covers unusually dry. The underbrush—blueberry and juniper bushes, tall grasses growing between the trees, branches that had been brought down by high winds and heavy snows, slash left from lumbering operations—was dry.

The leaf mold, pine needles, and moss that floored the forests was dry too, powder dry. Beneath that the topsoil itself had no moisture. Places in the woods that were normally wet and marshy all year were dry and dusty. Streams, lakes, and ponds had receded from their banks.

The wardens, who went regularly into the woods and who manned the state's lookout towers, were anxious about forest fire. They had been watching conditions gradually worsen since the middle of September. While a columnist for the Portland paper was writing, "It seems to me that the colors of the foliage are blended more splendidly this year. . . ,"[1] the wardens knew that because of the drought the leaves of the hardwood trees had turned color later than usual and remained on the trees longer. In southern Maine when they did fall it was because of the drought not frost, for even the nights were warm in September.

The leaves were so dry they could be crumbled easily in the hand. They lay lightly in the woods. If a fire started they would be a menace, for burning leaves carried by the wind would spread the fire. It was some consolation that fires, when they did occur, were small, but they burned deep into the ground, making them difficult and costly to put out.

An even graver concern for the wardens was the public's apparent unawareness of the hazardous fire conditions. Those who manned the towers felt that with the dry conditions they could not take a chance on even the smallest wisp of smoke. Using the telephone with which each tower was equipped, a warden would call down to someone to check on a spiraling column of smoke, no matter how small. Often the call would come back that someone was burning leaves or rubbish. The towns had not issued bans on outdoor burning. Sometimes the smoke was from a burning town dump.

On Friday, October 3, a crew working on a new state road in Yarmouth set a fire to clear some land. It got away from them, and the local fire department had to be called in to put it out. On Sunday the fire, which the firemen had considered out but which had gone underground, broke out again, burning up through the ground along the roots of trees. The firemen returned and put it out. On Monday it broke out again. This was just the kind of problem the wardens knew could develop, considering the drought, from even the smallest fire.

Most fires were unintentionally set and on their way before they were discovered. The sun shining through a bit of broken glass could start a fire, as could live cinders from a passing train. Alton Tracey, working on the blueberry plains near his home in Unionville, patrolled behind a truck that was spreading hay, to put out any sparks from its exhaust. His concern was realistic. At Sanford's town dump a fire was reported as having started from the hot exhaust of a truck dumping leaves. A cigarette tossed carelessly into the underbrush presented one of the greatest hazards of all. Even the heat in a just extinguished match was capable of starting a blaze.

Early in October, State Fire Inspector Lawrence Dolby stood in the yard of the Sweetser School in Saco with Saco's Fire Chief, Buck Emmons. Emmons was talking with a teacher about the fire department wetting down the school yard to lay the terrible dust. Emmons was a pipe smoker, and as he talked he filled his pipe. He carried his matches in a little blue Edgeworth tobacco can. Thirty years later Dolby said, "I can remember him to this day taking out the can and scratching a match on the bottom of it and lighting his pipe . . . puffing away, blowing smoke in the teacher's face. I stood directly behind these two people and watched Buck as he blew the match out and then he put it behind him and held it, and I looked at the match in his hand and it was out. He dropped it in a few seconds, and the match fell on some dry leaves on the ground and those leaves started to burn."

In Kennebunkport town Fire Warden Arthur Welch knew how dry it was, and warned the police and everyone he talked with to be on the alert for fire. "I guess," he said later, "some people thought I was crazy."

Farmers, who knew how dry it was, might have been concerned about fire, but the drought had brought them more immediate problems. They could not do their fall plowing because the soil was so dry it was impossible to lay it over into furrows. And their wells were going dry. This meant that water had to be hauled for household use and for livestock.

Neighbors, whose wells were still producing, shared, and cities and towns with a water system set up public water sources. In Springvale the fire department attached a hose to a hydrant so that farmers from outlying areas could come in to fill their barrels, wash tubs, jars, buckets, and milk cans. The Portland Water District, with abundant water available from Sebago Lake, opened two free fountains in Falmouth and one in Scarborough.

Watering livestock presented the biggest problem, especially for dairy farmers with large herds. In the Norway–South Paris area, Goodwin's Dairy borrowed a six-hundred-gallon tank from the Norway Fish and Game Association, and Roy Smith of Pike's Hill had an old army water tank in which to haul water for his thirty head of cattle. But other farmers were not as fortunate. They bought every empty vinegar and molasses barrel the local stores had to sell and made two or three trips a day to the nearest water supply. William Young from Crockett's Ridge in Norway had eighteen hundred turkeys and twenty head of cattle to water. His hundred-year-old well was dry for the first time in memory.

In Phippsburg Center one old resident said the pond there was lower than he'd ever seen it. In one section its bed was dry, and what appeared to be the remains of an old road was visible, a road no one had ever seen before. In Yarmouth Irving Daughty's frog pond was the lowest it had been in thirty years, and his cranberry bog wasn't a bog anymore. Rivers and streams were low too. Farther north, Moosehead Lake, Moxie Pond, Spencer Lake, Long Pond, and Brassua Pond, which feed the Kennebec River, all were at their lowest level in years. At Caribou the shortage of water at the Caribou Dam threatened an electricity shortage.

But lumbermen and potato farmers in northern Maine welcomed the dry weather. The absence of wind and rain made it easier to cut timber and dig potatoes. They felt little concern about forest fire—heavy frosts at night had kept the forests from drying out. Warden Charles Harriman, whose territory included the northern sections of Penobscot and Piscataquis counties and the central and southern sections of Aroostook said, "The woods aren't bad at all. It would take a lot of brimstone to start a blaze."[2]

Such was not the case in southern Maine, where, by the second week of October, the woods were in a Class 4 state of danger, which meant they were in a "high state of inflammability."[3] Maine Forest Service officials were worried. Unless it rained, and no rain was forecast, the woods would soon be in an explosive condition. The decision was made to reopen the lookout towers, which had been closed at the end of September as was usual, and to call back the watchmen who had been laid off, yearly economies that were dictated by the department's limited budget. Forest Commissioner Rendall and Austin Wilkins, the department's supervisor in charge of fire control in forests within the organized territory, went to Governor Hildreth and warned him that they might have to ask him to close the woods.

Wilkins also talked with Fish and Game Commissioner George Stobie whose department faced a potential loss of $250,000 in hunting license fees—its total source of revenue—in the event of a closure. Sporting camp owners would also suffer serious financial loss if the woods were closed. Stobie hoped a simple ban on campfires and smoking in the woods might be a suitable alternative, but he and his colleagues agreed that if keeping people—even hunters—out of the woods altogether was necessary to save them from destructive forest fires, it should be done.

By October 5, which happened to be the first day of Fire Prevention Week in Maine, all the state's lookout towers and storehouses had been reopened and were operating at full strength. It would seem that Fire Prevention Week presented a dramatic opportunity to impress upon the public the danger that existed because of the drought, but, although firemen did urge building ponds for rural firefighting, for the most part their speeches and posters were aimed at preventing house fires.

Programs were held to advise the public to have their chimneys cleaned regularly, and fire drills were held in the schools, but the only mention of woods fires came in an editorial on the front page of the *Portland Press Herald*. Calling attention to the fire that had been set by the road crew in Yarmouth, which had proved so difficult to put out, and was, in fact, still burning, the editorial writer admonished those concerned for not posting a watchman on the fire, adding, "Seldom has this part of Maine experienced such a tinder-dry season. There must be the greatest caution on the part of everybody. It is no time in which to start fires."

The Yanks won the World Series on October 6. In Bar Harbor the Jackson Laboratory announced that it had been awarded $64,550 by the federal government for its cancer research, and that the money would be used to build an addition onto the lab. President Truman was calling for meatless and eggless days; Americans would have to practice self-rationing to "head off starvation in Europe." Hope had failed for a peaceful solution to the problem of partitioning Palestine.

Happier news was the filming of the movie *Deep Water* at Vinalhaven. Twentieth Century Fox had sent Dana Andrews, Caesar Romero, Anne Revere, Dean Stockwell, Jean Peters, and a crew of fifty technicians to Maine to make the movie version of Ruth Moore's novel *Spoonhandle*. The local papers were full of pictures of the stars hobnobbing with natives in the little island town.

The temperature in Portland that day was eighty-four degrees, in Bangor eighty. "Indian Joe," a full-blooded Passamaquoddy Indian from Union who predicted the weather by the migration of geese and the quarters of the moon, was saying the weather would stay warm until October 20.

Reports of small woods fires here and there began to come in to the office of the Forest Service in Augusta. On October 7 fires were burning in the Topsham-Bowdoin area, on the Wells-Sanford Road in York County, and in Portland. A bulldozer had been called in on the Yarmouth blaze to dig a trench to contain it. It was still burning deep underground and had broken out in a three-acre, slash-covered area between Route 1 and the new highway. Wilkins, concerned because the fires were going underground, tying up men and equipment for long periods of time, and anticipating the need for extra help in his office to answer telephone calls for state assistance, arranged for staff people to come in from the University of Maine's Forestry Department. Radio stations were asked to alert the public to the explosive conditions, and town wardens were advised to stop issuing outdoor burning permits. Sunday, October 12, was the beginning of a week of nervous watching.

Violetta Wallace, who lived in Hollis and worked in the telephone office at Bar Mills, took a ride that Sunday afternoon and paid a visit to the lookout tower on Ossipee Hill (or "mountain" as it was apt to be called locally). Standing in the tower, looking down on the acres and acres of trees, many of them pines, which came right up the side of the hill to the foot of the tower, she said to Donald "Mike" Ferguson, the watchman, "What would you do if you saw a fire?"

"I'd get out of here in a hurry," was his reply. Neither knew that her thought and his reply were prophetic.

On Monday, the thirteenth, a fire broke out in the Pine Grove Park area of Lisbon Falls. The Topsham-Bowdoin fire was still burning, defying the efforts of two or three fire departments to put it out. A small fire of undetermined origin was burning on the Shapleigh Plains, and nearby residents, seeing the smoke, thought, "Oh, they're burning over the blueberry plains again." Working on these fires, digging out fire lines, firemen found that the soil was so dry it spilled off their shovels like loose sand. Bulldozers, brought in to dig trenches and to make firebreaks, often had to make second runs to lay up sufficient mounds of earth, and their blades raised great clouds of dust.

On the fourteenth, Vermont's Governor Gibson closed the woods in his state. It was the first woods closure in Vermont since 1941. Newspapers in York and Cumberland Counties carried front-page articles about the dry condition of Maine's woods, warning hunters to be careful. Commissioner Rendall told a Portland reporter that so far most of the fires were in the organized townships not in the heavily timbered regions of northern and western Maine where "everything was quiet." He pointed out that while Governor Hildreth was not prepared to close Maine's woods, forest and game wardens were reporting conditions daily. "I hope," said Rendall, "that the Lord sends us some rain." But the Portland weather bureau could foresee no such relief.

On Wednesday, the fifteenth, ten fires were burning in Maine. Monday's fire at Lisbon Falls had been brought under control that night, but had broken out again the next morning and raced to within five hundred feet of thirty houses.

The fire in Topsham was still burning, in fact had flared up on the same day the fire in neighboring Lisbon Falls gave so much trouble, and had burned more than a hundred acres of small growth and slash. Students from Bowdoin College had been hired to help dig trenches. Late that afternoon a fire started up in Gray in a field a short distance from some woods that were just over the town line in New Gloucester. There was a strong wind, and the fire quickly spread into the trees. Fire companies from both towns responded, following the fire deep into the woods where it was burning in slash that had been left from a cutting operation. Water had to be hauled in by tank trunk. When State Fire Warden Philip Barton arrived on the scene, he looked the situation over and went to the selectmen of New Gloucester and asked them if a bulldozer could be brought in. The bulldozer was already on the way. Barton credited its use with preventing the fire from becoming a serious one for the town, and commended the firemen from Gray and New Gloucester for working so well together. This was not always the case when a fire involved two towns, for deciding which chief would have authority over both companies was apt to be a problem, and sometimes firemen would take orders only from their own chief.

That day there was evidence that fires in Lewiston and Falmouth were started by hunters. On Thursday, the sixteenth, with twenty fires burning in the state—double the number reported twenty-four hours before—and the deer season only a week away in the northern counties, Commissioner Rendall and Governor Hildreth met to decide whether Maine's woods should be closed. While woods closures were not rare in Maine, they were never imposed lightly. The announcement of a woods closure in New Hampshire came that morning, and late in the day Governor Hildreth's office announced that at dawn on the seventeenth Maine's woods would close too. The governor went on radio that night to explain his decision. "Experienced woodsmen," he said, "have advised me that they have not seen such dry conditions in thirty years." The woods had been in Class 4 danger for two weeks, and weathermen still could not promise rain.

Actually the closing was only partial. Fires and smoking in the woods were forbidden, but both were allowed at state-maintained campsites. Hunting was forbidden in the woods, but was still allowed in fields and marshes, along the shores of rivers, streams, lakes, ponds, and on coastal waters. The governor had, however, asked the attorney general to give his opinion on imposing a total hunting ban.

The woods closure did not affect lumbering operations. The governor had no authority to deny this use of Maine's woods. But Rendall warned all operators of portable mills and woods tractors to screen their smoke stacks to prevent sparks from flying into the tinder-dry underbrush. Hildreth urged care and restraint upon the woodsmen, saying, "Upon these people rests a great responsibility to exercise every possible vigilance."

By the end of the day on the seventeenth, the first day of the woods closure, fifty fires were burning in Maine. Among them were fires at Bar Harbor's Fresh Meadow, an underground fire in North Kennebunkport, and a new fire at Shapleigh Plains. At 12:30 P.M. on the seventeenth, state Game Warden George Townsend, while patrolling his district, discovered a fire on a back road just north of Poverty Pond between Shapleigh and Newfield. It was burning a hundred feet from the road, but he could easily trace its start to the remains of a cigarette on the edge of the road.[4] Townsend made a futile attempt to stop the fire, which already was burning on a fifty-foot front, then drove a mile and a half to the nearest telephone to call the Shapleigh Fire Department. By the time the firemen arrived half an hour later, two acres had burned, and the fire had worked itself to a high ridge. The following day it was the largest fire in the state, having swept through twelve hundred acres of scrub oak. By evening it had split, one spur moving toward Waterboro, another toward Shapleigh.

But on the eighteenth the most serious fire in Maine was the Topsham-Bowdoin blaze. Already almost two weeks old, and having burned through a thousand acres of slash and timber, it was still out of control and had become a threat to Bowdoin Center. It came roaring out of the woods toward the small settlement. Twenty homes in the path of the flames had been evacuated. At others, families had loaded their furniture into trucks standing in their dooryards, ready to move if the wind shifted. But only one old log cabin was lost. Heroic bulldozer crews dug deep trenches to create firebreaks. Fighting forest fires with bulldozers was a new and effective technique.

About two hundred firefighters, some of them students from Bowdoin College and the University of Maine Extension in Brunswick, as well as firemen from three or four towns, fought the fire. Extra equipment—five thousand feet of hose and three power pumps, purchased with money made available from the state—was rushed from Boston. Fish and Game Department planes were brought in to plot the movement of the fire from the air, but communication with the men on the ground was a problem. Neither the planes nor the firefighters had two-way radios.

Even the Civil Air Patrol planes, called in that night as spotters for Maine's fifty forest fires, had no radio equipment. The Maine Wing of the CAP had had a wartime radio frequency, but had lost it in 1946, and been given in its place two other frequencies, meaning that new equipment was required. This had been shipped three days before from Chicago, but was not expected to arrive in time to be useful. Pilots spotting fires either had to devise ways to drop messages to the nearest town or had to land at the nearest airport and telephone their alarms. Such methods of communication were a severe handicap in fighting the fires.

On Sunday morning, October 19, the air in many of Maine's towns and cities carried a haze of smoke and the smell of burning wood. The Reverend Paul West of the West Falmouth Baptist Church called on his congregation to gather for a special prayer meeting on Monday night to pray for rain. "It's come to the point where that's the only answer," he said. "Miracles are possible if people are in earnest. Miracles do happen, and will happen if it is the will of God."

But Sunday was a day of optimism for forestry officials. No new fires were reported, and more than half of those that had been burning Saturday night were out. Most of the others were under control. The fire at Bar Harbor, which had burned a hundred acres, and the Bowdoin and Shapleigh Plains fires were "nearly under control." Most municipalities had finally realized the danger and had banned all outside fires.

There were disturbing reports of arson at South Paris, where a pile of kerosene soaked hay had been found in the middle of a barn floor. A "tall, thin man" was being sought after having been seen at a number of suspicious fires, and the aroused townspeople were patrolling the streets.

At the Topsham-Bowdoin fire weary firefighters, many of whom had not slept for forty hours, had a chance to rest, and there was time to tell some of their stories to the press. The blaze had driven twenty-five moose out of the woods. It was rare to see one moose; to see twenty-five was news. Firemen told how they had competed with a colony of beavers for desperately needed water, knocking down their dam to release the flow of water, only to find that overnight the beavers had built it up again.

There was satisfaction that "only one ramshackle shack" had burned at Bowdoin Center, where many houses had been threatened, but there was concern about how the fire bills were going to be paid. Town officials estimated that fighting the fire, which was still burning, had cost about $20,000. The town's total annual budget for all departments was $20,000.

On Sunday, the nineteenth, a 1910 heat record was broken in Portland with a temperature of seventy-eight degrees, but it rained that night; just a light shower, but rain, the first since October 3. The worst seemed to be over. But Maine's battle with wildfire had just begun. On Monday a fire that had been mulling underground at North Kennebunkport for almost a week broke out, and began to move.

NOTES

1. Mary E. McCrum, "Bittersweet," *Portland Press Herald,* October 14, 1947.

2. "Worst Drought in Years Continues to Spread in Maine," *Portland Press Herald,* October 16, 1947.

3. In his final report on the 1947 forest fire disaster in Maine, Austin Wilkins of the Forest Service explains that fire danger stations, which classify the conditions in the woods, "determine the fuel moisture content of various types of forest growth and under what condition certain types of forest fuels will ignite." The five classifications are: Very wet, wet but drying out, fires will start, fires will burn hard and from any fire burned, and explosive dry conditions.

4. "Warden Traces Devastating Woods Blaze to Cigarette," *Portland Press Herald,* October 29, 1947.

Chapter II:
The Race of Terror

Novelist Kenneth Roberts was worried about fire at his farm, Rocky Pasture, on the Wildes District Road in Kennebunkport. The house sat well back from the road, its drive curving over the spread of pasture land that gave it its name. An excellent spring supplied water for the house, and there was a pond for fighting fire, but the pond was low. Roberts knew if a fire like those burning at Topsham and on the Shapleigh Plains got into the woods near his house, he might lose it.

Hoping to find another source of water on his land, Roberts had called in a procession of water dowsers, who had among them located nine potential springs. On Monday, October 20, dowser Henry Gross of Biddeford, who had said there was enough water at Rocky Pasture to "supply two towns," began his search for a suitable spot for drilling. Roberts hoped he would agree with the findings of at least two of the other dowsers, for he never drilled until at least three had agreed. By noon Gross had ruled out one site, and declining lunch, saying, "I never eat lunch. You go in and get yours. . . ," he spent the noon hour "questing back and forth" with his forked stick.[1]

In Kennebunkport Village Thelma Burrows was getting lunch for her husband, Joe, when she heard the whistle blow on the firehouse across the street and saw the truck go out. She had counted the blasts and knew the firemen were headed for North Kennebunkport.[2] A few miles away at Cape Porpoise, Martin Wildes, who was carpentering at the head of the cove, heard the whistle blow too. It was the second call in a week for the North Kennebunkport fire, which was on the other side of Route 1 in a wooded, normally boggy area.

North Kennebunkport was a separate town, but it did not have a

11

fire company of its own and depended for fire protection on Kennebunkport, which had four small volunteer companies, one for each
section of the town: the village proper, Cape Porpoise, the Wildes District (or "Wildes Town" as some called it), and Goose Rocks Beach.
Their equipment was modest: a couple of pumpers and a vintage ladder truck in the village, a rebuilt Reo pumper at Cape Porpoise, a 1925
pumper at Goose Rocks, and only a hose reel at Wildes Town.

At the Ossipee Hill lookout in Waterboro, Mike Ferguson had had
a busy morning. He had called in a fire at Alfred, two at South Sanford, one at Saco, and one on the Kezar Falls–Cornish Road. At 1:02
P.M. he spotted the North Kennebunkport fire and put a call through to
Clayton Weymouth, state warden for District 1, which took in fifty-
one towns in southern Maine. Weymouth had just returned from
checking on the Shapleigh fire, which still required patrols, but he
told Ferguson he would head over to North Kennebunkport. From the
tower Ferguson could see that the fire was spreading. The race of terror had begun.

At first Chief John Eldridge of the Arundel Engine Company
from Kennebunkport Village and his crew did not consider the North
Kennebunkport fire serious, but by the time Weymouth got there it
was clear that putting it out this time was going to be a problem.
There was abundant fuel in the area where it was burning—scrub
growth, and peat deep in the bog. But Kennebunk had sent equipment and men, and although getting water in to the fire would be difficult, if they were not able to beat it down, surely they could stop it
at Route 1, the three-lane principal highway into Maine.

Juanita Spofford of Fortunes Rocks in Biddeford had gone to
Kennebunkport with friends that afternoon to have ice cream at
Miller's Drugstore in Dock Square. Hearing about the fire, they decided to go home by way of Route 1 to Five Points in Biddeford,
where they could pick up a copy of the afternoon newspaper before
heading down West Street to Fortunes Rocks. But they found Route 1
closed to traffic and were detoured down Route 1-A, the old, winding
road to Biddeford.

Later that afternoon Arnold Stinson, chief of the Cape Porpoise
fire company, who had taken his wife to Saco, stopped at the First National Store in Biddeford on his way home and heard there that the
North Kennebunkport fire had jumped Route 1.

Fanned by high winds, the fire had leaped across the highway in
an arc of flame that dwarfed firefighters, who stood helplessly by.

Even before the flames had jumped the road, flying embers had started a spot fire a hundred feet beyond it, and beyond the reach of the hose of the firemen. The new, small fire was spreading rapidly toward Route 1-A.

Now the firefighters had a new problem. Trying to contain the blaze was one thing; trying to keep it from burning houses was something else. The fire had reached a section of woods and fields crossed here and there by country roads. Along the narrow roads were scattered modest homes, small farms with livestock, and summer camps and cottages. Beyond lay the small city of Biddeford, for the wind was from the northwest, and blowing the fire straight toward the city. A stand would have to be made at Route 1-A, which provided the first break in the fire's path, and a call went out for more help.

Fire departments in nearby towns were alerted that a forest fire of serious proportions was out of control south of Biddeford. Appeals were broadcast over the radio for tank trucks—trucks that usually hauled milk or oil—to be rushed in to carry water to the firefighters, and for trucks and volunteers to help families whose homes lay in the path of the fire to move their furniture. In Augusta officials of the Forest Service and Governor Hildreth, who had been alerted, waited to hear that the fire had been contained.

But it was not stopped. The stand made at Route 1-A failed. The flames pushed on toward Biddeford, spreading in a widening arc. The fire crossed the Boston and Maine Railroad tracks. The 5:20 Kennebec Limited out of Union Station in Portland was delayed almost an hour on its run to Boston, but it did get through, as did freight trains (minus their oil and gasoline-carrying tank cars) later in the evening. In Boston newsmen picked up the story of the fire in Maine, and made plans to cover it. A crew for Paramount Pictures headed to Maine to film some newsreel.

Ordinarily, when the wind drops at night a forest fire will slow down and become manageable, but this one did not. It crowned—jumped to the tops of the tinder-dry trees and spread quickly from tree to tree—and while the crown fire raced on ahead, the slower ground fire burned what the overhead flames had missed. The tremendous heat of the flames as they fed on resinous pine trees and juniper bushes drove the firefighters back. More help was needed.

The Lane Construction Company, which was building the new turnpike, sent a crew with a thousand-gallon pumper and bulldozers. By the end of the week they were being called "The Lane Devils" because of their daring work bulldozing firebreaks in the path of the flames.

In Biddeford families on West Street, a rural, residential street on the outskirts of the city, evacuated their homes, and volunteers who had done Red Cross work during the war opened a canteen for the evacuees at St. Joseph's Hall. Martina Butler, who was given responsibility for buying food, was not sure just how much would be needed. She bought a pound of coffee, two or three loaves of bread, butter, eggs. . . . Later in the week, when coffee grounds were being taken away from the canteen by the truckload, she remembered with a wry smile that modest beginning.

That evening in Kennebunkport Thelma Burrows decided to fry up some doughnuts for the firemen, and put on a pot of coffee. They would be hungry when they came back to the station. Hers too was a modest beginning.

Mrs. Lafferty, whose Green Leaf Inn was across the street from the Kennebunk fire station, thought about the men who had been out in the woods off Route 1 fighting the fire since afternoon and decided to make some sandwiches and coffee to send out to them. Enlisting the help of some of her guests and buying extra supplies from stores that were still open, she prepared the food and drove out on the highway where the word was passed through the smoky woods that a lady was out on Route 1 with food. One trip was not, of course, enough: the women spent the night making sandwiches and carrying them to the hungry men.

Two days before, Kennebunk people had read in the evening paper about the scattered fires in York County. Now, as out-of-town firetrucks, full crews aboard, raced through their village, sirens sounding, the fires were more than a headline. They themselves were involved. That evening Aurele Tremblay, a thirty-six-year-old blacksmith from Kennebunk, was struck by a truck speeding to the fire. He was rushed to the Maine General Hospital in Portland—the ambulance making a dash along fire-bordered Route 1—but he died the next day, the first fire-related fatality.

The firefighters were hampered by a scarcity of water and by the unpredictable wind that carried the fire. At some point in the evening the wind changed course altogether, swinging from the northwest to the northeast. The mile-and-a-half-long side of the fire became its front. Leaving flames still burning toward the Proctor Road, Guinea Road, and West Street in Biddeford, the wind began pushing the fire toward the sea and the cottage settlements of Fortunes Rocks and Goose Rocks Beach.

The next day, the twenty-first, Kenneth Roberts was to write in his diary: "Cloudless again. A tremendous big fire burned all last night, a row of flames against the northern sky. A hurricane hit Bermuda. If only it would come near enough to bring rain. This state is on the verge of one of the greatest disasters that ever hit it. . . ."

NOTES

1. Kenneth Roberts, *Henry Gross and His Dowsing Rod* (New York: Doubleday and Company, Inc., 1951).
2. Today North Kennebunkport is called Arundel.

Chapter III:
"I thought it was the end of the world."

At 6:30 A.M. on the twenty-first, Mabel Emery left her home on the Guinea Road in Biddeford to go to work at the Saco-Lowell plant. Her husband; her adult daughter, Ruth; and her teenage son, Richard, were still sleeping. She hadn't turned on the radio, and she hadn't seen the morning paper, so she didn't know that in the night a house had burned on West Street. At eight o'clock her foreman told her she was wanted at home. John Henchey, a brother-in-law, who also worked in the mill, said he would drive her. She didn't know until she saw the two chimneys and smoldering rubble around them that her home had burned.

Mr. Emery and his children had had some warning. People had come to the door and told them that the fire was close by. "You'd better leave," they said. Ruth began to carry clothing, family pictures, and personal papers out to the car. Richard, who enjoyed woodworking, carried out a few of his prized tools, regretting the lathe he had to leave behind. Mr. Emery, with the help of Orison Davis, a friend from nearby Oak Ridge, brought the new refrigerator into the yard, hoping to get a truck to take it away to safety.

In the woods behind the house they could see the smoke, and they could hear the fire coming. It sounded like a freight train. Ruth had trouble starting the car, which heightened her fear, and she called frantically to the men who had gone back inside the house to get a couch. When at last they came out, they just had time to jump into the car and drive away before the fire burst out of the woods, setting the backyard field aflame. The house exploded. "It just blew," Ruth remembers. "It just blew apart."

There hadn't been time to save the refrigerator or the couch. There hadn't been time to look for the family pets, a cat and a dog. And there wasn't time, just then, to dwell on what had been lost, for another house three hundred feet away was in danger. The owners had gone to work, so the Emerys and Mr. Davis set to work to try to save the house from the flames licking toward it across the field. It was there that Mrs. Emery found them. They had taken blankets from the beds, wet them, and laid them around the foundation of the house where the clapboards came close to the ground. The house did not burn.

The Emerys did not seek shelter in town at St. Joseph's Hall. John Henchey said, "You come home with me," so they went with him to Goose Rocks Beach in Kennebunkport.

The Emery house was not the only one to burn in those early hours. The Thompson house on West Street had burned in the night, and Willie Ouellette lost his Proctor Road home and fifteen head of cattle. The Paramount Pictures crew was filming the blaze near the Ouellette farm when the fire jumped the road, and a tree in back of the house burst into flames—a frightening, blazing torch, high over their heads, crackling and throwing sparks and heat. The men ran for their car, which they had left on the road. It was gone. A *Boston Evening American* reporter had seen it in the path of the fire and, finding the keys in it, had moved it down the road. The men had an exciting story to tell when they got back to Boston. Almost everyone had a story to tell before the fire was out.

The flames followed an unpredictable, but inexorable course across the countryside that morning, heading for the sea, burning some houses, missing others—for freakish reasons or because families, sometimes just women and children, fought to save them, carrying water from wells, beating out burning debris that fell into dooryards.

Firemen from Kennebunkport who knew the area well, men like Chief Lawrence Ireland of the Goose Rocks Beach department and Arthur Welch from Cape Porpoise, drove frantically up and down the back roads, checking to see that every family knew the fire was coming, warning them to get away while they could. Some had already left, taking what household furnishings they could pile into their cars or even into horse-drawn wagons. Some, particularly old people, were reluctant to leave. Their fear of leaving lifetime homes was greater than their fear of the fire they hadn't yet seen.

Chief Ireland talked with one old lady who lived alone on the Fox Farm Road. She declared she wouldn't leave her home "even if I burn up." He argued with her, knowing how hopeless her situation was. The firefighters couldn't stop the fire—it was blowing right over their heads. Even with better equipment and more men, they wouldn't be able to stop the wind-driven flames that raced through the tops of trees.

The old lady was adamant until another fireman, who'd come along, asked, "Don't you have any relatives near here?" She did and at last agreed to go to them. The men loaded some of her furniture into a pickup truck, tied her cow on behind, and drove her away from her home. Fifteen minutes later the barn caught fire, and it and the house burned flat.

That morning at Biddeford Pool, a small peninsula community on the coast east of Kennebunkport and Goose Rocks Beach, Frank Handlen was painting a house with Bud LeGallee. They could see the smoke moving over the horizon to the west of them, and it became apparent as the morning wore on that this was no ordinary fire. They decided to knock off work and go over and have a look.

They followed Route 9 along the coast through Fortunes Rocks into Kennebunkport. Just over the town line was Roy Emmons's dairy farm. The front yard of the farmhouse was jammed with trucks, cars, and people, and poor Roy was pacing up and down in front of his barn wringing his hands. The fire was coming through the woods behind the house. They couldn't see it, but they could hear its roar. Just beyond the verge of trees behind the house and barn was an ominous wall of smoke, so high it blocked out the sun.

Emmons's cattle had been taken out of the barn and driven into a pasture on the other side of the road. Firemen were wetting down the buildings while others were loading the Emmons furniture into trucks to be taken to the casino at Fortunes Rocks for safekeeping. Everything was being done that could be done, but Emmons paced and wrung his hands. What hope was there against the wildfire that was running loose across the countryside? If it was not stopped, if he lost his barn—indeed, if he lost his cattle—his livelihood was gone.

Handlen and LeGallee did not stay long at the Emmons farm, where there seemed to be plenty of help. Just down the road at Donald Campbell's house, furniture was being loaded into a truck, and they stopped to help. Suddenly, from the woods on the other side of the road, the fire broke through. It came with astonishing speed, in a great burst of flame through the heavy smoke, and jumped the road. Furniture was dropped. Buckets, which some of the workers were using to throw water on the house, were tossed aside. Everyone scattered. Campbell shut the front door, let his pigs out of their pen, and drove away. Handlen and LeGallee jumped into their car and drove back the way they had come.

The fire had not broken through at the Emmons place. It had gone beyond it through the woods in back to jump the road farther along. Roy Emmons did not loose his farm or cattle, although a barn filled with machinery on the other side of the road was lost. But Donald Campbell's house burned. Less than an hour after fleeing, Handlen and LeGallee went back to see what had happened and were appalled that all that remained of the house was a chimney and "one small blue flame." It was frightening to see how quickly and thoroughly the house had disappeared. The next day Campbell told reporters, "I've been twenty-eight years getting this farm of fifty acres the way I wanted it. And now it's gone. I never saw anything happen as quick."

Beyond Route 9 and the Campbell house toward the ocean lay Goose Rocks Beach, a settlement of about two hundred summer cottages, many dating from the 1890s with wide piazzas, sheltered by tall oak and pine trees, and bordered along the sea by a fine beach. Most of the cottages had been closed for the winter. A few families lingered, and a few others lived year-round in winterized cottages. They had begun what they thought would be just another warm, sunny October day.

Those with children, like Dot and Fred Smith, had sent them off on the early morning school bus. It was unusual for the Smiths to be at the beach so late in the season, but because of a polio epidemic near their home in Virginia, they had stayed in Maine, enrolling their youngest daughter, Mimi, in the Kennebunkport school through October.

Shirley and Eliot O'Hara had stayed on longer than usual too. They had closed their art school at the end of the summer, and their son, Desmond, had gone off to his studies at Tufts College. But Mr. O'Hara was writing a book and had stayed at Goose Rocks to work on it. They had left just a few days before, heading for Washington, D.C., after stocking the school's cupboards with art supplies for the coming year, leaving behind about half of the pictures Mr. O'Hara had painted in his lifetime and his collection of paintings by other artists.

Dot Mignault was still at Goose Rocks, looking forward to a quiet winter in her house on the point after a hectic summer running her store, bowling alley, and dance hall there at the beach. The pace of life after Labor Day was slow and peaceful. With few people around, Goose Rocks seemed set apart from the rest of the town. It was easy to be out of touch with what was happening elsewhere. At about 9:30 that Tuesday night Dot Mignault looked at the red sky toward Biddeford. "I think there's a fire," she said.

Dot Smith first knew about the fire, and the danger, when someone came and said, "It's up at Tea Kettle Corner, the flames and everything, and it's gonna come down here." Tea Kettle Corner, which had earned its name in the days of the Stanley Steamer when residents of Goose Rocks had found on trips to Biddeford that their cars needed a teakettleful of water at that corner, was only a few miles away at the junction of the Fortunes Rocks Road and Guinea Road. During the summer Dot had heard farmers say how dry it was and that "it would be terrible if there's a fire." But they said that every summer.

The Smiths got out the garden hose and soaked their house completely. Dot packed their Studebaker with some of the things they wanted to save—her husband's telescope and paintings, her checkbook and income tax records. "But," she explained later, "your mind goes. You can't think what to save." She heard the roaring of the fire over toward the Campbell's. She too thought it sounded like a freight train, and that sound was one of her most ghastly memories of the fire.

At the Henchey's, a nice, old farmhouse that sat on a hill at the eastern end of Goose Rocks Beach, looking down on Little River and the ocean, it was Mabel Emery who heard the fire coming. Thirty years later she still remembered what Laura Henchey had served for lunch that day. "It was a fricassee of chicken put into the oven with biscuit. Oh, those biscuits were out of this world! And we had enough for supper, but of course we never ate supper."

Sometime after lunch Mrs. Emery heard the roaring of the fire. It was coming up the hill behind the house. She rushed to John Henchey. "John," she said. "The fire is here. What are you going to do?"

"The noise you hear is the freight train going through Kennebunk," he answered. But he was wrong. The barn caught first, and there was no way to save the horse stabled inside. Hens flew in every direction. The women tried to drive away, but no road was open. They left their car and fled toward the beach, Mabel Emery clutching a box of personal papers that Ruth had already rescued once from the fire.

Dot Mignault's house sat on a point of land closer to the water than any other house at the beach. It had appeared at first that the fire would not come that way. The wind was pushing it toward the western end of the beach, and houses there did burn. But the wind turned, sweeping the fire back toward the east where a small group—those who for one reason or another had not evacuated to some other part of Kennebunkport or to Biddeford—had gathered at Dot Mignault's for safety.

When it had seemed that the fire would burn only west, Dot Mignault drove down to the cottage at the western end of the beach where her seventy-three-year-old friend, Beatrice Seidel, lived alone and brought her back to the house on the point. "Mike" Annis and her two small sons had joined them, as had Dot Smith and others—about ten in all, women and children—and Dot Mignault's two dogs. Fred Smith and the other men had gone off to move cars nearer the water and do whatever else they could. The women decided that if the flames reached the house on the point, they would go to the beach and the ocean. They would take blankets and wet them and crouch under them and pray that they would be safe there where there were no houses and trees to burn.

The fire roared into the beach settlement, a maelstrom of wind, smoke, and flames. Mabel and Ruth Emery and Laura Henchey retreated to the beach and the water. Mabel Emery remembers, "We were walking in the water . . . there wasn't anyone else . . . except ahead of us, walking up the beach, quite a ways ahead of us, was a little old lady. She was carrying her pocketbook." That vignette of an old woman, calmly walking up the beach as she might on any normal day, stayed in Mrs. Emery's mind, in sharp contrast to the row of burning houses and trees nearby.

The air was filled with smoke, and embers fell on their heads. Ruth took off her white socks and wet them, and she and her mother put them on their heads so their hair wouldn't catch on fire. "With the fire going over us, I thought it was the end of the world," Ruth said later.

Neither knew how long they had been in the water before they saw that some houses in the middle section of the settlement were not burning. They came out of the water and huddled on one of the porches until a Red Cross worker came along and helped them get to Biddeford.

At Dot Mignault's the women and children watched the advance of the fire. Dot Smith had seen her house burn. It was the only time she cried. At last the heat became intense, and they all went out onto the beach. They wrapped themselves in blankets, first a dry one, then a wet one, and waited, praying, trying to keep their spirits up, reassuring the children, worrying about their men, who were off trying to save cottages. For Dot Smith there was the added worry of Mimi. Was she still at school or was she on her way home on the school bus, heading into the fire? (Mimi and two other children would be reported as missing and would be found at the home of the bus driver, who had taken them home when she couldn't get through to Goose Rocks Beach.)

When the women came out from under their blankets to see what was happening, they held wet pillowcases over their noses and mouths so they could breathe. They could see that trees were burning from the top, not the bottom, flames in the green pines and the copper-colored leaves of the oaks. They "heard the breaking of branches, and now and again an explosion as fuel oil tanks caught fire. Branches and burning shingles were dropping on the beach, carried there by the wind, which was now a gale."[1] Dot Mignault saw the side of the O'Hara cottage blown away when the house exploded into flames.

Terrified animals, fleeing the fire, came running onto the beach: squirrels, chipmunks, rabbits, and, when the beach grass caught fire, mice and rats, who tried to get under the blankets, frightening some of the women and the children, and sending the dogs into a frenzy.

The women had agreed that if they had to retreat again they would somehow swim to Timber Island, which lay just offshore. But Timber Island was covered with pine trees, and burning shingles, scaled by the wind from the roofs of the burning houses on shore, soon set it ablaze.

Their final refuge was, after all, Dot Mignault's house. Turning to look back into the burning wind, Dot could distinguish the silhouette of her house still standing against a background of flames. The back porch steps had caught fire. There was an oil barrel on the porch, but there was also a fire extinguisher there. She made a dash for it. As soon as the others saw what she was doing, they came running, and grabbing the mop pail, garbage pail, and every other available container they could find, they formed a bucket brigade to Little River.[2] They saved the house, and they sheltered there during the rest of the day and the long night. When the afternoon edition of the *Biddeford Daily Journal* reported "25 Homes Burned, Goose Rocks Beach Threatened," it was already obsolete news.

Even while Goose Rocks Beach burned the fire was racing toward Cape Porpoise. Carolyn and Frank Craig lived in Cape Porpoise, a part of Kennebunkport but a comfortable little community in its own right. On Monday when the fire whistle had blown for the North Kennebunkport fire, Frank was painting their house, a small 1829 Cape on the edge of the village. There didn't seem to be any reason for particular concern. The fire was ten miles away in another town. But Carolyn wondered about it. That autumn, walking out behind their house where a good many trees had been cut down during the war years, she had noticed the dryness of the debris left from the cutting.

That Tuesday morning she had looked out the kitchen window and said, "Frank, that column of smoke is a huge, great column. I've never in my life seen anything like it. Come and look." But the smoke appeared to be over the town line in Biddeford, and Frank went back to his painting.

As the day wore on cinders began to fall on his paint. "I'm going to have to stop painting," he told Caroyln, and she, having noticed the unusual amount of traffic going by the house—cars and firetrucks headed toward the fire station in the square, said, "I think we'd better get busy and find out what's going on." They hadn't heard about Goose Rocks Beach.

They drove down to the fire station where Carolyn waited with their infant son, Alan, while Frank rode out on Route 9 toward Goose Rocks Beach with some other men to see just where the fire was. When he came back, his face was white. "It's terrible," he said. "Houses are burning up there. It's burnt the Williams farm and it's running toward Goose Fare Farm. We'd better get home."

At Goose Fare Farm, a fine eighteenth-century house on Route 9 high above the Batson River marshes and the sea, Martin Wildes, Arnold Stinson, Charlie Nedeau, Frank Thompson, Cliff Seavey, and a whole crew of local firemen were wetting down the house and loading furniture into a truck. Even as they worked, a mattress on top of the pile caught fire from a flying ember. There seemed little hope of saving the house. Although the Clock Farm, a Kennebunkport landmark near Goose Rocks Beach, had been saved, the Hutchins house had burned and the Williams place. Thoady Goodwin, who lived at Goose Fare Farm, went to the barn and unhooked his cow and horse. He slapped each on the stern and said, "You're on your own." The next day when he was told his was one of the houses that had not burned, he couldn't believe it. When he went back, his horse and cow were waiting for him at the barn door.

In Cape Porpoise village, people now knew of the danger. The

Craigs backed their old Dodge panel truck up to their house and began loading it with some of the things they were least willing to lose. There would not be room in the truck for all of their furniture. But before they had finished, another truck pulled in off the road. "Can I help you move some furniture?" the driver asked. He was a stranger, one of the many people who had come to Kennebunkport to help evacuate families and their possessions. With his help the Craigs were able to take most of their furniture to a garage at Kennebunk Landing.

People from every city and hamlet within twenty-five miles of Kennebunkport had responded to its call for help. An army of firefighters had descended on the town, professional firemen from all over southern Maine and New Hampshire and from towns as far away as Amesbury, Massachusetts, and Skowhegan, Maine. Governor Hildreth had ordered out two National Guard companies. The navy sent men and equipment from Portland, and that Tuesday night eighty soldiers, medics among them, arrived from Fort Williams in Portland. The Coast Guard cutter *Laurel* came into the mouth of the Kennebunk River to evacuate people, if necessary, and to run fire hose lines ashore. Coast Guardsmen and equipment arrived from the stations at Cape Elizabeth, South Portland, and Biddeford Pool.

In the selectmen's office upstairs over the village fire station Road Commissioner Cliff Maling had gotten the job of directing men and equipment where they were needed. With the telephone ringing constantly, and only messengers to help him communicate with men in the field, his was a difficult task.

Across the street Thelma Burrows had made a corn chowder. Town Clerk Walter Goodwin, who also served on the Board of Health, had come to Thelma that morning with two or three elderly evacuees. "What am I going to do?" he had said. "These people have to stay somewhere. Could you take them in? Could you make a corn chowder or something for them?"

Later her neighbor Leona Thompson came in. She had been through a serious forest fire in Kennebunkport in 1930 and had some idea of what was going to be needed. "What are we going to do about sending food out to the firefighters?" she asked. Thelma was ready to help. Sandwiches would have to be made, and the men would have to have something besides coffee to drink. The women set to work, calling neighbors and friends, asking them to cook, asking them to help at Thelma's where hot meals would be ready for the men when they came in from the fire line.

Frances Landry taught at the Cape Porpoise school on the Mills Road, as Route 9 was known locally, between Cape Porpoise and Goose Rocks Beach. It had been a strange and upsetting day. Since mid-morning mothers had been taking their children away, first the women from Goose Rocks Beach, now those from Cape Porpoise. The village was evacuating. Efforts to turn the advancing fire away from the village toward the sea had failed.

Miss Landry waited until the last of her class had been taken care of and then in tears hurried home to the Cape Porpoise house where she and her eight brothers and sisters had grown up. Most of them had been born in the house, which their father built. The Landrys went to Kennebunkport village to stay with relatives and were not to know until the next morning that their house did not burn.

Many Cape Porpoise families had relatives or friends in the area who took them in, but some went to stay at the Nonantum and Old Fort Inn, summer hotels, which had been reopened, at the request of the Red Cross, to shelter them. Furniture was stored at the town hall and in garages, and in a Rogers Fibre Company warehouse in Kennebunk. Some Langsford Road families retreated to Pinkham Island in Cape Porpoise harbor. By late afternoon most of the inhabitants of Cape Porpoise had left. Those who were still there were there to fight the fire.

The fire burned along Route 9, reaching where there was fuel to burn—whether houses or trees, burning arbitrarily, taking Arthur Welch's house, leaving his neighbor's. It split, part of it burning off toward Nessler's Point. Some firefighters thought their prayers had been answered when advancing flames would suddenly veer away or even burn back the way they had come, but others believed it was their own grit that saved their homes and ultimately their village.

Firefighters were everywhere. The Portland and South Portland fire departments were in the square. The Kittredge brothers were out on the Pier Road to fight flames that came their way. About five o'clock a shift in the wind turned the fire from its advance on the square, and sent it into the woods behind a row of houses that lined Main Street from the junction of Route 9 to Crow Hill. One of these was the Craig house.

The Main Street houses and the woods behind them had been thoroughly wet down. When the water supply in the town system was exhausted from the demands made on it that day, water had been supplied by a Merrill Transport Company tank truck, which had come out from Portland. The Craigs were lucky: there had been just enough water to wet down their house and one more beyond it toward Crow Hill.

Frank Craig and six other men stood between his house and the edge of the woods where the fire was burning. He admitted later that if the other men had not stayed, "I don't think I'd have had the courage to." Roaring like a locomotive the flames hit the tops of the trees. The heat was so intense that the men threw themselves on the ground to save their faces. It looked as if the fire would take the Craig house, but instead it took a backward sweep along a little gully and then went on toward Crow Hill.

It left behind piles of burning debris and spot fires in the grass around the house. Where the fire had passed in the woods, flames sprang up in old tree stumps, having followed root systems underground. With no water, Frank, in desperation, brought ketchup, milk, vinegar—anything wet—from the house, even sopping water from the toilet bowl to pour on the more stubborn flames.

Althea and Frank Beard lived in Cambridge, Massachusetts, where Frank was studying at Harvard. Their summer home was at Cape Porpoise. They had heard that afternoon about the fire and decided to drive to Maine to see if their cottage and the neighboring cottages of friends and relatives were safe.

It was a beautiful, warm day. Coming north along Route 1, nearing Maine, they saw on the horizon what looked like clouds and thought, "It's going to rain. What is everybody worried about?" They soon realized they were not seeing clouds, but a bank of smoke.

It was late afternoon when they arrived at Kennebunk's Cooper's Corner and found the road into Kennebunkport blocked off and guards patrolling to keep all unauthorized vehicles out of the town. The curious had been flocking to the area, jamming the roads, hampering the progress of fire trucks and tankers bringing desperately needed water. The Beards left their car on the side of the road and set out on foot for Cape Porpoise.

They hurried through Kennebunkport Village: through Dock Square, up Spring Street, along elm-lined Maine Street with its fine homes of early nineteenth-century sea captains and merchants and the small, brick custom house, now a library, where they had registered their ships and cargoes. The Beards took the turn onto School Street, a two-mile stretch to Crow Hill and Cape Porpoise.

In the gathering dusk they could see the rosy glow of the fire ahead of them on the horizon. They were heading right for the fire; but, surely, if they could get to their cottage, on the water's edge, they would be safe. They could go into the ocean there if need be. They ran, walked, and jogged along School Street. Althea never knew her legs would go so fast.

Approaching Crow Hill, they saw a line of men silhouetted against the red sky. The firefighters had gathered on top of the hill with their trucks and hose to make a stand. The Beards hurried on, noticing as they passed two firemen on the roof of one small house putting out flying embers as they landed on the house. On the left behind the big, old Curtis farmhouse, beyond a field, beyond a grove of pines, the fire was coming. Hose crisscrossed the road. They stepped over it and went on down the hill toward the village, finding their way through the smoke to the Ward Road on the right, away from the fire.

Hap Smith, caretaker of their cottage, lived on Ward Road. They found him and his family in the dooryard of their little white house, their furniture loaded into two trucks, about to leave for a son's home in Sanford. "Don't go down to the cottage," said Hap. "It's gone." A tongue of the fire had found its way around the far side of Cape Porpoise and reached Fisher's Lane.

So the cottage was gone. It was a sad loss. The large, clapboarded house and another next to it had been built by Frank's grandfather. It had been a beautiful vacation spot there on the water's edge, with a tennis court, gardens, separated from the rest of the village by a stretch of wooded land. There didn't seem to be much point in going on to view the ruins, so Frank and Althea went with the Smiths back to Kennebunkport, taking the Wildes District Road, which was still open, past the turn to Land's End, down toward Turbat's Creek, following the curving ocean drive, past Walker's Point, and the impressive colony of turn-of-the-century summer homes on Cape Arundel.

Back on Crow Hill, Cliff Seavey and the other firefighters waited for the fire. They had a hose truck with a pumper on it and had been wetting down the pine trees behind the Curtis house for more than an hour. If the trees were wet enough—if the flames could not get started in the grove—the men thought they had a good chance of stopping the fire there.

But the fire came so fast, traveling with its own wind, that it could not be stopped. The flames hit the pine trees and swept right through them as if they had not been wet down at all. The firemen didn't even have time to reel in their hose. They cut it off with an axe and drove the truck back, away from the flames.

Cliff Seavey had watched the fire come. It had looked like a small tornado coming up the back of Crow Hill, a funnel of cinders, flames, and smoke. It had looked like a picture of a water spout he'd seen as a boy in a school geography book. It came over the brow of the hill and seemed for a moment to disappear into the air before it was over the hill and down into a cluster of houses on the other side, heading toward Paddy's Creek, Land's End, and the Wildes District. Beyond that it would have an easy run through Buttonwood into Kennebunkport Village.

Out at Land's End Anne Louise Perkins was packing her car. From overhead the pilot of a small plane had warned her with a bullhorn that she had about thirty minutes to get out before her escape would be cut off. What should she take? She chose warm clothing—winter was coming—leaving family heirlooms and treasures behind. The plane came back, the pilot warning her that she had twenty minutes, and then ten. "Take the back way if you can," he called down, seeing from the air that she had a choice. When at last she left, the smoke was so thick she could not see the front of her car, and she didn't know whether she would get through or whether she would meet a solid wall of flame. She got through and from Kennebunkport went on to the Rockingham Hotel in Portsmouth, New Hampshire, for the night. That night the moon shone blood red behind the smoke. It was to shine red for three nights, and every night she looked at it and prayed for it to go back to normal.

At 7:30 that evening *Portland Press Herald* staff writer Harry Foote took off from Portland airport in a plane piloted by Milton Smith. They flew down the coast toward Kennebunkport to view the fire from the air. Foote's account of what they saw appeared in the *Press Herald* the next morning.

"Ahead of us rose a long sweeping curve of rosy-tinted smoke. We approached at about 1,800 feet altitude. The air, clear over Portland, soon grew foggy with smoke." They flew in over Biddeford and saw a "wide, curving arc of flames . . . eating steadily nearer and nearer to the bright, blinking lights of the city." This fire front appeared small compared to the Kennebunkport fire, but "it was burning virtually unchecked, and along so long a line that a shift of wind could have sent it quickly sweeping in on the southwest side of Biddeford hardly more than a mile away." To the west "was a bright but broken line of flame in the town of North Kennebunkport. It marked the back side of the fire—the general area in which it gained its start Monday afternoon. It still had plenty of life."

Smith and Foote flew over the gray, no-man's-land of burned acreage between North Kennebunkport's fire front and the fire in Kennebunkport. No house lights blinked in the charred, smoking, deserted landscape, only, here and there, the "winking orange dots of fire scattered across it." The men were close enough to see "for the first time the full face of the fire. In a long, straight unbroken line that ran southeast-northwest, the fire was eating its way south." Smith estimated the line of the fire to be eight miles long without a visible break from its beginning to the coast, and that at the coast the smoke cloud rose seven thousand to eight thousand feet.

The plane made a pass over Cape Porpoise at about twelve hundred feet, and Foote saw a house on the outer edge of the fire burning. "The flames were going straight up, sucked up by the draft of the roaring woods around it." Through the smoke he could see other houses, behind the fire front, still burning, "big orange blobs of color in the gray and black. Over my shoulder, the moon, which had been a beautiful silver in Portland, had been turned a reddish yellow by smoke."

Smith turned the plane for a final run to look at the blaze, this time at only six hundred feet, and the "heavy [Grumman] amphibian bounced and shook in the hot rough air from the fire." Looking down, they could clearly see that since their last pass, the fire had jumped a hundred feet to another house, setting it aflame. In other places "the fire had leaped out about three hundred yards in front of the line of flame to set fire to patches of brush and woodland." The two men speculated about the desperate struggle going on below them and agreed that "the men who fought the blaze were doing a heroic thing." To Foote "it seemed impossible that men alone, without the help of God, could stop so huge a blaze."[3]

Below them Martin Wildes was fighting the fire. When he had heard that it was headed into Cape Porpoise, he had quit work and gone out to fight it. He had seen some amazing things since then: houses still standing while everything around them was burned, flames that seemed to be burning the very air itself—burning in the air over a creek from one bank to the other with no break, like a blowtorch. Later he didn't hesitate to admit he'd been scared. "Everybody was. Everybody thought the world had come to an end."

Althea and Frank Beard had gone to the Kennebunk Inn five miles from Kennebunkport and taken a room for the night. At dinner in the dining room at the inn, they talked about the good times they had had at Cape Porpoise. Thinking that they had better call Frank's Aunt Betty in Chicago, who owned the cottage next to theirs, they decided suddenly, "Let's go back and see if we can see the place." The fire would have passed by now.

They retraced their steps, leaving the car at Cooper's Corner, walking to School Street where this time they got a ride with Dick and Hazel Davis who were going back to see if their Cape Porpoise home had burned. No one knew yet just what had happened at the Cape, what had burned and what hadn't.

This time Crow Hill was deserted. The firemen with their trucks and equipment had gone around the hill to fight the fire on the other side toward the Wildes District. The big Curtis farmhouse and all of the houses on top of the hill were gone except the small house where the two firemen had been on the roof beating out falling embers.

But Cape Porpoise village itself was intact and surprisingly peaceful. The Davises found their house on the Pier Road safe. The Beards left them there and continued down the Pier Road on foot, turning onto the narrow end of Allen Road, which wound around the base of Stone Haven Hill. It was the back way to their cottage and beyond that Fisher's Lane.

It was dark and smoky, and then suddenly ahead of them they saw a flare-up of flames—bushes on fire—and a man whacking away at them. They raced to help him. It was George Gifford, a summertime neighbor. "The houses are standing! The houses are standing!" he cried. "Thank heavens you're here. It's all right. I'm so glad you're here."

The fire had taken a house on Fisher's Lane, but the wind had shifted before it reached Allen Road, sending it toward the Pier Road where one house burned. The Giffords had arrived from Massachusetts in time to fight the small after-fires and blowing, burning leaves and embers, which could still have set the Allen Road cottages on fire. That danger was not over.

The Beards and Giffords worked until dawn, beating out smoldering hummocks of grass at the edge of the marsh, battling flare-ups in bushes, watching for sparks that might land on the roofs of the cottages. The only water they had came from the ocean—faucets were dry all over Cape Porpoise. Luckily the tide was in, and they filled buckets and set them up and down the road, ready to douse erupting flames that the wind could whip into a raging inferno.

In the woods above Wildes Town, firemen were fighting the same weary battle. After crossing Crow Hill and burning seventeen more Cape Porpoise houses and reaching out to Land's End where it burned the Perkins place, the fire had moved on into a wooded area above the Wildes District settlement.

Less than a mile away Kenneth Roberts, who had not had time to get a new pond dug at Rocky Pasture, stood on his porch and told a New York City reporter, "It's terrible. There are caravans of people fleeing with their clothes and household goods from Cape Porpoise. The fire is almost impossible to get at because it's moving through the tops of the trees. Behind is another, slower moving ground fire. Both are going like Hell."[4]

If it was not stopped, if the wind did not shift, it would sweep right on into historic Kennebunkport with its fine, architecturally important houses. In the selectmen's office over the fire station Cliff Maling told newspaper reporters, "We've already lost the lower part of Cape Porpoise, and we need everything we can get to save this town."

At her father-in-law's house in Kennebunkport village Carolyn Craig stood on the lawn and looked at the red sky toward Cape Porpoise and the Wildes District. Every now and then flames would shoot up, just like a torch, and she would know another house had gone.

Families in the village, many of them sheltering friends and relatives from Goose Rocks Beach and Cape Porpoise, had packed their cars with important possessions. They too were ready to flee. Some hadn't waited to hear whether the firemen had been able to stop the fire, but had sent irreplaceable family heirlooms away to safety. Some of these were never to come back to Kennebunkport, remaining in the hands of family members who lived "away." The town waited.

A change in the wind and a backfire finally stopped the advance of the fire. Just before midnight an exhausted Cliff Maling cautiously reported that the blaze had "pretty well burned out." But Fire Chief John Eldridge pointed out that the fate of the town depended on the pre-dawn winds. "If the wind blows in toward the town, we'll be right back where we started before we fought the thing to a standstill. Right now it's temporarily controlled."[5]

Fresh volunteers, who were still arriving, were sent to relieve weary firefighters, who came into town for food and to sleep. At Thelma Burrows's and at the Arundel Grange Hall they found a hot meal—corn chowder, fish chowder, beef stew. They slept wherever they could lie down—on the floor of the selectmen's office, in the firehouse, on the lawns of nearby houses.

In Augusta Austin Wilkins said the Kennebunkport fire was "the worst in the history of the Forestry Service." It had damaged an estimated five hundred thousand board feet of young pine, as well as consuming many cords of wood that were already cut and ready for market. An early count of houses lost was shocking. About a hundred had burned at Goose Rocks Beach, half of the total number there. Thirty-two had burned at Cape Porpoise. Fifty had been lost in other parts of town. It was a terrible accounting. And the fire was not out yet.

NOTES
1. Gertrude Mackenzie with Ruth Goode, *My Love Affair with the State of Maine* (Camden, Me.: Down East Books, 1997).
2. "Graphic Description of Recent Disastrous Fires in 4 Kennebunks," a paper prepared by Caroline Wallace and read at the annual meeting of the Kennebunk Fire Society, November 11, 1947, and later printed in the *Kennebunk Star*.
3. Henry T. Foote, "Kennebunkport Fire Dwarfs Devastation Seen at Okinawa, Declares Eyewitness," *Portland Press Herald*, October 22, 1947.
4. *New York Herald Tribune*, October 22, 1947.
5. *Miami Herald*, October 22, 1947.

Chapter IV:
The Common Enemy

At midnight on that Tuesday, October 21, Forest Commissioner Rendall, looking back over the day, named it the worst in the history of forest fires in the state of Maine. It had been a Class 5 fire day, the highest classification for forest fire danger. Only four or five days of steady, drenching rain could relieve the hazard, but no rain was forecast.

Governor Hildreth had issued a second proclamation, which was to take effect at sunrise on the twenty-second, prohibiting all hunting, fires, and smoking in any of Maine's woods. Under this decree the hunting that had been allowed in open areas and along waterways by the proclamation on October 17 was prohibited. Hildreth's announcement came just as the deer season opened in Maine's six northern counties. Although the governor was careful to point out that "there is no evidence that the hunters caused the fire situation," still it was his judgment that "hunting is likely to increase such menace and fire hazard."

It was the first time in thirty years that the deer season had been interrupted because of forest fire danger. Sporting camp owners began sending telegrams all over the East canceling reservations that had been made months before. They stood to lose over a million dollars, but the fires that were burning in Maine justified the ban.

On Wednesday morning the *Portland Press Herald* devoted its whole front page to fire stories. Kennebunkport's incredible losses dominated the news, but there were other fires, many of them serious, covering wide areas, out of control, and burning houses. Newsmen were hard pressed to cover all the stories, and fires that would normally have rated lead stories were accorded brief articles.

The worst were in the southern and central parts of the state, but there were fires in the north too. There were ten in Aroostook County. One of them, at Madawaska, was heading toward the town of Grand Isle. A Caribou fire had started from sparks from a nearby field where potato tops were being burned, and had destroyed a fine stand of cedars.

Five fires were burning in Washington County. The worst of these, at Centerville, had been fought down after burning 250 acres, but broke out again and spread to within a quarter of a mile of the village of Jonesboro, where five hundred residents were evacuating. On another front this fire was reaching toward Whitneyville where a crew was standing by to wet down millions of board feet of lumber stacked in the Crane Lumber Company yard.

On Mount Desert Island where firefighters had patrolled the edges of a hundred-acre burn all weekend, a new small fire had started up outside the fire line early on Tuesday morning and had quickly become a fast moving, uncontrollable fire that by sundown was a threat to three or four island settlements, including Bar Harbor.

Down the coast at Lincolnville a fire was burning on the side of Mount Megunticook. At Wiscasset, where three small brush fires were thought to have been set, police were looking for "two young men in a car."

A dump fire in the town of Madison in central Maine had jumped its bounds and quickly spread into Norridgewock, burning three farms and sending deer and other wild animals racing out of the forest. Farther south, at Westbrook, sparks from the town dump set fire to a tool shed in a nearby quarry and spread from there into woods.

At East Livermore in Androscoggin County, a costly fire that began in the early afternoon on Tuesday was thought to have been started by a cigarette carelessly thrown from a passing car. Shortly after one o'clock Irene Randall had gone outside to tell her husband, who was splitting wood for the winter, that she had finished not only the lunch dishes, but her fall housecleaning as well. They stood talking, enjoying the sun and the beautiful afternoon, for it was another glorious, cloudless day, until he said, "I smell wood smoke." There was smoke on the horizon toward the schoolhouse a quarter of a mile away. Jumping into the car, they drove to the school and found a fire burning in the grass behind it. The fire department had already arrived, and the young teacher, Jacqueline Mitchell, with flames only thirty feet from the schoolhouse, had led her twenty-eight pupils from the building and sent them home.

Although the cause of the fire was to be officially listed as unknown, it had started near Jug Hill Road, and it was thought locally that someone in a passing car had tossed out a lighted cigarette butt. Although the firemen ran with their hose to try to stop the flames, the blaze spread to tall pine trees. Even so, the men kept the fire from burning nearby houses, which escaped with only a few burned roof shingles. Not until the water supply ran out did the fire have its way. By then the wind had shifted and was pushing the flames toward Highland Lake and the Maine Methodist Church Conference's summer campground.

Irene Randall had gone for safety with her children and the family dog to her in-laws' house a few miles away. That evening, looking toward the campground, she thought everything there must be on fire. It was: the beautiful pine grove and fifty buildings, including the tabernacle, were being destroyed. Five hundred firefighters, including men from Jay, Readfield, Fayette, Farmington, and Livermore Falls, as well as high-school boys, and even high-school girls, who under the leadership of the plucky Miss Mitchell coupled hose and manned hose lines, had not been able to stop the fire.

From the campground the fire raced on, leaping the Livermore-Fayette Road, burning six large farms—houses, barns, and livestock. At midnight when Kennebunkport firefighters were cautiously saying they had stopped their fire, the East Livermore blaze was still out of control and burning on a ten-mile front toward the town of Wayne.

Another serious fire had burned that day at Brunswick. Fifteen hundred firefighters from seven communities had battled a blaze that started around 11 A.M. in grass behind the town dump on the town's northern outskirts. The firemen had it almost checked when suddenly it broke away "like a scared jackrabbit," and with forty-mile-an-hour winds behind it headed toward Jordan Avenue, threatening homes there.

It was a vicious, unpredictable fire. Howard Sylvester and Kenneth Knight, experienced firemen from the Brunswick Fire Department, were laying the first five hundred feet of hose along Jordan Avenue when they were cut off by flames. Turning the nozzle on the end of the hose to get a fog spray so they could breathe, they worked their way out of the path of the fire. The hose had to be abandoned to the flames, but the men escaped.

Such danger, such heroism was not rare. Later that afternoon the wind veered, sending the flames toward the Brunswick-Topsham

Water District station where, despite smoke and flames and intense heat, employees Armand Lavoie and Alphonse Gagnon stayed on duty to keep pumps going to provide water for the firefighters. Two storage sheds and $18,000 worth of equipment were burned at the station, but these losses, and the hose given up to the fire on Jordan Avenue, seemed insignificant considering that two hundred homes on Jordan Avenue could have gone, as well as buildings at the University of Maine Annex and at the Naval Air Station, which were threatened. The fire was finally stopped at the air base about 5 P.M. where firefighters, aided by the closely cropped grass and wide runways, were able for the first time to make a stand.

Fires were burning in Oxford County too. At Welchville the Edmand Daniels family battled a grass fire with brooms to within twenty-five feet of their home before the fire department came. At Canton a Tuesday fire burned more than thirty-five acres of meadowland and was still burning on Wednesday morning.

Another Oxford County fire was at Fryeburg. About two o'clock Tuesday afternoon Carleton Merrill, state warden for District 2, received a call from the Pleasant Mountain lookout tower telling him a fire was burning in the Oak Hill section of Fryeburg. A week-old ground fire, burning in scrub oak, jack pine, berry bushes, and slash left by a logging operation five years before, which had been contained and patrolled by the Fryeburg Fire Department, finally had broken through the fire lines. When Merrill arrived, he found the fire burning fast before a strong wind.

Neighboring Brownfield was one of the towns to send men and equipment to the Fryeburg fire. Brownfield had organized a volunteer fire department just that spring, and at a special town meeting the townspeople had voted to raise $5,000 to equip it with a second-hand truck for transportation, two gasoline pumpers, three thousand feet of hose, portable one-man Indian pumps, axes, and shovels. With enough hose to reach any building in Brownfield from its nearest water supply, and supplementary equipment available from the state's storehouse at Lovell, the firemen felt they could serve their town well. And they had, putting out one forest fire that summer, and saving two homes.

The wind that drove the Fryeburg fire had also brought a fire into York County from Wakefield, New Hampshire. Mike Ferguson at the Ossipee Hill tower had seen it start up that morning on the New Hampshire side of Province Mountain, and after alerting New Hampshire officials, he tried to contact Clayton Weymouth whose district would be involved if the northwest wind brought the fire over into Newfield. It took Ferguson three hours to find Weymouth, who was on the Biddeford fire line.

Weymouth headed for the storehouse at Alfred to pick up the equipment he knew would be needed in Newfield. His home was in Newfield, so he knew the town's firefighting equipment consisted of a few Indian pumps. At the Alfred storehouse he learned that another bad fire had developed in Waterboro near Ross Corner. When Weymouth had been called to the North Kennebunkport fire, he had left the Shapleigh-Waterboro fire front under control. The blaze that had begun near Poverty Pond on Friday the seventeenth had been stopped and held on that first day, but the next day around one o'clock Mike Ferguson had spotted another fire near Shy Beaver Pond, three miles to the east of Poverty Pond. This fire, officially listed as of unknown origin, was thought to be an extension of the first blaze. It spread quickly, feeding on pitch pine and blueberry bushes on the Shapleigh and Waterboro plains. By evening the fire line around the twelve-hundred-acre burn was so long the firefighters on hand couldn't patrol it effectively. Bulldozers were brought in to create a firebreak, but before they could get all the way around the fire, it jumped again. Not until Monday did the firemen feel they had it under control, and by then it had burned about twenty-five hundred acres, threatening Newfield, and on the south reaching almost to Waterboro's Ross Corner. Now, on Tuesday, Ferguson was reporting a fresh outbreak near Ross Corner.

Weymouth drove to Ross Corner with shovels, grub hoes, and rakes, and then headed for Newfield, arriving around 3:30. He found that the Province Mountain fire had crossed the state line and burned about a mile into the west side of town. It was traveling fast and headed toward a bad slash lot.

Weymouth's first thought was to get help fast. He tried to reach Carleton Merrill, but Merrill was busy at the Fryeburg fire in his own district. Weymouth called six fire departments, but found all were either out on fires or unable to leave their own towns. Only nearby Limington was able to respond immediately to Newfield's need.

The fire had already passed through Stevens Corner and was headed for Mee's Corner. There at Drew Pond the Limington men and a group of men from Newfield, among them Arthur Moulton, decided to make a stand. They had a portable pump and there was plenty of water. It seemed a logical place to try to stop the fire.

The Newfield men had been fighting the fire south of their village at Poverty Pond when they had heard about the more serious fire that was coming in on the northwest. They left the Poverty Pond blaze, which was heading away from Newfield toward Waterboro and Shapleigh, to other firefighters, and drove to Stevens Corner and from there to Drew Pond. There they waited—an hour, two hours—for the fire to come through. Later Moulton admitted, "That was our first mistake. We should have backfired right there. If we had understood the thing, if we had backfired. . . ."

Backfiring—setting a controlled fire ahead of a wildfire and letting the two burn together, the principle being that the area already burned would not burn again—was an effective measure to use against forest fire, but it was not used without careful thought, for it was dangerous. Sometimes a backfire ended up burning more than the wildfire it had been set to control. (Given responsibility to start a backfire to stop a tongue of the Centerville blaze near Cherryfield, Alton Tracey found it "the hardest thing I ever had to do in my life." Considering the dry conditions, he understood the chance he was taking.) Many men were unwilling to backfire without the sanction of a town or state fire warden who would take responsibility for the consequences. Backfiring was also illegal. Since colonial days it had been against the law for anyone to deliberately set a fire on land near or adjoining woods without a permit.[1]

The men did not backfire at Drew Pond. They set up their pump and waited for the fire to come. It came, at a tremendous speed, crowning in pine trees, then falling to the ground to burn a distance and then, when it reached another stand of dry trees, crowning again and leaping forward. It burned with intense heat and sent clouds of smoke before it. The men at Drew Pond had no face masks. They began to choke. They didn't think they could survive without masks, and the fire was coming too fast. They shut off their pump, dumped it into the pond so it wouldn't burn, and ran for their lives.

Not until that night when the wind dropped were the weary men able to make an effective stand. They stopped the fire on the Sanborn Road south of Mee's Corner in open fields where it was manageable. Miraculously, no Newfield houses burned that day. Some had been saved by firefighters, but others had survived because they were surrounded by mown fields or pastures cropped close by livestock. With the flames under control, firebreaks could be bulldozed. The pump was retrieved from Drew Pond, and the men had time to get something to eat and to rest. The worst seemed to be over for Newfield.

That night neighboring Waterboro's trial by fire really began. Liz and Champ Gould had a dairy farm on the Ossipee Hill Road just north of South Waterboro village. Ross Corner lay to the west. To the north was Ossipee Hill, Waterboro Center, and North Waterboro, and to the northeast the settlement of East Waterboro. The Goulds were newcomers to town, who had bought their farm in 1946, so when Jim Roberts, a neighbor, had stopped by a few days before and told them, "There's a fire up on the blueberry plains near Poverty Pond," Champ had asked, "Should I go volunteer to help fight it?"

"No," advised Roberts. "Stick around here. When they want you, they'll call you."

The Goulds had driven over to see the place beside the road where the fire had started and then fanned out. They had seen the smoke where it was mulling away on the plains. It hadn't looked like much of a fire. So they were not concerned, although they knew how dry conditions were. Champ had been trying to plow the field below the barn and found the ground too hard to lay up proper furrows. And although they did not have water problems themselves, for their four-thousand-gallon system was gravity fed from deep springs, others did. Wells were going dry.

On Tuesday they knew that the Poverty Pond fire was still burning and had spread, and they had heard about the fire at Kennebunkport and the homes lost there, but they didn't see any reason to draw a parallel between the two fires. They went to Portland to do some errands.

That afternoon, coming south out of Portland they saw the smoke in the sky over Kennebunkport, and to the west the pall of smoke from what they thought was the blueberry plains fire. But when they reached Hollis and made the turn in the road toward home, they knew from the position of the smoke that the fire had burned on beyond the plains. "That's Ossipee now!" exclaimed Liz.

Indeed, the fire had spread and was out of control. If it was not stopped, it could go on to South Waterboro and to heavily-wooded Ossipee Hill. If it got to timber and crowned, it could go over the hill to North Waterboro, Waterboro Center, and East Waterboro.

The most immediate concern was for South Waterboro. Long-time residents there remembered the fire of July 1911 that had begun west of the village and been carried by the wind to houses on the outskirts where it had jumped from roof to roof, catching easily on the dry wood shingles. Fifty-four homes, stores, the post office, Grange hall, Baptist Church, and the railroad station had burned.[2] People remembered how little time there had been to save possessions. Now cars were packed with bedding, clothing, family silver—whatever was judged important.

The Goulds' farm lay between the fire and the village. Their first thought was to try to save their place, but they weren't sure what to do. Liz drove down the road to the Thompsons' to learn their plans. She found Lewis, Evelyn, and Gib Thompson raking leaves away from their house. They had ladders up against the building and were wetting down the roof with pails of water. "What should I do?" Liz asked, and was told: "Go home and do anything you can that you think will help when the fire comes close."

At home she and Champ got out the garden hose and hooked it up to wet down the house. They would have plenty of water, and luckily, except for the cupola, the barn roof was steel. They would have to watch the well house, the hog house, and the chicken coop. Liz telephoned her father in West Kennebunk and asked him to come for their two oldest children. She would keep the youngest with her. She asked her father to bring his rifle.

There were sixteen head of cattle in the barn. The Goulds had no way to truck them away or any place to take them. They had a choice of turning them loose to fend for themselves or shooting them and had decided to be ready to shoot them. The cows, smelling the smoke, were frantic, blatting, stamping in their stalls, and pulling on their chains. Champ closed the doors to the barn, gave them grain, and turned on the radio. They calmed down, comforted by the radio that was always played at milking time, shut away from the smoke and the confusion in the farmyard. A horde of firefighters had arrived with South Waterboro's firetruck.

Fire Chief Alva Werren thought the fire would get to within a mile of South Waterboro village by 1 A.M. A stand was to be made at the Gould farm. Werren said, "There's a good chance we can't stop it. If we don't, it will reach the center of the village about 10 A.M. Wednesday."[3] But the fire didn't reach the Gould farm that night. At 11 P.M. word came that it had broken through on the road farther on toward Waterboro Center, and some of the firemen raced off with the truck. Some stayed to watch through the long night with Liz and Champ. Nerves, excitement, and plenty of coffee kept them awake.

On Wednesday morning Champ took the tractor and plowed fire-breaks around some of the buildings. He carried four barrels of antique dishes out to the middle of the plowed garden and covered them with wet canvas. Liz put food and a milk can full of water in the back of their panel truck and went through their clothes, thinking, "Winter's coming. We've got to have coats. We've got to have warm clothes." She collected pictures, the kids' birth certificates, other legal papers, and the old English blunderbuss—that wasn't going to go up in smoke—and put it all in the truck. There was no way to take any furniture. If the house burned, it would too. There were things she'd hate to lose, but if they burned, they burned.

Another concern for Liz was feeding the firefighters. She had shopped in Portland so she had coffee and sugar and a big pot roast. She got out the copper wash boiler and made beef stew. She brought up canned vegetables from the cellar, and there was a good supply of their own bacon, ham, and eggs to feed the hungry men.

Some of the men were acquaintances from town, but many were from distant towns and cities. There were high-school boys from Portsmouth, firemen from Auburn, Cape Elizabeth, and Portland—strangers in unfamiliar territory. The driver of one truck wheeled into the yard and called, "Where's your hydrants, lady?" He'd never fought fire in a town without hydrants.

This lack of a town water system was critical. Waterboro covered a wide area, much of it forested, with small farms scattered on hillsides, along wooded roads away from any substantial supply of water. Even the people in the four village centers depended on wells. South Waterboro's selectmen had made a plea over the radio for help, and a hundred oil and dairy trucks and other trucks carrying water in vats, oil drums, and milk cans had converged on the town. When they had used up the supply they brought with them, they pumped water out of the mill pond at North Waterboro and out of Little Ossipee Pond at the bridge on Route 5 outside Waterboro Center.

Stan Littlefield of Alfred borrowed the new three-hundred-gallon septic tank that sat waiting to be installed in a neighbor's yard. Littlefield and a group of men from the Alfred Fire Department loaded it onto a flatbed truck, filled the tank with water, and with a hand pump borrowed from the Sanford Water District, where Littlefield was superintendent, had a workable, if unusual, way to haul water to hot spots on back roads far removed from any water supply.

Waterboro desperately needed men to fight the fire that was

spreading north, south, east, and west. By the end of the day Wednesday, the burned area would total between four and five thousand acres. Volunteers poured in. They came from Auburn, Gray, Portland, South Portland, Cape Elizabeth, Gorham, South Windham, North Berwick, Ogunquit, Sanford, Springvale, Alfred, Kittery, and Portsmouth, New Hampshire. They included professional firemen, men who didn't know anything about firefighting and were just willing to do what they were told, college and high-school boys, and soldiers from Portland's harbor defenses.

Fire Chief George Stevens of the New England Shipbuilding Company in South Portland came with three pumpers, fifty men, ten thousand feet of hose, gasoline and oil to run the trucks, first aid supplies, and even sandwiches made by plant employees.

But equipment and men were not in themselves enough. Firefighting in Waterboro was severely hampered by problems that, while not unique, were magnified by the size of its fire. Firefighters were everywhere, on all sides of the blaze, but the effort of a crew battling to stop it at a particular road or field or to save a set of buildings or even a village, was all too often an isolated effort. As one veteran fireman said afterward, "It was little bunches of fire departments here and there and the other place cuttin' holes in it. But it always managed to go 'round."

No one had time to devise an overall plan for fighting the fire. No one person, or group of men, was in charge or coordinating the firefighting because no one knew who had that authority. Who had the ultimate responsibility? The selectmen, who were responsible by state law, or the chief of the local volunteer fire department, none of whom was trained to deal with a large fire or a large number of men? The state warden, who had no local jurisdiction, and who had to visit other fires in his district? The professional fireman, chief of a large city fire department, who knew more about fighting house fires than forest fires? The veteran firefighter, who understood forest fires and knew the local terrain, or the natural leader, who might have had military training and knew how to organize men and delegate authority? And who had responsibility for supervising the college students and high-school boys who arrived by the busload? In each town, on each fire front, men fought fiercely and well, but there was confusion, duplication of effort, and lost opportunity.

There was also no quick way to communicate along wide fire fronts. The men had no walkie-talkies or two-way radios in the firetrucks and cars. The only way to pass word from man to man and crew to crew was to travel the distance on foot or by car. This wasted precious time. Again and again men would just escape enveloping flames they hadn't known were moving in to cut off an escape route.

For two days Mike Ferguson had watched the fire spread. Wednesday was, as he wrote later in his official report, "a day of horror as the Waterboro fire raced out of control on the north side of Ossipee Hill." At 3:30 that afternoon he stood in the lookout tower with a radio technician, who was manning the tower transmitter for the state police radio network in York County, looking down at the flames racing up the hill. It was, they decided, time to leave their post. The radioman went first. Ferguson lingered about twenty minutes putting his record book and a few other things into the pack basket he carried to and from work every day. By the time he had climbed down the long tower ladder, flames were roaring through a nearby pine lot. Ferguson raced to his car. In his excitement he couldn't get the door unlocked. When at last the door was open, he couldn't get into the car: he had forgotten the pack basket on his back. When he told the story later to friends, he laughed about it.

From the top of Ossipee Hill the fire roared down toward North Waterboro, Little Ossipee Pond with its shores clustered with cottages, and Waterboro Center. One of the firefighters who fled before it was sixteen-year-old John Kelley.

Kelley lived in Portland and was a Junior at Deering High School. He had read in the newspaper about the forest fires, and one day word was passed in his industrial arts class that volunteers were needed to help fight them. Recalling his experiences years later, he said, "You can imagine the appeal this had for a high-school boy." He and some of his friends arranged to be excused from school and signed up at the Caldwell Post of the American Legion near Woodfords Corner. From there buses took volunteers to the fire areas.

On Wednesday Kelley was bused to Waterboro, and late that afternoon he and about a dozen men volunteered to go into the hills above a settlement that was probably North Waterboro. (Kelley, like many men who fought in Waterboro, was never sure afterward just what part of the town he'd been in. As Esther Smith wrote in her *Maine Life* article "The Two Waterboro Fires," "Even today people say, 'Waterboro . . . oh yes, I was out that way fighting fire in '47 but don't have any idea just where. . . .' ")

The small group of men was to make a firebreak to save a set of farm buildings. They were taken in an old dump truck up a dirt road, past some fields and a series of woods. The farm sat on top of a hill in a two-hundred-acre field. All around the field grew mature white pines. Fire was coming up the far side of the hill and, if not stopped, would reach the pine trees, crown, jump out across the field, and burn the buildings. The men were told that their job was to set a backfire, which would go down over the hill to meet the wildfire.

They set to work making a fire line on the far side of the hill down into the edge of the pine wood, scraping away flammable material down to mineral soil. After a couple of hours they had their line pretty well established and were ready to start their backfire, but the boss of the operation came rushing up and ordered everybody out of the woods fast. The fire was about to encircle the whole top of the hill, cutting off their escape.

They grabbed their tools and ran up into the field where they saw that the fire was already burning on all sides. They reached the farmhouse and their truck just as the fire came up over the edge of the hill where they had been working and crowned in the fifty- to sixty-foot pines. A crown fire is impressive. It moves like a giant ball of flame rolling across the tops of the trees, consuming them, throwing up sparks, smoke, and flame.

With the fire rolling around the perimeter of the field, the men held a hurried consultation, deciding they would have to try to break out down the dirt road, which they hoped had not been cut off. As a precaution, they doused a heavy tarpaulin with water on both sides with their Indian pumps and, after climbing into the back of the old steel-bodied dump truck, they pulled the tarp over them.

The driver started the truck down the road, going as fast as he could without losing control, careening down the narrow, bumpy, dirt road. Under the tarp the men bounced up and down, back and forth. It was a hair-raising ride. But the men in the back of the truck didn't know just how hair-raising it had been until it was over. When they reached safety at the bottom of the hill, they discovered that the paint on the front fenders and the hood of the truck was blistered and burned off, and the tarpaulin was burned full of holes. The shaken driver told them that he had driven right through the fire.

That night weary but determined men fought the fire all over Waterboro. A crew stopped it short of houses on the outskirts of Waterboro Center and, shortly after midnight, rushed to North Waterboro to cope with a fresh outbreak there. The most spectacular battle was at East

Waterboro where an estimated two thousand firefighters set a mile-long backfire to save the village. On the other end of Waterboro, off the West Road out of South Waterboro, another crew worked all night to stop and beat down a fire front that threatened that village. Not far away Liz and Champ Gould were keeping another all-night vigil.

All over Maine home owners kept watch, and crews of weary men battled to hold hard won lines at more than forty different fires. Fire had become the common enemy. The Centerville fire had burned three thousand acres, and its front was ten miles long, but it had been stopped at the edge of Jonesboro. Three thousand acres had burned in Newfield too, but only three homes had been lost, and Wednesday night the firemen there had it "mostly under control." Firefighters in Fryeburg had had a harrowing day that began at 1 A.M. when that fire, which had been considered well under control, flared up again. Five hundred men fought that stubborn blaze, and by late evening it was again under control.

The Kennebunkport fire was still not out, but was being held. The people of Kennebunkport were anxious and pessimistic. They had seen what fire could do. The destruction at Goose Rocks Beach was shocking. Evacuees and summer residents who hurried back, found row upon row of blackened chimneys rising out of smoldering ash heaps. Goose Rocks Beach looked like pictures they'd seen during the war of bombed out European cities.

National Guardsmen patrolled the streets and had set up road blocks. At the request of the selectmen, Governor Hildreth sent in the guard when it was discovered that looters had come into town and were taking plumbing from the cellars of burned houses. Only those who could prove they owned property or had relatives in town were allowed through. Mary McLean and her mother, whose cottage had burned at Goose Rocks, got past the guards only because they had had the foresight to bring the deed to their property with them.

Among those who came back that day were Shirley and Eliot O'Hara. They had been in New York when they had heard over the radio, "Eliot O'Hara School of Watercolor wiped out." They had rushed back to Maine. The completeness of the destruction of their property was hard for them to believe. Even the foundations of the studio and gallery, the dormitory and dining hall, and their own cottage had been hard to identify. Eliot's paintings—his own and others in his collection, the stacks of paper and the many boxes of painting supplies already bought for next summer's classes; indeed, everything they had left behind, was gone. In the ruins they found one small cloisonné vase, its enamel melted and blackened by the fire, which they kept. Sitting in the ashes of his studio Eliot painted a picture of Timber Island still burning, smoke spiraling into the sky, with the black chimneys and blasted trees of Goose Rocks Beach in the foreground. "Goose Rocks Beach is gone. It will never be rebuilt," predicted one year-round resident. "It will never be much of anything any more."

Wednesday night, state officials were actually encouraged because most reports coming in to them were of fires "surrounded," "deadened," and "controlled," if not out. But there were still trouble spots. The fire that had burned into Kennebunkport was still spreading on the northeast toward Biddeford. Residents at Biddeford's Five Points, among them the Emery family who had found temporary shelter in an apartment building, were warned to evacuate. And there was fear that if fire lines on the Newtown Road and the Guinea Road were not held, the fire would burn to the Saco River and jump it. If that happened, Saco's Camp Ellis would be in danger. In the Madison-Norridgewock area more than twenty-five hundred acres had already been burned, and thirty-mile-an-hour winds had brought the fire almost to the Skowhegan line. At Wayne firemen had no water and were using bulldozers and backfires to create a firebreak, but the fire was still racing out of control.

Then there was the fire on Mount Desert Island: that day it had advanced rapidly before freshening winds. By evening it had covered more than two thousand acres, causing a thirty-mile smoke trail in the sky. So far only one or two buildings had been lost to it, but Wednesday, at 2 A.M., the wind veered and began to push the fire straight for the town of Bar Harbor.

NOTES

1. Philip T. Coolidge, *History of the Maine Woods* (Bangor, Me.: Furbish-Roberts Printing Company, 1963).
2. Esther L. Smith, "The Two Waterboro Fires," *Maine Life,* October 1974.
3. "Waterboro in Path of Raging Fire," *Portland Press Herald,* October 22, 1947.

Chapter V:
Down Millionaires' Row

Christine Rowell had been coming to her summer home, Barberry Ledge, in Bar Harbor since 1918. Hers was not one of the grand houses of the town that millionaires had made famous, but it was a fine house, with five bedrooms, a separate wing for the servants, and a stone terrace shaded by pine trees and bordered by a natural garden and woods. From the terrace there was a view to the mountains of Mount Desert, and the view of Frenchman Bay from the third-floor study—a gem of a room with low bookshelves under the eaves and a fireplace—was considered by the family to be one of the best in Bar Harbor.

In 1947 Mrs. Rowell came to Barberry Ledge early, arriving the last week in May at "my dear place,"[1] as she called the house she had helped design, and where she and her husband had summered for twenty years before he died. She entertained a succession of house guests that summer, sharing with them "many a gay time." Her last guest left her at 6 A.M. on October 5. Alone and free at that glorious time of the morning to do whatever she liked, she drove to the top of Cadillac Mountain. There, with what seemed the whole world spread before her, she saw "three leaping deer taking their morning exercise." In later years her memories of that morning were to be among her most vivid of Bar Harbor. She would remember how from her terrace she had seen the first rays of the red sun strike through the green pines and the brilliant, flame-colored autumn leaves. She would remember the "beautiful and exciting" drive past fields covered with white frost, and how she had shared the view of Frenchman Bay with the graceful deer.

October was hot and dry on Mount Desert Island. Bar Harbor people knew the woods were dry, but those who thought about forest fires must have felt confident of their town's ability to cope. Unlike many Maine towns, Bar Harbor had a permanent fire chief, and its firemen were well trained. Just that May the National Park Service had held a firefighting school in Acadia National Park, which made up a large part of the island. Members of the Bar Harbor Fire Department had attended the school, whose instructors were experienced firefighters from Yellowstone Park. The Bar Harbor men had used their training in August at a Hulls Cove forest fire, and when on October 16 hunters started a fire on the northwest corner of the island, the firemen had it out before it had burned an acre.

At 4 P.M. on Friday the seventeenth, the fire department received a call from a Mrs. Gilbert, who lived on the Crooked Road near Dolliver's Dump, about seven miles from Bar Harbor. She said there was smoke coming from the cranberry bog between her house and Bill Dolliver's dump. She had seen cranberry pickers there earlier in the day and had noticed that they were smoking cigarettes. Dolliver's Dump was on the south bank of Fresh Meadow, a large bog with a heavy growth of marsh grass. Aware that the vegetation on the heath was so dehydrated that even a small fire, if not controlled immediately, could get out of hand, Fire Chief David Sleeper dispatched a 150-gallon tank truck to the scene.

The driver found the fire thirty to fifty feet off the edge of the bog directly in front of the dump. It had already burned about an acre of the dried marsh. He emptied the water in his truck on the flames and then drove to the nearest phone to call the firehouse. Chief Sleeper ordered a general forest fire alarm sounded and sent every man he had to the heath. He also called officials at Acadia Park. Although the fire was not burning in the park, they were ready to help and sent a pumper and a crew.

The fire spread rapidly. Getting water to it was difficult. The firemen were well equipped, but it was hard to drag the hose through the thick grass, and refilling the trucks was time-consuming. Learning from a nearby resident that a woods road through the Shea farm on the east side of the bog led to a brook that bordered the bog on the north, a pickup truck loaded with hose, a pump, and a crew of men was ordered to the brook. The road was already enveloped in flames, but the truck went through.

By midnight the firemen had contained the fire, which had burned a hundred acres. It was not out: there were still hot spots deep in the bog, and there was much mopping-up work to be done; but, they had stopped its spread. For the rest of the night and through the weekend water was pumped continuously on the edges of the burn and on hot spots in the bog. Around-the-clock patrols were set up.

Mrs. Rowell had heard the whistle blow and learned that the fire was near Mr. Shea's farm. Later when she saw him in the village, she asked him if he was anxious about his farm. "Oh, no," he replied. "It's not burning in the timber."

"Then I don't have to worry about you, Mr. Shea," she said.

At dawn on Tuesday morning, the twenty-first, a brisk wind sprang up from the northwest, whipping up clouds of smoke from the center of the bog. The men on duty, among them Chief Sleeper, were pumping more water onto the bog when one of the men who had been patrolling the edge of the burn came running up to report that a small blaze had sprung up about two hundred feet outside the fire line. Chief Sleeper went immediately to the spot and found a fire about a hundred feet wide, spreading with terrifying speed before the wind through a thick growth of spruce and pine. Leaving his crew to do what they could to stop it, he ran to his truck a quarter of a mile away and drove another quarter of a mile to the Shea farm where he put in a call for help to every fire department on the island. He also called Dow Field in Bangor, headquarters of the 14th Fighter Wing of the United States Army Air Force. At 7:55 A.M. the general alarm was sounded in Bar Harbor. At 8:30 a convoy of two hundred men and equipment left Dow Field for Mount Desert.

In Bar Harbor Dorothy Stanley had heard the fire whistle blow. She had already noticed the column of smoke rising high into the sky to the west. It didn't seem particularly menacing. But at the scene the firemen could not lay hose fast enough to head off the flames that spread rapidly through the spruce and pine trees, crowning forty to fifty feet in the air. By the time reinforcements arrived, the fire was completely out of hand. Bar Harbor's Great Fire was on its way.

It was headed toward the Hugh Kelly farm on Norway Drive to the southeast. There, because of several large pastures and the road, the firefighters hoped they could stop it. The men from Dow Field set up headquarters at the farm.

But the wind had filled the air with flying embers. Before anyone realized what had happened the roof of the Kelly barn was ablaze. "Run for your lives," someone shouted as the barn burst into flames, which shot high in the air. The main fire was still two hundred yards away on the west side of Norway Drive.

From the burning barn the flames spread into heavy growth on the east side of the road and from there into several acres of dry, three-year-old slash. It was mid-day. "Now," Chief Sleeper was to write in his official report, "we had a two-pronged fire of gigantic proportions. We had a fire that was a fire."

That afternoon Mrs. Rowell and a friend drove around the island. They made a circuit of the fire area, stopping to speak to men on guard along the road. All of the men were frank, saying, "We can't stop this fire." They were trying to guide it to Eagle Lake where there was plenty of water and hoped to hold it there. "If we can't, it will go to the ocean." If it went to the ocean, it would burn over Great Hill above Bar Harbor village. Barberry Ledge was on the south side of Great Hill. If the firefighters couldn't turn the fire or stop it, Barberry Ledge would be the first house on the outskirts of Bar Harbor to burn.

After dropping her friend at home, Mrs. Rowell drove back to Barberry Ledge by way of the Mountain Road. Later she wrote, "I will never forget the view as I reached the high point on the Mountain Road that looks toward the sunset at Blue Hill. A red sun was disappearing over the horizon sending up long brilliant red streams over a heavy, purple cloud. Just over my head was an enormous mass of purple, pink, orange, black and gray smoke, brilliant in the light of the setting sun, a whirling mass, funnel-shaped, driven by a strong northwest wind and beyond this whirling mass a glimpse of the peaceful background of the mainland, with the bay and the mountains like an Italian primitive painting. McFarland's Hill and Great Hill were between my house and the fire, which meant about five or six miles."

Firefighters and equipment were massed at the Eagle Lake Road to try to stop the fire there. But at four o'clock it crossed the road into Acadia Park. By 4:30 the flames appeared over the crest of McFarland's Hill. At five o'clock they were burning on a three-mile front, threatening farms along the Eagle Lake Road. While the firemen were able to save most of the buildings in its path, they could not stop the fire.

On the north it posed a threat to Hulls Cove, a small settlement of about 250 inhabitants. One of the oldest houses on the island, the Hamor house, was at Hulls Cove, as was Farnsworth's Boat Yard, where many yachts were stored for the winter. If the fire burned south, it could take the famous Jordan Pond House and Cadillac Mountain would be ravaged. It could also go to Seal Harbor, a pretty little town of white houses scattered along a blue harbor, and to Northeast Harbor with its comfortable year-round homes and summer estates on the hills above its harbor, hidden from public view by stands of pine trees, palisaded fences, stone walls, and impressive carriage houses. If the wind shifted to the east, these towns and landmarks would be spared, but the fire would go to Bar Harbor.

For years Bar Harbor had been the most famous summer resort in the state and one of the most famous on the eastern seaboard. At the height of its development in the 1890s it had rivaled Newport, Rhode Island, as a summer retreat for the wealthy who stayed in its elegant hotels or built storybook homes on the high, wooded hills and along the shore of Frenchman Bay. Railroad magnates, Turkish princes and ambassadors, as well as people like A. Atwater Kent, the radio magnate; former U.S. Representative James G. Blaine and his son-in-law Walter Damrosch, the composer and conductor of the New York Symphony; Mary Roberts Rinehart, the writer; and the Pulitzers of Pulitzer Prize fame, all owned property at Bar Harbor.

Among the grand houses were an Italian villa, a replica of a French castle built all of granite and called The Turrets, and Victorian mansions that bore deceptively simple names like The Farm, Geranium Cottage, Strawberry Hill House, and The Doll House, each with its own setting of beautifully terraced lawns approached through large tracts of natural forest.

One of the show places of Bar Harbor was Wingwood House, home of Chicago banker A. T. Stotesbury. The Stotesbury estate was on Bay Drive, the shore road between Hulls Cove and Bar Harbor, with five hundred feet of frontage on Frenchman Bay. The fifty-room Georgian Colonial (some said it had sixty rooms, some a hundred) had cost more than a million dollars to build in the 1920s. It had been designed for entertaining, with a movie projection booth, an elevator, a loudspeaker system for piping music throughout the house, and a concealed stairway leading from the Garden Room, the largest room in the house, to the owner's suite.

The Stotesburys entertained lavishly. Once they hired an orchestra and brought it by train from New York City to play for their guests. A Bar Harbor youth, walking by that afternoon on his way to Duck Brook for a swim, heard "the beautiful music," and when he passed by again later after dark on his way home, Japanese lanterns were strung out over the lawn, and he could still hear music. Perhaps the guests were dancing on the terrace that looked out over formal gardens sloping down to Frenchman Bay.

As night came on, from the mainland it looked like most of

Mount Desert Island was ablaze. Flames, bursting high in the air as they crowned in tall fir or pine trees, lit up the sky, outlining huge clouds of smoke. Shortly after dark the fire reached the Bangor Hydro-Electric Company transformer serving Mount Desert, and power went off all over the island.

Mrs. Rowell had promised to play bridge that evening with a group of women in Bar Harbor village. When she learned that they intended to meet despite the threat of the fire and the loss of electricity, saying they would use kerosene lamps and candles, she joined them. She would not be outdone by "those brave and cheerful ladies," and besides, it would be better to be with friends than to be alone. But as the evening wore on, she became restless. She was glad when at last it was time to go home. She was anxious to know what progress the fire had made. Driving home, she stopped at the turn from Eagle Lake Road to her own street, Cleftstone Road, where several men were on guard, and asked, "Where's the fire?"

"Half a mile along Eagle Lake Road." She explained that she and her cook, Mrs. Pritchard, and her maid, Elizabeth Davis, were alone at Barberry Ledge. Mr. Nolan, her gardener, and his wife lived over the garage at the end of the driveway, and they were elderly. Mrs. Rowell felt responsible for them all. "Will someone give us warning if the fire comes nearer?" she asked. The men were not sure.

She went home. In her room she lit two candles, and then proceeded to pack. She folded her dresses in one bag, put her shoes in another. She collected her important desk things, and made a package of precious photographs. She carried one bag after another down to the car, which she had left at the front door. When this was done, she opened the door into the back hall that led to the servants' quarters, but not hearing anyone stirring, closed it again, and went to her sitting room. There she lit a tiny fire in the fireplace, and "said goodbye to [her] adored things."

That night at the Mount Desert Hospital in Bar Harbor, Mrs. Welch Forbis of Southwest Harbor gave birth to a baby girl. Portable equipment had been brought in to light the delivery room. The rest of Bar Harbor was dark, except for the ominous glow in the sky. Those who had gone to bed slept uneasily.

Mrs. Rowell did not go to bed. Around 3 A.M. she heard the firehouse whistle blow again. She did not know the wind had shifted and was now driving the fire toward Bar Harbor, but she got into her car and drove again to the corner of the Eagle Lake Road. No one was there, so she waited. When a jeep filled with young men came along, she blew her horn to stop them.

"My house is there in the wood," she said. "Shall I wake the other women and be ready to leave? Will anyone give us warning?" One of the young men told her she would hear the firefighters with their equipment retreating down the Eagle Lake Road. That would be her warning. And, he added cheerfully, "I don't think the fire will get here until about noon tomorrow."

Again she returned home and this time went to the Nolans. She found them awake and frightened and wondering what they should do. "Pack at once," she told them, and helped them carry their boxes and armloads of clothing down to the car. When it was full, she wondered where she could take the things for safekeeping. They could not stay in the car, which she would need to evacuate the Nolans, Miss Davis, and Mrs. Pritchard when the time came. She wondered if the gardener of her friend, Mrs. Max Farrand, would let her leave the things in the garden house at her ocean-side estate. She drove through Bar Harbor in the morning light and found the gardener just sitting down to an early breakfast. He helped her unload the boxes and clothing from the car into the garden house.

By the time she returned to Barberry Ledge the sun was up, "a fiery red ball through the heavy smoke," and she found "poor, little Mrs. Pritchard up and dressed and feeling that the last judgment had arrived. Two young men had been to the house on motorcycles and left word to evacuate." She directed Mrs. Pritchard and Elizabeth Davis to tie up their clothing in sheets. There wasn't time to pack properly. "We'll leave at once."

But before they could leave a miracle happened: the wind shifted. Stepping outside, she discovered that "the air was sweet and the sky was blue. Birds [were singing] and a great white cloud had blown to the west." They were saved. It was an unforgettable moment. The wind shift had stopped the fire along a ten-mile front just behind Great Hill.

The Reverend Anson Williams of Bar Harbor's Maine Sea Coast Missionary Society and his wife, Margaret, lived on Pleasant Street in the village. They had slept fitfully, hearing the fire whistle blowing in the night, calling for more firefighters. Around 4:30 A.M. Mr. Williams turned on the radio and heard that the fire was burning on a wide front toward Cadillac Mountain and Bar Harbor. He got up immediately and dressed in heavy boots and an old coat and hat. He would go to the firehouse and offer his services. Before he left he told his wife, "Keep the radio on. You may have to be evacuated."[2]

Margaret Williams tried to collect her thoughts. She was terrified, but knew she must make some preparations for evacuation. She would be able to take only a few things with her. What should she pack? When it was all over, her husband would need a good suit of clothes, for he would have to make pastoral calls to comfort those who had lost homes. She went upstairs and packed a suit, a shirt, tie, socks, and a good pair of shoes. What else should she take?

She opened the cedar chest where one of their sons and his wife had stored some things. In it was her daughter-in-law's wedding gown. How often Mrs. Williams had heard her say, "If we ever have a little girl, I'd like her to be married in my wedding dress." She hesitated, knowing there were more practical things she could take, but then gave way to "sentiment . . . and carefully rolled the dress in tissue" and laid it in the suitcase.

Firefighters had been pouring into Bar Harbor. They came from Ellsworth, Brewer, Bangor—from fourteen fire departments in all, including Dow Field. So many men were sent from Dow that all but essential business was suspended on the base. The soldiers brought equipment: shovels, back tanks, trucks, bulldozers, medical supplies, canteen units, and a spotter plane with radio connections to a jeep on the ground. But one Dow pilot who flew over the fire expressed the opinion that, "It would take all the firefighting equipment of New York City . . ." to put it out.

The National Park Service flew specially trained firefighters from other states to Acadia Park. At a meeting Wednesday afternoon with Chief Sleeper it was decided that the Park Service personnel would have full control of firefighting within the park, and that their most immediate concern should be to try to hold the fire on its southwestern front at Aunt Betty Pond. By late afternoon they had achieved that, but only after setting a backfire against the advance of the flames that were being pushed by a freshening wind.

As the fire advanced, leaving behind it more and more acres of smoldering trees, spot fires, and roots burning underground, a larger and larger burden was placed on the firefighters. Every able-bodied man on the island was needed on the fire front. Few were left in the villages to advise and lead the women, children, and old people. As the fire continued unchecked, plans were made for moving them out.

Late Wednesday night a spokesman for the Bar Harbor Fire De-

partment told a *Bangor Daily News* reporter that there was little hope
the fire could be stopped. "All effort must be concentrated on saving
the towns if possible," he said. Somesville was now directly in the
fire's path, and residents there had been told it would reach them in
three hours. On the outskirts of Bar Harbor, people like Mrs. Rowell
had been warned that morning to be ready to leave and to listen for
seven blasts of the firehouse whistle, the evacuation signal.

Among the volunteers who rushed to help Bar Harbor were Howell
"Burnie" Burns, son-in-law of Dorothy and George Stanley, and five
other Bar Harbor boys, all students at Bowdoin and the University of
Maine Annex in Brunswick. They had been fighting the Kennebunkport-
Biddeford fire when they heard that their own town was threatened. A
friend from Bangor, Ed Herlihy, had driven them up in his car. They
arrived about five o'clock and went right out on the lines.

For the firefighters Wednesday had been a day of weary battle in
the wooded valleys and mountainsides of Mount Desert Island. For
the people of Somesville and Bar Harbor it had been a day of waiting.
For Mrs. Rowell, who understood that her home would be spared only
if the "miracle"—the wind from the northwest—held, it had been a
day to decide which among the furnishings with which she had filled
Barberry Ledge during half a lifetime, she should try to save.

She knew if she began to pick and choose among them she might
not be able to keep herself together, and this was no time to give way
to emotion. She was grateful when friends came by during the day offering to take things to safety. Early in the morning Harriet Ogden
took a few small boxes, among them a box of Christmas presents Mrs.
Rowell had already bought for her grandchildren in New York. Later
Mr. Sprague, who had painted her house that autumn, came to the
door with two of his helpers and said kindly, "Is there anything we can
do to help you?" She had already packed the amber glass that she "had
carried in my own arms from London long ago." She had always, at
the end of each summer, packed it in a special box and stored it in a
special place in the house. Now she said to Mr. Sprague, "I can live
without this glass, but I do love it, and perhaps you would take it for
me to Mrs. Farrand's garden house."

In the afternoon she drove into Bar Harbor to the Express Office
to have other small, easily-packed items shipped to New York. She
also wanted to get gasoline for the car, but found that without electricity the pumps were not working.

With gray army vehicles and firefighters everywhere, the village looked like an encampment. Driving home she caught "one magnificent view" of McFarland's Hill covered with smoke and flames and learned from a guard on the road that the fire was still being held. There was no wind that night so she went to bed and slept.

In the village the Stanleys went to bed too. Burnie, they knew, would be out all night, and with the wind holding northwest Bar Harbor was in no immediate danger. It was 3 A.M. when Dorothy heard the back door open. "Is that you, Burnie?" she called sleepily.[3]

"Yes," he answered, and came to their bedroom door. He was black with soot and "all done up in bandages."

"Stan!" cried Dorothy. "Burnie has got burned!" But the bandages were not for burns. Burnie and a group of firefighters working in the woods had found themselves in danger of being cut off by the fire. Quickly they piled into a pickup truck, with three of the younger men riding on the running boards, two on one side and Burnie on the other, and headed out a dirt road. They were traveling "about forty miles an hour when a frightened deer leaped out of the woods, hit Burnie in mid-leap, and knocked him off the running board." Burnie was lucky. He was badly shaken, but he escaped with only cuts and bruises.

The fire had brought terror to the deer of Mount Desert Island. Some escaped by swimming to the mainland. But many did not escape. Four had been found by wardens that afternoon suffocated in a bog where they had taken refuge and been trapped by the flames. Allen Salisbury, a volunteer firefighter from Bar Harbor, told of standing in a long line of men near the Eagle Lake Road, waiting for the fire to break out of the woods. Suddenly a deer, racing before the flames, sprang through the trees. Seeing the line of men, it hesitated for just a moment and then turned and ran back into the burning forest. Man was to be feared more than fire. Salisbury, a hunter himself who went out each year to get his deer, said, "I never could get over that."

Thursday morning, the weekly *Bar Harbor Times* was printed on schedule. Its headline was "Entire Island Menaced by Fire," but as the *Times* went to press, Hulls Cove, three miles from Bar Harbor, was the most severely threatened. The wind had shifted again, driving the fire away from Somesville, saving the Jordan Pond House, but sending the fire toward Hulls Cove. By ten o'clock the wind was so strong that the fire line on the north could not be held. Men and equipment were rushed to Hulls Cove, and the people there began to evacuate.

Some Hulls Cove families carried their furniture into open fields, thinking it would be safe there. Others took theirs across the causeway and bridge to the Bar Harbor Airport in Trenton on the mainland. Owners of some of the big estates at Bar Harbor had chartered planes and flown to Maine to try to save some of their belongings. Landing at the Bar Harbor Airport, they must have observed the clusters of refrigerators, couches, mattresses, chairs, and other paraphernalia of modest households scattered in the open fields beside the runway.

Allen Salisbury had gone to Hulls Cove to help his sister evacuate. Since Tuesday he had been out fighting the fire, helping to save homes and farm buildings along the Eagle Lake Road. Now its threat was more personal. His own home was on the other side of Bar Harbor in one of the caretakers' cottages on the grounds of the Jackson Laboratory. Salisbury worked in the lab and was also night caretaker. His wife cooked for the students who came in the summer to live in platform tents in the grove of great pine trees beside the laboratory buildings.

Worried about Hulls Cove and the unpredictability of the wind, Salisbury told his wife to take their daughter, Nancy, and get off the island to her parents' place in Trenton. Florence Salisbury didn't stop to pack. She took her pocketbook, grabbed a few clothes from the clothesline, put Nancy in the car, and went. She didn't even take the time to scoop up the presents Nancy had gotten on her fifth birthday a few days before.

When she reached Trenton and told her parents that Hulls Cove was being evacuated, her mother said, "Then we must go to the store and buy all the milk we can." They lived on the main route off the island, and she felt sure that many of their Bar Harbor friends would come to them. She would feed them chowder made with clams her husband had dug.

In Bar Harbor Dorothy Stanley watched the cloud of black smoke to the northwest and prayed that the wind would not shift again. Stan and Burnie (who had gotten some rest and had his wounds dressed) were fighting the fire at Hulls Cove. Jeeps, trucks, and fire engines, their sirens wailing, rushed through the village streets. She waited.

Mrs. Rowell knew that the fire was at Hulls Cove. She too waited for more news. At two o'clock her electrician, Mr. Lymburner, came to the door. "Is there anything I can do for you?" he asked.

"What is the latest news?"

"I've just heard that a strong northwest wind will come late this afternoon."

"Then, Mr. Lymburner, my house will be the first to go." He agreed.

She and Elizabeth Davis had packed a few more things—some

linens and a set of new china. Putting the box in the car, she told the women and the Nolans to be ready, and drove to the village to the Express Office.

At Hulls Cove a few houses on the outskirts of the settlement had burned, ignited by sparks blown ahead of the main fire. One of them was the old Hamor place, a fine brick house, home for generations of one of Hulls Cove's shipbuilding families. By mid-afternoon the wind was blowing a gale, turning the fire into a giant blowtorch aimed at Hulls Cove. But at approximately three o'clock, "to the amazement of the firefighters, there was a dead calm, and for approximately five seconds no fire of any type was visible. Then every tree and every bush burst into flames."[4] The wind had dropped completely, and then, with a roar, it rose again and veered from the southwest to the west and finally to the northwest.

One fireman who found himself suddenly in the path of the fire told later how he "looked up and it looked as though two gigantic doors had opened and towering columns of roaring flames shot down" upon him.[5] He and his crew had seconds to flee.

This "terrible blast caught up the front of the fire that was reaching Hulls Cove, and threw it back, saving all but the houses the advance . . . sparks had ignited. It also picked up the flames all through the woods, and threw them southeasterly and then southerly. Even before the flames shot over from Hulls Cove to Bar Harbor, flames . . . came over Great Hill and tore up Cadillac . . . , from there striking down the east side of Cadillac to Sieur de Monts Spring"[6] not far from the Jackson Laboratory on the south side of Bar Harbor.

When the wind shifted, Allen Salisbury went straight to the Jackson Laboratory. Now it seemed certain that the people of Bar Harbor, many of whom worked at the lab, would have to be evacuated, and it was even possible that the lab was in danger. As an employee, Salisbury would be needed to do whatever could be done to protect the irreplaceable cancer research records and the 90,000 mice, bred over a period of thirty-five years through 208 consecutive generations in the study of various strains of cancer, influenza, yellow fever, rabies, and other diseases.

At the lab another employee, Elizabeth Fekete, had already begun to move microscopes and centrifuges to a fireproof wing, placing them in the aisles between the rows of mice cages. At the direction of business manager Dale Foley other employees were putting a supply of food into the cages of the mice and filling their water bottles. If the lab workers were evacuated and could not get back for a day or two, the mice could survive.

Salisbury went to work helping feed the mice and clean out their cages. Knowing the conditions on the fire front, he said to Foley, "You want to get these girls back up town, Dale. The fire's headed, and it won't be too long before it's here." Foley said he had asked Fire Chief Dave Sleeper to let him know if they would have to evacuate. "Dave Sleeper is so tied up right now he can't let anyone know anything," said Salisbury. The women were sent home.

Mrs. Rowell was in the village. She had been able to get gasoline for the car and had stopped at the Express Office to see if the packages she had left the day before had been shipped. Mr. Graves, the agent, told her, "The driver is collecting now. We expect to send everything by Eagle Lake Road, which has been opened again."

"Then I will give you another package to send," she said, and crossed the street to get it out of her car. But suddenly she "heard a roar, and down Cottage Street came dancing dry autumn leaves from every direction, and dust and dirt and then heavy smoke. Over Great Hill at the end of the street a steady fiery red light appeared." She jumped into the car, and drove back to Barberry Ledge as fast as she could.

At the house she called to Mrs. Pritchard and Miss Davis and Mr. Nolan, who was in the yard, to be ready, and then went back down the drive to get Mrs. Nolan. She found her frantically trying to collect a few last things. "I am going," said Mrs. Rowell sternly. "You can follow me." The time for saving things was past.

Flames were creeping up on both sides of the drive when she drove back to the house. Mrs. Pritchard was ready at the door, weeping, and saying Elizabeth wouldn't come. "Get in the car," shouted Mrs. Rowell, and took "one flying leap" up the stairs to the maid's room. Miss Davis was just putting on her hat. "Come," ordered Mrs. Rowell. "Leave everything."

At the car Mr. Nolan saw the women safely inside and then, over Mrs. Rowell's protests, closed the door, saying, "I will walk down." As gardener at Barberry Ledge for thirty-two years he had traveled the path from the main house down through the woods to his home over the garage at the foot of the driveway hundreds of times. He wanted to do that just once more. Mrs. Rowell tried to grab him, to pull him into the car, but he was already out of her reach, and she did, after all, understand the need for last goodbyes.

Again she drove the car down the drive through the fiery gauntlet. At the bottom, where the path through the woods came out, she waited for Nolan, who had not appeared. For one awful moment she wondered if she would have to go into the flaming woods to find him. Had he "stumbled on the way down and died surrounded by flames on his lovely path?" But at last "the poor, frightened man appeared . . . just able to stand . . . and to climb into the car."

Mrs. Rowell turned onto the main road where flames were already advancing on either side. "And so," she wrote later, "I left my perfect house, after thirty-two years of comfort and happiness." She had looked back once and seen it burst into flames.

At 4:10 the signal for the evacuation of Bar Harbor came. The whistle on the firehouse blew seven blasts and then seven more. Policemen and soldiers were sent to outlying roads where residents might not have heard the signal to tell them to leave. Those without their own transportation were brought to the Athletic Field on Main Street to be taken out in buses and trucks.

Bernard Hawkes and his wife and three children and an elderly woman who lived with them were brought to the Athletic Field in an army truck. He had been at work at the North Atlantic Packing Company on West Street until three o'clock, when the wind had begun to rise, and his boss told everyone to "take off for home, 'cause it's lookin' bad."

Hawkes had gone to the fire station to see if there was anything he could do to help. He had been told, "You'd better get t'hell out of here and get home, because we're gonna blow the evacuation whistle."

At home he found his wife in the middle of doing a washing. "Pull the plug on the thing. . . ," he told her. "Leave it. We've got to leave." They hastily packed a few things and were out in front of their house when an army truck came by to take them to the Athletic Field.

Everyone did not leave willingly. Mrs. Hawkes's father refused to leave his home at all. Eighty-four-year-old Mrs. Margaret Blanchfield was finally prevailed upon to leave hers, but was adamant about staying in Bar Harbor. She was taken to the firehouse. Firemen coming in and out during the night saw her there, sleeping, sitting upright in a chair.

Seventy-nine-year-old Irving Young, his pet cat in his arms, was lifted into the truck for evacuation. The cat sprang away. Young climbed back down to look for his pet, was brought back to the truck, managed to get down again, and this time, in the confusion, was not seen or missed. After the fire, relatives waited a week for news of him and then asked that a search be made. Bones thought to be Young's were found in the rubble in the cellar hole of his house.[7]

One woman, who was doing her weekly ironing, said she wouldn't leave until she had finished and would come along in her own good time, which she did.

When Josephine Higgins's neighbors told her everyone was to be evacuated, she said, "I'm not going till Bob comes." Her husband was fighting the fire at Hulls Cove. Before he had left home that morning he'd told her, "If they evacuate you today, I'll be back." He did come back to see her and their six children, the youngest fourteen months old, safely to the Athletic Field.

Dorothy Stanley and her husband decided that with the wind blowing as it was, north-northwest, it would be safe to drive their car to the foot of their street to The Bar, a short road connected at low tide to Bar Island. It would be safe there near the water, and the tide would soon be turning so they could cross to the island if the fire came into the village.

Charlotte Stuart was a telephone operator. Her sister and her family and Charlotte's own small daughter had left. When the whistle sounded for evacuation, Charlotte called her supervisor to see if she was needed. The answer was, "Come at once." She walked from her home to the telephone office on the third floor of a building on Main Street in the center of the small business district.

Across the street the owners of Tripp's Restaurant ignored the evacuation signal. They were busy preparing food for the firefighters. They had closed the restaurant for the winter a few days before and were on their way to Florida when they had heard about the fire on Mount Desert Island. They had returned and reopened their restaurant to help feed the firemen.

At the Mount Desert Island Hospital all movable patients were sent home or to the hospital in Ellsworth. Among those who had gone home was Isabelle Forbis, but her baby daughter was kept at the hospital. All the patients who could not be evacuated were moved into a new fireproof wing along with food, oxygen, and medical supplies. The nurses who remained on duty were given responsibility for specific patients. A medical detachment from Dow Field stood by, ready with litters if the need for complete evacuation came, and Dr. Larrabee stayed at the hospital.

With the main route from Bar Harbor through Hulls Cove shut

off, the evacuees were sent by the longer, southern route through Otter Creek, Seal Harbor, to Asticou, Somesville, through Town Hill, and then to the bridge to the mainland. People were also fleeing from these communities, and as darkness came on a great, slow-moving caravan of cars and trucks wound its way off the island. Just over the bridge on the mainland at Trenton, cars of sightseers, who had come to watch the evacuation of Mount Desert Island, lined the road and overflowed into the fields.

Margaret Williams had made arrangements with the Reverend Bousfield, superintendent of the Sea Coast Missionary Society, and his wife to leave Bar Harbor with them when the time came. After the long day of uncertainty, when the signal for evacuation sounded she was almost relieved to know something definite at last. Her packed suitcase and a briefcase filled with important papers were near the front door, and now she waited for her friends to come.

When the bell rang she opened the door expecting to see Mr. Bousfield. Instead, a tall soldier stood on the porch. He told her he had been ordered to take people to the Athletic Field. Before she could explain her plans, he seized her by the arm and took her "protesting every step of the way to a huge army truck parked by the walk. Before he left the porch he opened the front door clear back and also the storm door, leaving the house open to the terrific gale. He said it was to prevent the heat from concentrating and blowing the house up."

Lifted bodily into the truck, Mrs. Williams was given no chance to explain that she had made her own arrangements to get off the island. What would the Bousfields think when they got to the house and she wasn't there? Would they waste precious time looking for her? At the field one of the officers in charge saw that she was upset and asked, "What's the matter here?" She explained what had happened. Turning to a driver, the officer said, "On your next trip take this lady and drop her off wherever she wants to go." She asked to be taken to the Mission House.

From the Mission House Mrs. Williams and her friends joined the caravan of about seven hundred cars leaving Bar Harbor and the island. Later she described the ride. "It was terrifying. There was a long line of cars . . . and they were bumper-to-bumper. The roadway was pitch black as all of the electric lights were out, but you could see flares of fire overhead. We had to have the car windows tightly closed as the sparks and flaming bits of material were hitting the car everywhere, and we were afraid they would get inside. We simply *crawled* for three miles, closely packed in with luggage and coats, very hot, our eyes and heads full of smoke, and everyone tense for fear the fire would come up on us from the rear and we'd be burned to death in this creeping caravan." For Margaret Williams there was the added worry of not knowing where her husband was.

Anson Williams had spent Wednesday as a volunteer working on a canteen taking food to the firefighters. Thursday morning he had been sent as a firefighter to the Duck Brook area between Hulls Cove and Bar Harbor. He worked a hose line with a young soldier from Dow Field, wetting down the forest floor. In mid-afternoon the soldier left to return with his unit to Dow, and Williams worked on alone.

Suddenly, he "heard an ominous sound. Except for an occasional slight breeze it had been very calm until then." Listening closely he "realized that it was the sound of a mighty wind coming from the northwest. The fire, which had been confined to the ground, was swept up into the evergreen trees." Knowing there was nothing he could do against such a blaze, and that "in a very short time [he] could be burned to death," Williams dropped the hose and started out of the woods as fast as he could go. In the dense smoke he followed the hose line. Veering once to avoid a huge pine tree that "suddenly burst into flame as if it had been doused with gasoline," the heat around him intense, he finally reached a narrow road.

On the road he found three young men waiting for a truck to come by to pick them up. He told them of the inferno behind them. There could be no waiting for trucks. "I believe our only means of saving our lives is to get to the Duck Brook Bridge," he said. The bridge was a mile away. They ran. They got to the bridge, legs weary, streaming with perspiration, out of breath, and took refuge under it, hoping that they would be safe there when the fire went over.

"I never knew what was passing through the minds of the other men while we were waiting," Williams said later, "but I remember scarcely a word was spoken." The fire came on with a frightening roar. Williams hoped that if they were to die in the fire, it would be quick. He knew from his pastoral work that "anyone who is badly burned, but still lives, endures excruciating agony."

The fire came, but with a "mighty whoosh" went overhead, showering the men under the bridge with sparks, which they beat out on each other's clothes. They had survived.

At the Jackson Laboratory Allen Salisbury called his mother, who was working at a canteen at the Odd Fellows Hall in Bar Harbor, to tell her he would be there shortly to get her. But first he went to his home on the lab grounds to pick up his dog and the family cat. On the kitchen shelf stood a row of pies and cakes that his wife had baked to send to one of the canteens. He decided to take them to the hall where he would pick up his mother and carried them to the car. He was to discover that the pets and the food were a bad combination: before he reached the canteen he stopped to throw the trampled pastries out of the car window.

Salisbury's boat, an Old Town Sea Cruiser, sat in the yard on its trailer, but he didn't stop to hitch the trailer to the car. He did take his gun, a box of family pictures, and the new suit hanging in the front hall that he had bought recently to wear to a Masonic "time." "But," he said later, "I slipped up." He forgot to get the box containing his collection of old coins. When he came back after the fire, he found the coins in the ruins of the house, melted together into a mass.

At ten minutes of five the fire crossed the road to Seal Harbor, closing off the last overland escape route from Bar Harbor, and swept into the grounds of the Jackson Laboratory. The wing of the lab that housed thirty thousand mice; research offices of the staff with their personal collections of mounted slides, charts, and records; and the library, with its meticulously gathered collection of journals and books, correspondence files, and old lab reports was totally destroyed.

Two-inch fire doors separated this wing from another that was considered fireproof. But it was fireproof in the sense that it had been built to withstand a normal fire, not "a wave of flame already generating terrific heat which would hit the whole surface of one side of the building on all three floors simultaneously."[8] The fire doors held but buckled in the intense heat, and although the walls of this wing stood, its roof burned and sixty thousand mice perished.

A third wing was under construction. The basement had been finished and roofed over with concrete. Wooden forms had been raised for the walls and upper floors. This framework and the lumber and supplies stacked nearby were destroyed, and the concrete floor above the basement crumbled.

In the grove of fine, old, fragrant pine trees nearby, a frame summer laboratory, mess hall, kitchen, recreation room for the summer students, platforms for their tents, the two caretakers' houses (and Allen Salisbury's boat on its trailer) were leveled. The grove as well as all but three or four trees in a thirteen-acre tract of spruce, fir, pine, oak, and birch beyond it burned. In sections of this forest the fire burned with such intensity that it not only consumed the humus under the trees, but the soil beneath that, exposing bare rock.

With Bar Harbor village now threatened on all its landward borders, Chief Sleeper made plans for defending it. From the beginning, ultimate authority over all of the fire companies and volunteers had been his. Now he quickly gave them their assignments.

He abandoned the town's outskirts as indefensible. The firefighters retreated from Hulls Cove along Bay Drive, which *Life* magazine was to dub "Millionaires' Row." All streets between the main section of town and Great Hill, Kebo, Cadillac, and Champlain Mountains were left to the advancing flames. Sleeper was being realistic: the flames were racing before a wind clocked by the Coast Guard at four o'clock that afternoon in Penobscot Bay at between sixty-three and seventy miles an hour.[9]

Sleeper put one crew, under the direction of the fire chiefs from Camden and Surry, at the junction of Eden and West Streets where the DeGregoire Hotel stood. Their job was to keep the fire from advancing along Eden Street or down West Street, which led to Main Street and the center of town. Chiefs from Bucksport and Brewer were assigned a larger crew at the other end of Eden Street where the Eagle Lake Road entered the village as Mount Desert Street. Their job was to keep the fire from sweeping down Mount Desert Street into the village.

These positions placed the men on the side of the fire, not in front of it, for the wind was blowing from the north-northwest. Because of this, and because Bar Harbor had hydrants and a good supply of water, Sleeper thought there was a chance to save the main section of the town. But if the wind shifted even slightly to the west, all of Bar Harbor would be lost, for it would lie directly in the path of the wind-driven flames, an inferno no one could face.

At the Athletic Field on Main Street twenty-five hundred people, who had not had time to evacuate before the Seal Harbor Road was cut off, waited to be told what to do. Eventually one of the roads out of Bar Harbor would be open again, but if the fire came into the village before this happened, the twenty-five hundred people would have to be evacuated by boat. Among those waiting at the field were Mrs. Mary Helen Cormier (called Helen by her friends) and her daughters, sixteen-year-old Helen and eleven-year-old Jane. They had walked to the Athletic Field from their home on Rodick Street a mile and a half away, carrying a suitcase, blankets, and with their fox terrier dog, "Tippy," on a leash. Mr. Cormier—Edward—and the Cormier's college-

age son Robert, who had managed to get home from the University of
Maine in Brunswick, were somewhere on the island fighting the fire.
Jane Cormier had been off playing with friends that afternoon when
her mother sent word that she must come home immediately. Jane
never forgot the smell of the smoke that hung over the village. It was
an "acrid odor. . . . When you smell it, you know it's a forest fire." It
was distinctive from the smell of a comfortable blaze burning in a
fireplace or woodstove.[10]

As darkness came on they watched the advance of the fire, for it
lit up the sky. They could tell when it hit the hundred-room Malvern
Hotel on Kebo Street. On its grounds stood eleven two- and three-
story cottages, some with as many as fourteen rooms, all large enough
to have servants' quarters. The hotel was advertised as being "for people of refinement," and its furnishings—Oriental rugs, antique furniture, a magnificent Steinway piano—were considered the finest of
any New England resort hotel. When the fire reached the huge hotel
and its cottages, the sky glowed with a new brilliance. Among those
who watched from the Athletic Field and mourned the loss of that Bar
Harbor landmark was its owner, Chester Wescott.

At six o'clock the fire was still out of control. A decision was
made to try to evacuate the people at the Athletic Field by boat from
the Municipal Pier at the foot of Main Street. If the boats did not come
in time, the rocky shore or the ocean itself might provide escape.

A soldier told them of this new plan by megaphone, asking all
who could walk to the pier to do so. Charlotte Stuart looked out of the
window of the telephone office and saw the crowd streaming down
Main Street, men and women leading or carrying children and family
pets, pushing baby carriages, carrying suitcases and bulging shopping
bags. Piles of personal belongings and furniture were left at the field.
Those who could not walk the distance were loaded back into the
army trucks and onto buses.

The withdrawal was orderly. Every account of Bar Harbor's Great
Fire speaks of the control of these people who could so easily have
panicked, for they knew just how precarious their position was. They
would have to wait at the pier for the boats to arrive, and no one knew
how long that would take or if enough boats would come. For some,
escape by boat was almost as terrifying as facing the flames, especially
when they saw the angry wind-whipped waters of Frenchman Bay.

Many were worried about the safety of husbands and sons, among
the firefighters, and wives and daughters, who had been working at

canteens and had been taken off the island in the first evacuation with no chance to call home.

Some were worried about family pets, not knowing where they were, hoping they would escape the fire. One woman who had had to leave home without her cat, had brought along the metal tray she always banged to call it home and at the Athletic Field had banged it diligently until the cat had appeared and jumped into her arms.

They did not know if their homes, indeed their town, could be saved. Much that they valued had already been lost. They had reason to weep, and there was weeping. But there was no panic. They gathered at the pier, some taking shelter in the nearby Shore Club, once an exclusive social club for men of the summer colony, and waited for the boats.

Helen Cormier and her daughters, Helen and Jane, were among those who took refuge at the Shore Club. There was no electricity. Using a flashlight, they spread blankets on the floor. Eleven-year-old Jane felt fear, but not panic. Her mother and sister, as well as all the neighbors and friends gathered around her, set a good example for the children among them. Jane had seen her sister embracing friends at the Athletic Field, speculating together about whether or not they would have homes to go back to; emotional, as high-school girls would be expected to be, but not hysterical. And her mother was calm, had been calm even when, walking down Main Street to the pier and shelter in the old Shore Club building, she had looked over toward their home two blocks away and, seeing the flames of the advancing fire against the sky, had believed their home was surely lost. "There goes the house," she had said, perhaps not even aware that she had verbalized her thought. Jane, helping to arrange their blankets, was thinking, "This must be what people in England went through in the blitz." They too had lined their blankets up, on the floor in the London subway. That was how they had gotten through the war, sleeping in the subway every night, and now surely this was like going through a war, their own war.

Bar Harbor's contact with the outside world was precarious. The police had radio cars, and the army had radio contact with Dow Field, but only one telephone line out of Bar Harbor was still functioning. The rest had been silenced, one by one, as the fire advanced. The open line went to Southwest Harbor and from there to Ellsworth. The Southwest Harbor operators, like those at Bar Harbor, had stayed on duty to keep the vital link with the mainland open.

Now the Bar Harbor police called the Coast Guard station at Southwest Harbor asking for boats. At the Bar Harbor telephone office Charlotte Stuart was told "to call every boat." She relayed the message to the Southwest Harbor operator. "Call the Coast Guard," she said. "Send them. And anybody you know who owns a boat, a workable boat—lobster fishermen, anybody who has a boat. Send them over. We need them."

The Coast Guard called Rockland, Portland, and even Boston stations, and the cutters *Bibb, Snohomish, McCulloch,* and *Laurel* set out for Bar Harbor. Closer to home the guard radioed Captain Bill Berry, standing offshore on the Sea Coast Missionary Society ship *Sunbeam,* which had already taken on the families of the crew, and asked him to bring his passengers into Southwest Harbor, where they would be sent on to the mainland, and then to proceed to Bar Harbor.

Around eight o'clock at the office of the *Press Herald* in Portland, an Associated Press wire dispatch came in saying four thousand people were trapped on the wharf at Bar Harbor. Reporter Roger Snow reminded his editor, Bill Chapin, that the navy destroyer *Perry* was in Portland harbor for Navy Day. "Destroyers are fast. Maybe that one could get to Bar Harbor and help," said Snow.[11]

Snow knew the commander of the First Naval District, Admiral Deyo, and called him in Boston, reaching him at a dinner party. Snow suggested he order the *Perry* to Bar Harbor. When the *Perry* left Portland harbor soon afterward with less than half a crew because the rest were on shore leave and couldn't be rounded up in time, Snow was aboard to get the story of the Bar Harbor fire. From Boston the destroyer escort *Powell* started for Maine.

While the ships of the Coast Guard and navy were racing through the night toward Bar Harbor, small craft of all kinds from Lamoine, Hancock, Sullivan, Sorrento, and all the other small harbors in and around Frenchman Bay had responded to their neighbors' need. Fish-packing companies in Southwest Harbor, Hancock, and Gouldsboro had sent their fishing fleets. Many other boat owners made their own decisions to face the rough work of getting women and children and the elderly off the pier and across the choppy waters of the bay.

On the pier the people waited, cold now, for the temperature had taken a sharp drop after dark. If they looked toward the town, they saw the fire burning in an arc around it. If they looked toward the water, they saw the angry waves. Rumors abounded. Someone had heard that three men in a rowboat had been run down by a larger boat.

They heard that people were trapped in burning houses, and that seventy-five firefighters had been enveloped in flames. When the fire set off a construction company's store of dynamite at How's Park on the edge of town, rumor on the pier had it that the firemen were dynamiting houses, the business district, the DeGregoire Hotel to stop the fire. Some of these rumors were to be reported later as fact.

But the evacuees had one worry that was real: someone remembered that there were oil storage tanks at the Clark Coal Company about seven hundred feet from the pier. If fire reached them, they might explode. Father Edward Fitzpatrick of the Holy Redeemer Church was on the pier offering what comforting words he could, but, "We had some terrible thoughts," Bernie Hawkes remembers. Fifty-one-year-old Raymond Karst was stricken with a heart attack and died on the pier. One Bar Harbor historian has written, "That night on the wharf will pass into legend as stories of it are handed down from generation to generation."[12]

At The Bar, not far from the pier, Dorothy Stanley sat and watched what, as she wrote later to family, "was probably the most awful and in its way awfully, horribly, beautiful sight that I ever saw. We were facing the water and the wind blowing right in our faces was driving the water—deep blue, for by this time darkness had come—into enormous whitecaps. To our left from Hulls Cove all down the shoreline and away around in back of us to the mountains was the line of fire, buildings and thousands of evergreen and hardwood trees all blazing at once, with flames leaping high into the sky. In front of us was the whitecapped bay without a trace of smoke over it, and in the distance the calm mainland with its twinkling lights and bright stars in the sky above it. Off to our right were all the islands in the bay, brilliantly illuminated by the orange glow from the fire. And up above it all, the moon shone. It is a scene I shall never forget, and I wish I had words to make you see it as we did. It was not real. It seemed something we watched with complete detachment and a quite impersonal interest, as one might watch such a scene in a moving picture. The odd part of it to me was that it was so silent because the wind blowing so strongly carried almost all sounds away from us."

Miriam Pottle, a reporter for the *Bangor Daily Commercial,* was at the Coast Guard station at Southwest Harbor, waiting there for a chance to get to Bar Harbor by boat. She had tried more than once to get through by road, following an army truck, following a police car, only to have to retreat each time because of smoke and fire. Welch

Forbis was at the station too, hoping to get on board a boat to Bar Harbor where his infant daughter, Judith Ann, was still at the hospital. But every available craft had already left. Pottle was deeply moved by the anxiety of the "frantic father."

Forbis knew there was still one boat in Southwest Harbor. It had just been completed for a New York man by a local boatbuilding company and had not yet been completely outfitted or taken for a trial run. Forbis appealed to two of the men who had helped build it. They agreed to take responsibility for outfitting the boat and using it to take him to Bar Harbor—there was no time to get permission from the owner in New York. The boat made its trial run in heavy seas on a mercy mission.

The first boats arrived at the Bar Harbor pier, and the evacuation began. Down into the lobster boats climbed young mothers carrying babies, older children with dogs and cats, and nuns from St. Edward's Convent. Elderly women, blankets over their shoulders, wearing their best hats and clutching their pocketbooks, were helped into the small boats. Some of the people on the pier like Bernie Hawkes and his family and Josephine Higgins and her brood (who had been told by her husband not to leave Bar Harbor by boat if there was any chance left of getting out by road), decided to wait a while longer. Many who chose to go were seasick on the crowded boats before they reached land on the other side of the bay. About four hundred got off by boat before the word was passed that the road through to Hulls Cove had been opened.

For three hours the firefighters had waged what Chief Sleeper was to call "the battle for the vital heart of Bar Harbor." The fire came down out of the hills and burned everything on the west side of Eden Street. At the junction of Eden and West Streets, just a few short blocks from the pier, the DeGregoire Hotel had caught fire and been consumed, but it was here that the first successful stand was made. For the first time the fire was stopped.

On the other end of town it was finally held at the junction of Mount Desert and Spring Streets, but only after a heroic crew went forward with hoses under wet blankets to play streams of water right on the point of the advancing flames.

As soon as it was certain that the fire would not spread down West Street, an army bulldozer was brought in to push the bricks and rubble from the burning DeGregoire out of the road and to clear downed wires, burning debris, and boulders, opening the Hulls Cove road.

Some of Bar Harbor's finest homes still burned on both sides of the road. Telephone poles hung by their wires; black chimneys stood out against the light thrown by the burning rubble of the massive summer homes. But the people on the pier were going to be taken through. At 9:10 P.M. they were given their instructions by the police. Led by an army jeep, the second evacuation of Bar Harbor began.

Bernie Hawkes was on a bus near the head of the line. Everyone had been warned not to open windows because of flying embers and the heat. As they turned the corner near the burning remains of the De-Gregoire, Hawkes put his hand on the bus window and found that it was so hot he couldn't keep it there.

Chester Wescott drove his own car, taking two women with him. With flames seemingly all around them, although not across the road, he was scared, but the caravan got through to the Trenton bridge, and beyond that the road was clear to Ellsworth.

The success of the daring evacuation was marred by a traffic accident. When it had become clear that there was a choice between leaving Bar Harbor by boat or by land through the fire zone, Mrs. Cormier had chosen the land route. She was terrified of going out on the rough sea in one of the small boats waiting to evacuate the people. She and her daughters were among thirty or so people who climbed into the open back of a U.S. Army truck. They sat approximately fifteen on each side and were given a wet tarpaulin to hold over their heads for protection from flying embers. The Cormiers were the first three sitting on the left side, young Helen on the end by the tailgate, her mother next, then Jane holding tightly to the leash of Tippy, who sat on Jane's lap.

The road past the steep rise called "The Bluffs" by local people, where the land dropped away on the other side to the ocean, was just wide enough for two cars. It was a narrow road for the truck to maneuver. From where she was sitting Jane could peer out to see embers flying from The Bluffs over the truck and down over the embankment on the other side to the ocean. It was a tense, frightening ride, but then they were through the danger zone, almost into Hulls Cove. Everyone was breathing a sigh of relief when suddenly another vehicle rammed a back wheel of the truck, overturning it.

It is difficult to reconstruct just what happened. Even those who were involved and survived were never sure whether the second vehicle was a station wagon or an army jeep, or from which direction it was coming. Jane Cormier remembered the truck being hit from the side, that is, from behind her where she was sitting and leaning back against the side of the truck. Her sister Helen was thrown out and under the truck. She suffered a fractured skull, and died three days later, a great loss to her family and the shocked community that remembered her as an outstanding young woman, exciting in her promise, and liked by all. The other fatality in the crash was forty-one-year-old Dow Field Warrant Officer Walter Coates, who died at the scene.

Jane and her dog Tippy also were thrown from the truck. It was Tippy, tugging on the leash fastened to his harness and still clutched tightly by Jane, who dragged her free of the wreckage. She and her injured mother, like others who were hurt, were carried to a nearby home. Jane asked again and again for her sister and was told Helen was being cared for in a house across the street. Years later it was to be Jane's judgment that she and her mother were not told the truth—that Helen had been rushed immediately to the hospital in Ellsworth—because Mrs. Cormier was already in a state of shock. It was at the Ellsworth Hospital the next day that the family was reunited (the father and brother having been located and brought in from the fire lines) to begin their sad vigil.

At Ellsworth the Red Cross had organized a center at City Hall for receiving the Bar Harbor evacuees. They were registered, fed, and sent on to families in Ellsworth, Brewer, and Bangor, who had offered to take them in, or to churches where cots were set up for them.

At City Hall newspaper reporters went among them, taking down their stories. A reporter for the *Bangor Daily Commercial* wrote:

> The story at the evacuation center at the Ellsworth City Hall at midnight last night was a story of faces. In came the victims of the inferno at Bar Harbor to register and then seek food and shelter . . . or to search for missing friends and relatives. The terror they had experienced was on their faces. The eyes of many had a glazed look, and the lines around their eyes and mouths were deep.
>
> They were grimy, many of them, and a few had tear-stained cheeks. For the most part, though, they were too stunned and too taut to find release in tears.
>
> The vast majority of people coming in off the big army evacuation trucks were older men and women and children. They came in wheel chairs, with canes, and supported by friends. Many of the children were carried in someone's arms.

One little old lady, with her hair straggling over her white face, came in on the arm of a grimy, unshaven, tobacco-chewing army sergeant. He left her at the registration table and asked where he could get a cup of "java" before he headed his truck back to the island.

A father held a tired child on his lap. He kept one eye on the door and tried to reassure his child. "Your hands are cold, darling," he said, as he rubbed them. Then he saw the face he had been waiting for. He smiled and said very quietly, "Here we are, my dear." His wife sat down beside him and kissed the child.[13]

A reporter for the *Boston Globe* interviewed evacuees at a Bangor hotel and was told by Colonel Joseph Wholean, whose mansion on Bay Drive had burned, "I got this thing on both ends. I have a house at Delray Beach, Florida. The hurricane swept that. They tell me there isn't a tree or bush left. At least there's a roof though. I have a place to live." Then he added that in the hotel dining room he had met the former ambassador to Costa Rica, Hallet Johnson, whose home at Bar Harbor had not burned. "I offered Johnson the key to my wine cellar," said Colonel Wholean, and laughed.[14]

In Bar Harbor reporters like Miriam Pottle and Roger Snow came in on navy and Coast Guard rescue boats that reached the harbor around midnight to find the pier deserted. The crews were sent ashore to relieve weary firefighters who came in to the canteens and sat and stared at their food, too tired to eat. At the firehouse Mrs. Blanchfield awoke from a restful nap and was told that the fire had been stopped three houses short of her home.

At the telephone office Charlotte Stuart and Lillian Ingalls, both of whose young daughters had been evacuated, heard that a Bar Harbor girl had been injured and waited anxiously to learn her name.

National Guard troops and police patrolled the dark streets, and Sewall Brown kept his small store open all night, making coffee by candlelight for the patrols and reporters.

The fire still raged, threatening Otter Creek, Seal Harbor, and Northeast Harbor, but Bar Harbor's ordeal was over. The back-breaking job of putting out after-fires and patrolling fire lines still remained, but there was time to count what had been lost. Police Chief George Abbott's first quick assessment was that more than two hundred houses had burned, including between sixty and seventy fabulous summer homes like those of Mary Roberts Rinehart and Walter Damrosch. The business district was intact, but all the hotels and the Jackson Laboratory had been destroyed. It was not known yet how many acres of Acadia National Park had burned. Bar Harbor had suffered a stunning blow, but its losses did not equal those suffered by the town of Brownfield in Oxford County that same day.

NOTES

1. All quotes and details concerning Christine Rowell's experiences at Barberry Ledge in 1947 are taken from an account written by her after the fire.
2. All quotes and details concerning the Williams' experiences during the fire are taken from "The Big Fire" by Anson R. and Margaret Williams as told to Mary Wilkes Haley, *Down East*, October 1962.
3. Dorothy Stanley's experiences during the fire are taken from a letter written by her to family members on October 26, 1947.
4. LaRue Spiker, "Like a Giant Blowtorch," *The Ellsworth American*, October 19, 1972.
5. Chief David A. Sleeper and Lieutenant John Heath, "The Bar Harbor Fire," Bar Harbor Fire Department, n.d.
6. Richard Hale, Jr., *The Story of Bar Harbor* (New York: Ives Washburn, Inc., 1949).
7. "Bones Found in Bar Harbor Cellar," *Portland Press Herald*, November 1, 1947.
8. "19th Annual Report of the Roscoe B. Jackson Memorial Laboratory: 1947–48, Developments During the Year."
9. Sleeper, "The Bar Harbor Fire," p. 5.
10. All the details of the Cormier family's experiences during the fire are taken from an interview with Jane Cormier Obermeyer on October 11, 1980.
11. Roger V. Snow, Jr., "The Reporter: The Man Who Covered the Bar Harbor Fire Also Brought a Ship," *Maine Sunday Telegram*, October 23, 1977.
12. Hale, *The Story of Bar Harbor*, p. 32.
13. "At Ellsworth—A Story of Many Sad Faces," *Bangor Daily Commercial*, October 24, 1947.
14. Amasa Howe, "What Four Men Went Through at Bar Harbor," *Boston Sunday Globe*, October 26, 1947.

Chapter VI:
"We knew we were doomed."

Brownfield is in the foothills of the White Mountains where the Saco River runs through a wide, sandy valley on its way to the sea, an area of much natural beauty, enclosed by the forested mountains of the Presidential Range, with gently rolling uplands, and ponds and streams running through wide meadows. The town sits in a valley beside Shepard's River, a tributary of the Saco, sheltered on the north by Frost Mountain and on the south by the Burnt Meadow Mountains. To the north is the town of Fryeburg, to the east Denmark and Hiram, to the south Porter, and to the west the New Hampshire state line.

In 1947 its population of about 750 lived in two small villages, Brownfield Center and East Brownfield, and on scattered outlying farms. Its village streets were lined with elm trees. Many of its houses were more than a hundred years old, and at least one, the old Ichabod Merrill place, a Cape, was thought to be nearly two hundred.

There were many Cape Cod–style houses in Brownfield. They looked like toy houses under the giant elms. Some, like The Birches, which faced the village green at Brownfield Center, had picket fences. The spacious grounds of The Birches were bordered on either side by white birch trees. To the rear an open porch looked over meadows that ran down to Shepard's River.

Perhaps the grandest house in town was the Stickney Mansion, a 147-year-old white colonial with a sunburst fanlight over the front door. It stood about a hundred yards east of the historic Pequawket Trail, a path that tradition says had been used by the Indians. The house had "Indian shutters," large fireplaces, and was filled with antiques and treasures gathered over the years by its well-traveled owners.

One of Brownfield's most interesting houses, The Sundial House, was a fourteen-room, two-and-a-half-story yellow frame building with an ell and barn. A large wooden sundial mounted over the front door was known to have been in place as early as 1824. The owners, Mr. and Mrs. Frank Harmon, took pride in the two-foot-wide clear pine boards on the floor of the master bedroom and the big old pine beams that had taken on the gleam and almost the color of mahogany. The house had been owned by Mrs. Harmon's family for generations.

Perhaps Brownfield's most distinctive landmark was the soldiers' monument on the village green. Every New England town has such a monument, usually of a Civil War soldier, but Brownfield's was different. The seven-foot-high bronze statue, mounted on a granite boulder, was of a young man, broad army belt across his chest, a long-visored Grand Army of the Republic cap in one hand, the other raised as if answering a roll call. It was Daniel Bean, a local boy who had enlisted at the age of fifteen, his likeness reproduced from a daguerreotype. Bean was eighteen when he died during the North's drive on Virginia, the first of Brownfield's soldiers to be killed in the Civil War, "one of the bravest and brightest sons of Brownfield" they had said in 1911 when the whole town had turned out to see the statue unveiled by his sisters and dedicated by the town fathers. Since then another soldiers' memorial had been raised on the green—an honor roll topped by a gold eagle, listing Brownfield's World War II dead.

Brownfield was mainly a farming community, although it had four sawmills and a one-man baseball-bat-making business and a one-man wood-turning business. It had an inn, three stores, three garages, the usual public buildings—schools, churches, a town hall, and, at East Brownfield, a railroad station. It was a nice little town and just that. There wasn't anything special about Brownfield unless your roots were there. Its history paralleled that of all the neighboring towns. It had no famous native sons. (Dr. Philo Farnsworth, a pioneer in the field of television, spent his summers in Brownfield, but he had been born in Utah.) Its houses were not architecturally unique; houses like them were scattered all over Maine. Brownfield was just a typical Maine town. That was its charm.

On Tuesday, October 21, the day the week-old ground fire in Fryeburg's Oak Hill section finally got away from the patrols set to watch it, Esther Boynton of Brownfield Center had taken her crewel work to a friend's house. It was a hot day, and the two women sat on the porch sewing. Looking north, they saw a trickle of smoke going up against the sky. As the afternoon wore on they watched it, and when a power line crew came by, Esther called to them, "Where's the fire, and how big is it?" It was, the men said, in Fryeburg, and while they didn't think it was "too bad," conditions were "awful dry."

The fire, fanned by a strong wind, was primarily a ground fire, burning in berry bushes, slash, and scrub oak. The Fryeburg Fire Department had called in help from Brownfield and Denmark. District Warden Carleton Merrill, who had been alerted by the Pleasant Mountain watchman, was there to help and had brought a thousand-gallon tank truck. He had come upon the truck at a road construction site on his way to the fire. It was hauling water to wet down the dust on the road. Merrill had told the driver that the water might be needed at the fire.

The fire was fought in the usual way with hand tools and portable tanks. Fryeburg had a tank truck and a booster tank. Brownfield had a couple of portable pumps and some hose. A bulldozer was brought in. The fire was brought under control shortly after dark when the wind fell.

During the evening most of the firefighters went home, confident that the situation was well in hand. But at 1 A.M. the people of Fryeburg were awakened by the continuous blowing of the village fire siren. The wind had come up again, fanning the edges of the burn, bringing the fire to life. Returning firefighters found that the flames had gained headway in all directions and that help had been sent for from Hiram. Before Wednesday was over Lovell, Harrison, and Porter would also send men and equipment.

All day Wednesday they battled the fire with limited success. A crew would think it had a section under control only to discover that the fire had burned underground in root systems and come up outside the line they were holding. Again, as in Waterboro, the work was made difficult by the tenacity of the fire, the size of the burn, and the lack of coordination among the fire companies.

That day about two thousand more acres burned over. Even a swamp, which was still wet, failed to slow the fire. By late evening it had been contained again, but now it was at the edge of Brownfield.

Wildfire is no respecter of town lines. The Brownfield firemen wanted to backfire and some of the others agreed it should be done. Others did not. It was finally decided that a backfire should be set at daybreak along the Brownfield Road (Route 113). All night long pumpers from several towns wet down both sides of the road from treetop to ground. At daybreak the decision was made not to backfire.

A Red Cross relief center to provide food and medical attention for the firemen had been set up at the Philo Farnsworth house. Esther Boynton had made doughnuts and sent them over. Thirty years later she remembered that on Thursday, "I really fried doughnuts."

The wind was changeable that day. It began in the southwest and kept swinging. About 9:30 in the morning it really began to blow, whipping the fire into new fury. During the morning it pushed the fire toward Fryeburg village. But by eleven o'clock the wind had swung west and was driving the main fire back toward the Brownfield Road. Four fire companies with pumpers were stationed there, but the wind carried the fire across the road and toward the Saco River. An attempt was made to drive it to Lovewell's Pond, but when it was clear that this would fail, men from the town of Denmark were sent to try to keep it from reaching the river where it might jump across, endangering their town. The fire raced before the wind, burning faster than a man could run through the tall, dry marsh grass on the bank of the river. By the time the Denmark men reached the river, the fire was already on the other side.

In Brownfield Center Esther Boynton had begun to fuss. She had grown up in Thomaston on the coast and was wise to the ways of wind. "When it comes afternoon, the wind's going to change," she told her husband, Guy. "That fire's coming back here."

"Oh, don't be foolish. You know better'n that," he said.

"I tell you the wind'll change. Will you take those oxen out and plow around this field. Plow ten rows, ten furrows at least. And then you go down on the Intervale and plow that whole thing up. Get one of the neighbors to hold the plow. Why those oxen will almost go themselves."

"It would only make a mess. All that land would only have to be laid down again."

"I don't care. You do it." Guy was not convinced.

The wind shifted suddenly. It swung to the north, and the fire, which had been traveling hard and fast, held a moment, then turned, crowned, and headed for Brownfield. A frantic attempt was made to gather men and equipment from the now less critical Fryeburg fire fronts.

The fire burned along the ground almost as fast as it burned in the crowns of the trees. Fields and roads were not barriers—they were no obstacle to a fire that could jump a river. The wind scattered embers for a quarter of a mile and blew jump fires as much as a mile ahead of the main fire. The firefighters retreated and made a stand, retreated and made a stand, until it was clear that nothing they could do would stop the fire.

By mid-afternoon a mass evacuation of East Brownfield and

Brownfield Center was under way. Cars, trucks, wagons, even wheelbarrows were hastily loaded with mattresses, tables, mirrors, tools, and clothing. Possessions were left behind to make room in a car for neighbors without transportation. Livestock was turned loose or herded down the already clogged roads to Hiram and Cornish, South Hiram, Porter, and New Hampshire. Overhead the sun behind the smoke looked like a full harvest moon.

From the tower on Pleasant Mountain the warden watched the fire. It seemed to leap over East Brownfield and then close in from both sides like a hand closing on a ball.

Charlie Harmon was one of the men who pulled back to help with the evacuation when it was obvious they could not stop the fire. As the afternoon wore on, they thought the worst might be over and Brownfield might be spared. "Then up through the valley came great clouds of smoke . . . and then flames. The fire was everywhere at once. One minute [there was only the] dense smoke to which [they] had become accustomed, the next minute flames and searing heat [were] everywhere. It was unbelievable."[1]

Esther Boynton had fried doughnuts all day long, one batch right after another. In the afternoon two elderly women, who had been evacuated from their homes, were brought to Esther, and her brother-in-law had brought his furniture and left it in the dooryard. The fire was almost certain to reach his house, but probably not Guy and Esther's on the far side of Brownfield Center where the main road branched west to New Hampshire and south to Porter.

Word came that East Brownfield was burning, and the fire was traveling up the valley. Brownfield Center would be next. Esther remembers, "Finally it was dusk . . . I can't place the time . . . , and we knew we were doomed."

Guy and Esther helped the two elderly women to the car. They picked up a few clothes, a few things around the house, but, Esther said later, "I did a dumb thing: I took good things and left ordinary things." After the fire she was to regret that she took pieces of silver and china and left behind her favorite wooden spoon, the black "spider," the cooking dishes she used every day.

The last thing she did before leaving was to walk through the house. It had been their home for seventeen years, since they had been burned out of their first house. They had worked hard, raising most of their food, keeping cows and pigs. Guy had worked in the woods during the winter months, and at last, just this year, they had decided they could afford to make some improvements on the house. During the summer

Guy had gone into his woods and marked for cutting trees that were tall enough and large enough to replace the old, rotted sills under it.

Esther walked through the house. She didn't try to gather up the loved books like Holman Day's *Up In Maine*—how she did love to read aloud the poem "Aunt Shaw's Pet Jug." She left behind all the pieces of crewel and cross-stitch she had worked over the years. She knew she was seeing for the last time the furniture she had helped save in 1930 when their first home burned. Nothing would survive this time. She and Guy knew there was no way the fire would miss their farm, which was at the end of the village street, pocketed by hills. The house and everything in it—the books, the handwork, the furniture, dishes, the bushels of potatoes, the jars and jars of fruit and vegetables and all the other food she had stored in the cellar—would be consumed by the flames. When she went out to get into the car, she didn't even close the door behind her.

Standing by the car, she heard Guy go into the barn, which stood near the house. Earlier he had brought their oxen and cow in from pasture and shut them up there. Now he took a lash whip and drove the frightened cattle out of the barn where they wanted to cower, but where he knew they would have no chance of survival. He drove them out with the whip, shutting the barn doors behind them. Esther heard him say, with emotion in his voice, "That's all I can do for you. I hope to God you can take care of yourselves." In the pasture there was a brook. Perhaps they could find safety near it. Calling to their dog, Esther and Guy climbed into the car and drove away.

The fire had burst from the wooded foothills into the valley where the houses of East Brownfield and Brownfield Center were clustered. There were fewer trees in the valley, but the fire spread. The wind carried burning pine boughs and shingles to the roofs of houses. As the fire burned its way through the valley, building up great levels of heat, houses exploded. As a house and the trees near it burned, another house nearby, would suddenly explode into flames the way a ball of paper tossed into a fireplace, and falling just short of the burning logs, will suddenly burst into flame, hot enough at last to burn.

Some houses burned from the ground up, grass fires catching in clapboards close to the ground. Trees, picket fences, telephone and utility poles caught fire. As the poles fell, pulling the wires behind them, the snapping and cracking of the breaking lines could be heard over the roaring of the fire.

Most of the people of Brownfield fled, but a few home owners and one or two valiant firefighting crews stayed, and they were able to save a few houses. Perley Walker, a Chevrolet dealer in East Brownfield, stayed to try to save his garage and his house across the street. Using wet burlap bags and brooms, he and one other man saved his buildings. They were the only two to survive in East Brownfield.

Mabel Stone did not leave. She lived alone on the Dugway Road that ran up out of Brownfield Center into the Burnt Meadow Mountains. She had planned to evacuate with a niece, but when the time came there was not room in the car for her dog too. She would not leave without her dog, so she stayed. Across the road from her house was a stone wall and beyond that a large, plowed field. She brought blankets downstairs and hung them on the newel post at the foot of the stairs in the front hall. If the fire came too close, she would take the blankets and the dog across to the middle of the field and crouch down under the blankets. She filled buckets with water and set them outside around the house. When sparks set fires in the grass near the house, she stomped them out with her feet or beat them out with a wet broom. Houses up the road and down the road burned. A nearby church burned, but Mabel Stone's house did not.

In Brownfield Center, the Harrison Fire Department, drawing water from Shepard's River, saved some houses, among them The Birches. Another group of four houses near the river was saved by four men with a pumper and four ladders. They went from house to house putting out fires. But in all only twenty houses survived in Brownfield Center. The Boyntons' was not one of them.

By the time the fire had passed, moving on toward Porter and Hiram, 75 percent of Brownfield's taxable property had been destroyed. Among the houses lost were The Sundial House and the Stickney Mansion. The Farnsworth place and $75,000 worth of electronic equipment were gone. Every public building—the churches, the schools, the post office, the Grange hall, the library, the town hall—had been left a pile of rubble and ashes.

Reporter Robert Crocker drove through Brownfield that night. He found what had been a pretty little town now a deserted wasteland of scorched ruins. By the flickering light of burning debris, he saw one old man "walking with his dog down streets littered with fallen wires, peering into the yellow heat" of cellar holes.[2] Two horses plodded unattended down the road. Cows standing in a blackened pasture lowed fitfully. Half-burned telephone poles and trees still smoldered, and here and there he saw a dead rabbit and the scorched carcass of a pig.

Reporters who came the next day and the day after described Brownfield's blackened chimneys, burned-out farm equipment, elms still standing but with the bark peeled away by the intense heat of the fire. "This," wrote Franklin Wright for the *Portland Sunday Telegram,* "was scorched earth at its worst. Virtually nothing was spared."[3]

What was spared was the statue of Daniel Bean and the honor roll of Brownfield's World War II dead. Both still stood on the green at Brownfield Center where nearby only a rectangle of stones, split apart by the heat of the fire, and broken stained glass marked where the Congregational Church had stood.

That night to the west toward Hiram, Cornish, and Limerick every ridge was outlined in dull red by the fire, which had raced on. The warden in the tower on Pleasant Mountain watched the fire all night. In the dark the smoke cover above it looked like a black lake. Now and then the flames would boil up through the smoke like lava welling out of a volcano, and sometimes it would look as though great balls of fire were leaping right out of the earth.

At Hiram, men who had fought to keep the fire out of Brownfield now tried to keep it out of Hiram village. Some houses had already burned near the town line. The firefighters organized themselves well. Men from Denmark were stationed on the northeast side of town, Baldwin on the east, Cornish on the south, Fryeburg and wardens from New Hampshire on the west, Kezar Falls on the northwest. Men from Baldwin and Sebago went up Rattlesnake Mountain above the village and split the fire as it came over, making it more manageable. Although eleven thousand acres, thirty-seven houses, and one sawmill burned, the firefighters' coordinated effort and a competently handled backfire saved Hiram village.

On that same day and night in neighboring York County a score of towns were under siege. Some, like Hiram, came through with the loss of only a few houses; others, like Brownfield, went down to the flames.

NOTES

1. Franklin Wright, "Scorched Ruins All That Remain of Brownfield," *Portland Sunday Telegram,* October 26, 1947.
2. Robert M. Crocker, "Limerick Countryside Lies Desolate in Ruins," *Biddeford Daily Journal,* October 24, 1947.
3. Wright, "Scorched Ruins."

Chapter VII:
The Day of the Big Wind

Veteran wardens and firefighters call Thursday, October 23, 1947, Red Thursday. It was the day of the big wind.[1]

At dawn between forty and fifty fires were burning in Maine. Some, like the North Kennebunkport and East Livermore fires, had already caused terrible damage to homes and communities. Others had burned vast stretches of timber and come threateningly close to settlements. As Thursday began, each of the fires was considered under control, but on every fire line weary men understood that they faced another long, anxious, potentially disastrous day. Probably no one would have predicted just how disastrous.

At 6:45 A.M. Linwood Staples and Arthur Moulton of Newfield were at the town hall in West Newfield. In two days three thousand acres of woods and fields had been burned in their town, and on Wednesday some houses had been lost. Except for one hot spot about a quarter of an acre in size off the Old Parsonsfield Road the fire was out.

Moulton called the weather bureau in Portland. "We're up here in a fire area in Newfield," he said. "Can you give us some idea what the weather conditions are going to be today?" The reply was not reassuring.

"It looks like you're going to get some wind. It's going to start picking up around nine o'clock. It will be from the southwest, but it will swing around to the northwest by the middle of the afternoon. And it's going to gradually increase all during the day. By two o'clock it will probably be a forty-mile-an-hour wind." A southwest wind would take the fire toward Parsonsfield. A forty-mile-an-hour, northwest wind would blow it right into the heart of Newfield.

Arthur Moulton had no official title or position. But he was a natural leader with a strong interest in his town, where he had lived all his life. He and his father owned a large sawmill and board yard on Route 11 between West Newfield and Newfield's Lower Village. His wife, Marion, was the town's doctor. He saw the need for a firefighting command post to coordinate the men and equipment that had come in to help fight the fire. If the wind blew the gale the weather bureau was predicting, they would have their work cut out for them.

The town hall at West Newfield seemed a logical headquarters. There was a telephone there and maps of the town. Moulton telephoned Arthur Baker, who lived in the Maplewood section and owned a small plane with a radio. "How about flying observation for us today?" he asked. "I think we're going to get a lot of wind. Let's see if we can keep track of what's going on." Baker was willing, but a way had to be found for him to get word to the men on the ground. A shortwave radio that would pick up the frequency of the plane's radio was located and brought to the town hall. Now Baker could call messages into the command post. Although the men there could not send messages back to him, they could relay his observations to the fire line by messenger.

Moulton, Clayton Weymouth, and some others got together to plan their strategy. Some wanted to go out immediately and backfire along the Old Parsonsfield Road between the fire and the Maplewood Road and, beyond that, Newfield's Lower Village. "If we can burn all this along here before the wind gets too strong," they argued, pointing to the map, "we've got it made. We can do it with a good-sized crew and stop the fire before it even begins to come this way." Some of the men were strongly opposed to backfiring: it was dangerous; technically it was illegal. Their alternative plan was to bulldoze along both sides of the narrow road, wet down the area thoroughly, and deploy a large crew of firefighters armed with shovels, grub hoes, and hand pumps along this firebreak. They won out. One hundred and fifty men with bulldozers and eight or ten makeshift pumpers were sent up the Old Parsonsfield Road.

At ten o'clock the wind came up. Baker was overhead and saw it drive the fire across the road, splitting the crew of men who had hoped to stop it. The fire came so fast that trucks were driven away with their hose dragging, and men just ran. "It was then," Clayton Weymouth was to write in his official report, "that we lost control of the situation."

Baker radioed Arthur Moulton, who was manning the command post, and then flew back over Stevens Corner where he'd seen a crew of men working on the back line of the fire. On a paper bag he scribbled, "Fire has jumped road and is burning like hell toward Maplewood. Send everything you've got." He weighted the bag with stones and dropped it to the men below.

As soon as Moulton knew that the fire was on its way, he telephoned people who lived in the Maplewood section and Lower Village and told them it was coming. The evacuation of Newfield began.

Marion Moulton, who was eight months pregnant, left by way of the road to Limerick. On a hill on the outskirts of Limerick she stopped her car and looked back. A great column of smoke rose in the air over Newfield. Toward Brownfield there was another, and another toward Waterboro.

Seventy-four-year-old Fred Sprague loaded a few things into a wagon, hitched up his horse, and was fleeing along the Maplewood Road into West Newfield. But the fire came too quickly. The back of his wagon caught fire. Sprague jumped from the seat to the side of the road, and the terrified horse raced on, pulling the flaming wagon behind him. Farther along the road near Long Bridge some men were filling a pumper with water from Adams Pond.[2] They managed to stop the crazed horse and went back along the road where they found Sprague. He had a broken leg and other injuries. They brought him out, but he died a few hours later.

Albert Smith kept to himself, living alone in a small house in the woods on Dunnell's Mountain in Newfield between the Maplewood Road and Lower Village. He kept a couple of cows and a horse named Jim. Warned that the fire was coming, he said he would leave as soon as he turned his cattle loose. This done, he hitched Jim to a light, four-wheeled cart and started for Lower Village. His way lay along the Gertrude Hall Road, which curved and climbed up- and downhill through woods and past stone walls.

No one ever really knew what happened, except that Smith did not get out. His body was found at dawn the next day lying beside a stone wall, a few charred pages from a small Bible he was known to carry scattered around him. Nearby were the charred remains of the cart and the horse Jim. The road there climbed sharply. Evidently slowed by the hill, Smith and the horse had been overcome by smoke and had died of asphyxiation before the flames got to them.

The fire spread through Newfield, burning with incredible speed and heat before the wind, which did indeed blow forty miles an hour. The firefighters worked on its sides, trying to keep it from widening out. Overhead, Arthur Baker put in the roughest flying hours of his lifetime. Thermal draughts alternately threw him against the roof of the plane and drove him down into the seat.

Radio contact with the town hall at West Newfield was useful for a while, but as the situation worsened, knowing the progress of the fire didn't help. There were not enough men, there was not enough equipment to fight such a fire. The listening post was abandoned in favor of efforts to keep the fire out of West Newfield.

Moulton, Weymouth, and a crew of men worked desperately at West Newfield village. Bulldozers dug firebreaks along the edge of the settlement and around almost every building. There was water, and there were pumps and hose. Home owners, feeling little hope that their village could be saved, evacuated. The owner of a store on the ground floor of the Masonic hall threw his keys to Weymouth. "Here's the keys," he said. "Anything you want . . . help yourself. Tomorrow mornin' it won't be here."

The telephone exchange was in the West Newfield home of Doris Hannaford, one of its operators. Linesmen for the company came in, dismantled the switchboard, and trucked it to safety.

Arthur Moulton was with a crew of men near the town hall when the fire broke through from the woods with a roar that sounded like a freight train. The smoke was so thick they could hardly breathe. Afterward Moulton described the situation. "The boys were practically lying on their faces. They couldn't get up to fight. You stand up to even load a pump on a truck and you'd choke and have to get down. That's how bad it was. We stayed there with our hoses. The shingles on the little building on the back of the town hall caught fire, and the fire had practically gone around us. 'Boys,' I said, 'Let's get out.' " They pulled out, leaving some of the hose behind. Moulton says, "My feeling was—the loss of another life was not worth the hose."

Clayton Weymouth and five or six men stayed in West Newfield with an old tank truck and another truck with a tank on it that wouldn't run and had to be towed. The town hall, a schoolhouse next door, and a number of houses burned, but Weymouth and his crew managed to save the Masonic hall and a score of other buildings.

In other parts of town, house after house was destroyed. Summer camps burned. The fire jumped Adams Pond, skirted Moulton's Mill on the other side, and then backed into the mill's board yards, sweeping them clean of thousands of feet of stacked lumber. Another mill farther down Route 11 on Poor Farm Flats was completely destroyed. Lower Village was devastated: the Methodist Church; the two-story Ethan Stone School; the post office; an auditorium; the store; the Dunnell family's combination home, garage, and filling station; almost sixty homes—all were lost.

Chief John Morrill of the Limerick Fire Department, who with his men and equipment had tried to defend Lower Village, said, with tears in his eyes, "I've never seen anything like this in fifty years of fire-fighting."[3]

Sixty percent of the town's valuation was gone, and although the main fire had blown on toward Shapleigh and Waterboro, Newfield still had miles of fire line to patrol and dig out. Weymouth, who had hardly slept and hadn't had a hot meal for four days, said, "I don't know where this is going to end."[4]

In Waterboro things seemed to be under control that morning. Battles had been fought the day before for North Waterboro, Waterboro Center, and East Waterboro, and the fire had been held away from South Waterboro. At the East Waterboro post office and store a man had told Franklin Wright of the *Press Herald* how the settlement had been saved the night before. "Yesterday," he said, "I wouldn't have given a nickel for our chances." He sighed with relief, thankful that the crisis had passed.[5]

In South Waterboro Wright talked with a group of men clustered around half a dozen firetrucks. They were not complacent. They had turned back the flames the night before, but they knew they couldn't relax yet. "If the wind holds," a chief said, "the town's safe." The wind did not hold. It blew a gale all over York County that afternoon.

Reporter Malcolm Barter and photographer James Callahan had come down from Boston Wednesday to cover the Maine fire story for the *Boston Globe*. They had seen the aftermath of the Kennebunkport fire, where an estimated eight hundred people were homeless. Goose Rocks Beach had looked like a battlefield. Only chimneys and foundations of houses and twisted iron stoves, plumbing, and tools remained. Looters had come in during the night to steal the iron, so the National Guard had been called in to patrol the streets. Barter had seen women weeping in front of the ashes of their homes and had talked with firefighters, one of whom had said, "Lord, I wish it would rain." Barter had interviewed Governor Hildreth, who had arrived late Wednesday afternoon to view the damage.

Wednesday night Barter and Callahan had stayed at the Kennebunk Inn where trucks hauling water stopping and starting up at the
traffic light on Main Street below their window kept them awake.
Thursday morning they heard that the Maine State Pier in Portland
was on fire and had gone to cover that story.

The Portland Fire Department and fireboats in the harbor had
brought the blaze under control, but not before half the pier and mixed
cargo stored in two sheds had been destroyed. Portland's Fire Chief,
Oliver Sanborn, gave it as his opinion that the fire "might have started
from petroleum products," but doubted if the cause would ever be
pinned down closer than that. Speculation along the waterfront was
that someone had flipped a cigarette onto the pier where it had landed
on a spot of oil.

From Portland, Barter and Callahan headed for Waterboro where,
they had heard, a strong wind was rekindling Wednesday's fire lines.
They drove back to Biddeford and from there followed Route 111
through Lyman toward Alfred and Route 202 from Alfred to Waterboro.

Arthur Roberts's home was at the junction of Route 111 and the
Day's Road. As a member of the volunteer fire department at Goodwin's Mills, a settlement that straddles the line between Lyman and
Dayton, he'd been acting all week as liaison man between Fire Chief
Ray Burbank and the crews out in the field. On Wednesday they had
had a couple of fires on the end of town near the Waterboro line to
worry about. Six or eight men were stationed at each with tank trucks
and pumps, beating the fires down when they flared up again and
again.

Roberts and Burbank had been keeping an eye on the smoke from
the Waterboro fire in the sky to the northwest, knowing that a strong
wind could bring that blaze into Lyman too. On Thursday about mid-
day they had felt the wind come up and could tell from the smoke that
the Waterboro fire had begun to move. Burbank told Roberts, "Get
over there and check the time the fire comes across the Boston and
Maine railroad tracks. Find out how fast it's moving. Then get to a
phone and call me."

Using back roads, Roberts got close enough to see the fire, coming fast, cross the tracks where they ran along the edge of a large heath
near the Waterboro-Lyman line. He hurried to the nearest house to
telephone Burbank, but the line was busy. Everyone was trying to get
a call through to someone. Roberts drove back to Goodwin's Mills,

knowing that precious time was being wasted. "Ray," he said. "You'd better let me go up and get our men out from the Andrews farm." The Andrews farm was in a back area near Roberts Pond in front of the fire.

"Does it look that bad?" asked Burbank.

"Yes, it does," answered Roberts. Arthur Roberts was always polite and soft-spoken, but Burbank knew him well enough to know that he was giving a warning that a less controlled man could not have delivered calmly. Burbank also knew that Roberts's judgment was good. Lyman was in for real trouble.

By the time Roberts reached the crew at the Andrews farm, and they had gathered up their equipment, the air around them was filled with embers, cinders, and smoke. They headed out to safety, Roberts first, the crew with their pumper and a tank truck behind. The last truck out was almost cut off by flames.

Roberts again drove back to Goodwin's Mills, this time to tell Burbank, "Ray, I'm sorry, but I'm going to have to go home." There was nothing to stop the fire from sweeping right through Lyman. His own family and home were in danger now.

Roberts and his wife, Lorraine, and two children lived in a big, old farmhouse with a large barn on the Day's Road, a short connecting road between Route 111 and Route 35. Next door Rob and Eva Merrill had a big farmhouse and barn, and across the road was a sawmill and a board yard stacked with about 900,000 feet of lumber, which Roberts had sold just six months before to the Gillies Lumber Company.

At home he told his wife, "Grab your clothes, whatever you think you need, your valuables, and get in the car. I'm going to send you to Alfred." She did not want to leave without him. "Hon," he said, "I think it's the only thing to do. I want you to go to Alfred to my aunt's house. If they try to evacuate the village up there, go to Wells Corner and stay there until you hear from me." All Lorraine Roberts could think of to take with her and the children was an old sweater and her pinking shears. They were to laugh about that later.

Roberts was not to defend his house alone. A small group of men gathered, among them his brother-in-law; his nephew; his hired man, Claude Emmons; and Emmons's son. Emmons had fled his own house in a wooded area on the Kennebunk Pond Road. "We're with you," the men said to Roberts. "We'll help you all we can. What can we do?" He thanked them all, then turned to Emmons. He was anxious that his hired man not feel obliged to stay. "Claude, do you want to stay?" he asked.

"I wouldn't be happy going anywhere and leaving you here," Emmons replied.

The men scattered to do what they could toward protecting the Roberts house and the Merrill farm, where no one was at home. They filled pails, tubs—whatever they could find—with water. Until the pressure died, they used the garden hose to wet down the Roberts house. Suddenly Roberts remembered a box of dynamite stored in his barn. He ran to get it, carried it to a nearby brook, and buried it. Later, he realized that he had forgotten to bring the caps, the most dangerous part of the explosive.

Malcolm Barter and Jimmy Callahan arrived at South Waterboro at four o'clock, just after a frantic call went out to Sanford for more help, and the order had been given by the state police for everyone in South Waterboro Village—home owners and firefighters alike—to evacuate. At almost every house people were carrying out furniture and bedding. The street was clogged with fire engines, oil trucks carrying water, army trucks, and buses brought in to help evacuate the people. Barter stopped to question a state trooper who was directing traffic in the center of the square. "I'm afraid it's coming," the trooper said.[6]

A couple of miles away on the Ossipee Hill Road, Liz and Champ Gould, who had been on watch for the fire for two days and nights, prepared again to defend their farm. On Tuesday night and all day Wednesday, when the flames had come dangerously close, they had had scores of firefighters with their equipment to help them, but now with the fire headed on all fronts, most of the men had pulled out to help defend other areas. Seven men from the Springvale Fire Department, with their new pumper, were working the Ossipee Hill Road where there were three other houses besides the Goulds'. Lloyd Davis and his brother-in-law, Orel Jones, were helping, as were Sid Emery, Carl Hansen, Colby Ricker—about fourteen men in all.

The fire came as a crown fire down the wooded foothills from Ossipee Hill. Four of the men stood in the field behind the Goulds' barn and watched it come, "roaring four barrels coming down the mountain, scary as hell." They had a 150-gallon tank of water and a length of 1½-inch hose. It was primitive equipment for meeting such a fire. One of the men said, "Let's get out of here." But another said, "We ought to save Champ's barn," and they stood their ground. The fire came out of the woods with a crashing roar into the open field and seemed to disappear in the air over their heads. Behind it came the ground fire, "meandering out of the woods" toward them through the grass.

Carl Hansen and three other men were wetting down the big hen house with a hose. Liz Gould watched them. "I can see them now . . . ," she said thirty years later, "four guys on that hose, just dipping and undulating like a snake. As smoke and flames would come, they would duck down, and then it would go over their heads and they'd get up. Course they had handkerchiefs—no masks, the fire department didn't have any masks—so they had handkerchiefs over their noses."

The wooden cupola on the barn caught fire. One of the men climbed up into it with a hose. The pressure in the gravity fed water supply was just strong enough to force the water out over the end of the nozzle. He stuck it up in the burned hole in the shingles and put the fire out.

Wood lots above and below the Gould farm were on fire. There was no way out by road. Although they felt sure the flames would eventually burn themselves out or move on, Colby Ricker and the Goulds made plans for their safety if the fire swept in on them. Ricker would spray them all with water from a tank on his truck, and they would make a run for a field that had burned over the day before.

It was night now, and below them the fire had swept into South Waterboro. Champ stood on a stone wall and looked down. It looked like everything—houses and woods—was burning. On his barn the steer on the weathervane was spinning "faster than a merry-go-round," he said later. "It was circling. Then it would stop and go the other way."

Lloyd Davis and Orel Jones were waiting for the last of the fire to clear the road so they could get out. They knew the main fire was headed toward Alfred, and that's where they wanted to go. Davis had a farm there with cattle, pigs, geese. . . . While they waited, they looked out over the fire. They were high enough above it so they could see its spread. To the southwest they could look for a mile straight through the forest and see nothing but one rolling ball of fire. Jones, a veteran of World War II, said he'd never seen anything like it during the war. He'd fought from North Africa clear to Germany. He'd seen ammunition dumps blow up; he'd seen a lot, but "I never saw anything like this," he told Davis.

Bessie and Ruel Ricker lived in Saco where Ruel ran the home farm for the Sweetser School, but both had grown up in Waterboro where their parents still lived. Ruel's parents, Harold and Mame Ricker, lived on Ricker Hill, east of South Waterboro village toward Lyman, in a fine old farmhouse that had belonged to Harold's father. Bessie's parents, Ivory and Ruth Smith, lived on another hill on the West Road west of South Waterboro village. Their house was old too, a gem of a Cape Cod, furnished with antiques, well loved by all the family, but especially by Ivory.

Bessie's sister, Esther, and her husband Everett Smith lived in part of the house with their two small daughters, Nancy and Midgie. Someone needed to be near the elder Smiths, for Ivory was a severe asthmatic and had a heart condition, and Ruth was blind.

Since the beginning of the week, when the Shapleigh Plains fire had begun to seem menacing, Bessie and Ruel had traveled to Waterboro every day to check on their parents. On Thursday they had driven up again, leaving their eight-year-old son in Saco with a cousin. He had come with them on Tuesday and, seeing Ossipee Hill outlined in fire, had had nightmares.

Every time they came to Waterboro they found that the fire had spread. From the height of land where the Smiths' house stood, it was possible to watch its progress. They would have liked to have taken Bessie's frail parents to Saco, but Ivory was reluctant to leave. "He just loved that old homestead so much," Bessie remembers. "He just couldn't get up his courage to leave it."

Despite her blindness, Ruth Smith was a person who planned. She had said, "We must get out our Saratoga trunks." She had directed her daughters and their husbands to bring two enormous trunks from the attic. They sat in the middle of the living room, and as Ruth thought of things that should be saved, Bessie and Esther packed them in the trunks. They had packed pictures, papers, a set of flow-blue china that their mother particularly prized, and other things.

On Wednesday Bessie had tried to talk to her father-in-law, hoping to lead him to make some plans for possible evacuation. "Have you your papers and have you your pictures?" she had asked.

"My dear girl," he answered. "That fire isn't going to come anywhere near us."

"I know," answered Bessie, with a conviction she didn't feel, "but if it should. . . ."

On Thursday Ruel left Bessie with her parents before going on to Ricker Hill. "Now I'll watch," he promised, "and if you need me, I'll be here."

Bessie and Esther and Everett Smith spent an anxious day. The fire was moving toward the house from several directions. From a window in a chamber on the second floor of the barn they could see it coming and coming. In the afternoon the wind rose, and it hurried the flames.

Bessie said to her father, "Don't you think we should leave, Dad?" But Ivory Smith could not bring himself to make the decision, even though by then the air was so smoky he was having difficulty breathing.

It was dusk when Bessie went to him and said quietly, "Dad, we have just one road to get out. We have to go." The decision was made. Bessie was to drive Everett's car and take her parents, Esther, the two little girls, and whatever clothes and other things they could fit into the car. Everett had been able to start up an old school bus that Ivory had made once from an ambulance, which had been sitting in the barn, unused, for years. Everett packed it with as many things as he could. But there wasn't room for the flow-blue dishes. When he told Bessie she said, "Well, Everett, we have done the best we could. Just don't tell her." When they finally left the house, Ruth Smith thought they were taking her prized dishes with them.

By the time they were ready to leave, the fire was almost upon them. "When we went out that night," Bessie remembers, "we went so quickly that we left lights on, doors open. We didn't think about anything like that; the fire was coming so fast, and in the dark it was much more frightening."

They drove east toward South Waterboro, but at Old Corner they found the fire had already come between them and the village. They turned onto the Lindsey Road and headed for Alfred. The road was jammed with people fleeing in every kind of vehicle piled high with household goods.

Bessie looked to her left and saw Ricker Hill burning. No buildings were silhouetted against the flames. The Ricker farm was gone. The ten-room house, the barn, the carriage house, the garage, the little blacksmith shop, the hen house—it was all gone. Where were Harold and Mame Ricker? Where was Ruel?

And then, as she drove along the crowded, smoky road, worrying about her husband, worrying about her father who was having such trouble breathing, grieving for the farm that was gone, wondering if her father's would burn too, and wondering where Everett was, for they had become separated on the smoky road, something went wrong with the steering wheel of the car. Suddenly it just went around and around. The car slid off the road. They were in the ditch, and they could see, hear, and smell the fire coming, coming. "I can't tell you the feeling that I had," Bessie said thirty years later, weeping as she remembered her anxiety.

No one hurrying by would stop to help. As each vehicle came along, Bessie and Esther would try to flag it down, but the people would call, "Sorry, we can't stop. Sorry, we can't stop," and keep right on going.

"I shall always believe," says Bessie now, "that it was an act of God that my cousin from Rochester came along." He had heard about the fire in Waterboro, and he and his wife had driven over to see if the Smiths needed help.

"Bess," he called. "What's the matter?"

"Oh, Oscar, something's happened to the steering wheel and it just lifted up and turned right 'round and 'round in my hand, and I can't steer."

"Get in," he said.

Ivory and Ruth, Esther and the girls, and Bessie all managed somehow to get into the car with Oscar and his wife. They took what things there was room for out of Everett's car, leaving everything else behind. One of the things they did not take was money belonging to the Smiths' church. Everett, who was treasurer of the church, had put it in the car at the last minute, without mentioning it to anyone. (They would find the car and the money and everything else intact the next day when they returned, for some friend who came along later, saw the car in the ditch beside the road, recognized it, and towed it into a nearby field that had already burned over.)

They went on to Alfred. Back on the West Road just outside of South Waterboro village, Ruel Ricker was trying to get through to Bessie, but had been stopped by the state police. "I have to get through," said Ruel.

"I wouldn't go through," the grim policeman told him. "It's your life, Sonny, but I'm telling you . . . don't try it."

Ruel turned back. Bessie would not know until she got home to Saco and found him there that he and his parents were safe, but that on Ricker Hill all they had had time to do was turn the animals loose and load an old kitchen desk into Ruel's truck before the fire overran the farm.

Betty Littlefield, of Alfred, worked for the Red Cross. For two days she had been helping in Waterboro, taking coffee and sandwiches to the men in the woods, bandaging cuts and bruises. Late Thursday afternoon she was at the Grange hall on the West Road just a block or so outside South Waterboro village. On the ground floor a canteen had been set up. Upstairs she had laid out bandages and ointments to provide first aid.

It seemed ridiculous to her when without any warning someone from the kitchen crew had come to the foot of the stairs and hollered frantically, "We're evacuating. Don't stop for anything." Surely the situation was not that desperate. No doubt the fire was coming their way, and this was just notice that they had to leave. She began packing her supplies, but then, deciding perhaps she had better find out exactly how close the fire was, went to look out the window at the back of the building. A Gillies Lumber Company sawmill and its sawdust pile were behind the Grange hall. Betty Littlefield looked out onto a wall of fire.

She was the last to leave the hall. "I ran out the door," she remembers. "I ran out the door with my things—I still took my things. Well, I had to set up somewhere else so I had to take my equipment. I got out, and I just couldn't believe the wind. It almost tore the clothes right off me. I ran to the car. It was probably fifty feet or more from the door. I got in and stalled the engine. I flooded it. No one was there. Everyone had gone.

"Cool down," she told herself, "and start it." She waited a minute and then started the car. She drove to the corner a few hundred yards away where Route 202 led off to Alfred. A group of people, who had watched her flight, were standing on the corner "just wringing their hands, their faces perfect blanks, absolutely in shock." When the Grange hall went, it literally exploded.

Seven hundred people fled South Waterboro, clogging the road to Alfred where the town hall, the Grange hall, churches, and private homes were opened to receive them. Malcolm Barter and Jimmy Callahan were among the last to leave. They had seen the fire, a ball of flame like a big moon, coming up behind the sawmill and the sawdust pile from the northwest. It cut through the main street, leaving most of the houses on the northern end intact but sweeping down Lower Main Street toward Alfred, taking just about everything in its path.

The firefighters who had been in the square with their trucks and equipment that morning had been ordered out like everyone else when it was clear that others making a stand on the northwest side of town had failed to stop the fire. Only a handful of men ignored or didn't hear the order. Old Myron Huff was one of them. His own house burned, but he managed to save his daughter's and two others, working so frantically that he didn't notice until afterward that his shoelaces were burned away.

By a fluke, the Springvale pumper and its seven-man crew arrived in the center of town in time to save a large business block and a number of other buildings. The crew had waited an hour and a half to get off the Ossipee Hill Road, coming out at last by the back way to Old Corner on the West Road. They had been following Lloyd Davis on the way to Alfred to head off the fire there, but on the smoky road had lost him, and instead of following Davis by the Lindsey Road to Alfred had turned down West Road and driven straight into the square at South Waterboro village. There, with the sawmill burning, they had set up at the mill pond and saved eight nearby buildings.

Two-thirds of South Waterboro village burned, including the sawmill and a box shop, but not a leather factory, a church, or the town hall. At East Waterboro, which had escaped once from the fire, the flames advanced again and this time took three-quarters of the village. Only four houses were lost at Waterboro Center, but twenty-five summer cottages were destroyed at Little Ossipee Pond. It looked for a time as though North Waterboro—where on Wednesday night the fire had spread into the board yard at Johnson's mill, but had not burned the mill, the church, the school, or anything else in the small settlement—might be wiped out, but a "miraculous backdraft" diverted the flames.

Meanwhile, to the west the Newfield fire was racing on past Poverty Pond where the Waterboro fire had started on the blueberry plains. The Newfield blaze had started near Province Lake in New Hampshire. Now it joined the Waterboro burn, sweeping down around it and on to Ross Corner on the Waterboro-Shapleigh town line. There thirteen houses would burn before it went on toward Alfred.

Reporters Barter and Callahan had driven on through Alfred, down Route 111, heading for Biddeford to file their story about the evacuation of South Waterboro. At the junction of Route 111 and Route 35 in Lyman they stopped at a gas station for a can of oil for their car. Barter had just stepped inside and told the attendant what they wanted when a man burst through the door. "You'd better get out of here! The fire has come past Kennebunk Pond and is headed this way."

"Guess you're my last customer," said the attendant, throwing Barter a can of oil. He grabbed his cash register, threw it into his car,

and fled. Barter and Callahan weren't far behind, heading for Biddeford.

The northwest wind had driven the fire from Waterboro with incredible speed. It had split around Kennebunk Pond, burning cottages
and trees on both sides of the water, traveling so fast that it went right
by a group of cottages in a pine grove on the end of the pond. Later
the flames backed in toward them, but seventy-one-year-old John
Littlefield, who lived year-round at the pond and did not flee the fire,
saved them single-handedly.

The main fire swept on to the junction of Route 111 and Route 35,
where it burned the gas station. Then the wind shifted. It swung into
the northeast.

About a mile down the road, Arthur Roberts looked across the
field behind his house and watched the wind swing the fire around. He
couldn't see flames, just a red glow through the smoke. Soon even
that was obscured. The wind picked the fire up and brought it through
the air across the field. "When that came over the field," Roberts said
later, "all I could think of was a big, rolling wave, a mixture of gas,
ashes, flames, and everything else, just rolling, making the most weird
roaring sound I ever heard in my life. And when it hit the ground, right
in the middle of the board yard, it looked as though there was a big
wave just cascading, opening out, full of fire, right onto those board
piles." It had passed within sixty feet of the corner of his house.

Nothing could be done to save the lumber and the mill—in less
than an hour they were gone. The small group in the field behind the
Roberts and Merrill houses fought spot fires. A manure pile at the Merrill farm exploded into flames. Then they realized that the back of the
Merrills' barn was burning. Ground fire had spread quickly along a
hedgerow that ran across the field to the barn. The men hadn't seen it
through the smoke. They managed to get two horses and a cow out of
the barn, but didn't know there was a calf. Only later did they understand why the cow paced back and forth, back and forth, while the barn
burned. From the barn, the fire spread to the Merrill house. But Arthur
Roberts's house did not burn. It was one of the few to survive in Lyman
which lost 192 year-round dwellings and 100 summer camps.

NOTES

1. Austin Wilkins, Deputy Forest Commissioner, "The 1947 Forest Fire Disaster," State of Maine, 27th Biennial Report of the Forest Commissioner,
   A. D. Nutting, 1947–8.

2. Today Adams Pond is called Rock Haven Lake.
3. Sanders R. Johnson, "Fire Leaves Newfield an Eerie Ghost Town," *Portland Press Herald*, October 24, 1947.
4. *Ibid.*
5. Franklin Wright, "Maine Looks Back on 1947: Burned-Out Families Living in New Homes Year after Big Fires," *Portland Sunday Telegram*, October 24, 1948.
6. J. Malcolm Barter, "Inferno in Maine," *Boston Globe*, October 24, 1947.

On Monday, October 20, a fire that had been mulling underground at North Kennebunkport for almost a week broke out and began to move. Late in the day, fanned by high winds, the fire leaped across Route 1 in an arc of flames that dwarfed firefighters, who stood helplessly by.

Ted Dyer photo

On Tuesday, the 21st, the fire swept into the summer colony of Goose Rocks Beach in Kennebunkport, burning almost 100 houses, forcing residents to retreat into the ocean.

Ted Dyer photo

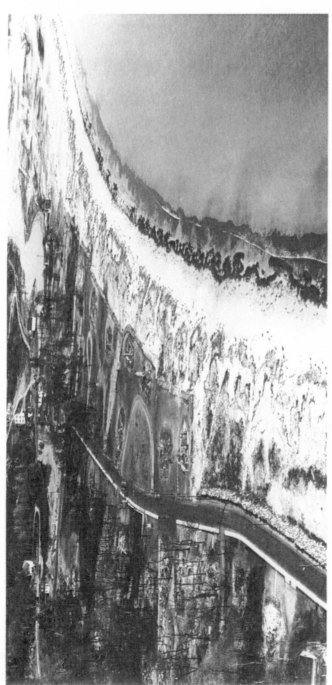

This aerial photo of the eastern end of Goose Rocks Beach shows how thoroughly the fire consumed most of the houses. At the far end of the beach stands the Mignault house, which was saved by a handful of residents who formed a bucket brigade to Little River.

Edward Hipple photo

Armed National Guardsmen were brought in to patrol the ruins at Goose Rocks Beach after looters stole plumbing from the cellars of burned houses.

Portland Press Herald photo

Farmers in Waterboro plowed firebreaks around their houses and barns to save them from a fire that spread from the Shapleigh Plains throughout the town.

Portland Press Herald photo

On Thursday, the 23rd, a fire that had gotten away from firefighters on Mount Desert Island swept into Bar Harbor burning mansions and modest homes. 2500 people were trapped for three hours on the Municipal Pier. This aerial view shows the path of the fire, which was kept out of the center of the town by courageous firefighters.

Bangor Daily News photo

As at Goose Rocks Beach, the complete destruction in the wake of the Mount Desert Island fire was shocking. Here a Bar Harbor man returns to survey the ruins of his home.

Bangor Daily News photo

Chimneys were all that remained of palatial summer homes at Bar Harbor.

Bangor Daily News photo

One of the victims of the Bar Harbor fire was the 100-room Malvern Hotel and 11 cottages on its grounds, well known as one of the finest and most elegantly furnished resort hotels in New England.

Bangor Daily News photo

The greatest loss at Bar Harbor was the Jackson Laboratory, a world-famous cancer research lab whose research records and 90,000 specially bred mice were destroyed.

Bangor Daily News photo

At every fire, firefighters, like these in York County, battled towering flames with primitive equipment—brooms, hand pumps, shovels, and makeshift face masks.

Photo courtesy The Brick Store Museum, Kennebunk

A scarcity of water was one of the problems for firefighters. Here a pumper is filled with water brought in in barrels.

Ted Dyer photo

Firefighters, like these on Mount Desert Island, carried water into the burning woods in Indian tanks, small, hand-operated pumps strapped onto their backs.

Bangor Daily News photo

Home owners evacuated before the advancing flames. An East Waterboro family, whose house was to be one of those to survive in that hard-hit community, prepares to take its furniture to safety.

Photo courtesy The Brick Store Museum, Kennebunk

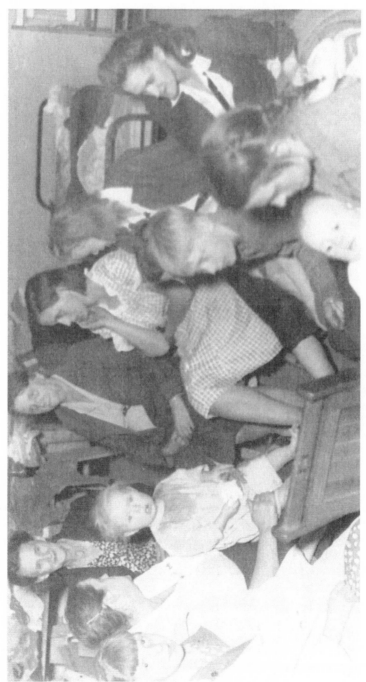

In York County, Biddeford was a center for evacuees. These refugees from Waterboro sheltered at Pepperell Hall, one of the centers set up to receive them.

Ted Dyer photo

Used clothing for burned-out families and firefighting tools were collected at Red Cross centers like this one on State Street in Portland. Transportation for supplies and firefighters was provided by local businesses.

Photo courtesy The Brick Store Museum, Kennebunk

The Red Cross, Salvation Army, American Legion and others carried coffee, soup, and sandwiches to firefighters. Salvation Army workers were particularly anxious to serve men on the fire lines.

Gannett Publishing Company photo

Canteens like this one at the Richmond Grange Hall were set up in every fire area to feed firefighters.

Gannett Publishing Company photo

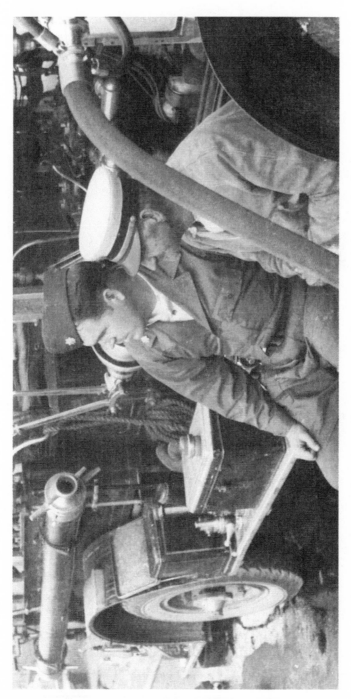

Men went without sleep to battle the relentless flames. Fire Chief Frank Cantara of Biddeford, haggard and unshaven, confers with a National Guardsman about the fire that threatened Biddeford for almost a week.

Ted Dyer photo

Newfield was one of the York County towns swept by fire on Red Thursday, October 23. This aerial view of Newfield's Lower Village shows how few houses were spared.

Portland Press Herald photo

Albert Smith of Newfield was one of 15 people to die as a result of the fires. Here arrows indicate where his body was found (left), the pages of a Bible scattered around him, the remains, of his horse, Jim, nearby (right). Game Warden George Townsend holds up a burned wheel of Smith's wagon.

Gannett Publishing Company photo

Another York County town swept by fire on Thursday was Lyman, which lost 192 year-round dwellings and 100 summer camps. This gas station at the corner of Route 111 and Route 35 went down to the flames.

Photo courtesy The Brick Store Museum, Kennebunk

The crossroads community of Goodwin's Mills on the line between Lyman and Dayton lay in the path of the fire. On Thursday afternoon home owners waited for news of the progress of the fire. Goodwin's Mills was saved by a shift in the wind and a firebreak bulldozed around the settlement.

Ted Dyer photo

At sundown Thursday night flames roared into the seaside settlement of Fortunes Rocks at Biddeford. That night people at neighboring Biddeford Pool could look across the water and see houses burning.

Ted Dyer photo

On the morning of October 24, only six houses were still standing at Fortunes Rocks. Around them lay burned rubble and gray ash.

Ted Dyer photo

Other sections of Biddeford were threatened too. Here firefighters have gathered on the Pool Road to try to stop the fire there.

Ted Dyer photo

Dayton was the last town to suffer severe losses. Roy Meserve was one of those to lose his farm on Saturday, the 25th. He stands by the ruin of his new $1500 tie-up where 12 cows died because he did not have time to set them free.

Gannett Publishing Company photo

Although homes were lost and communities were threatened in Norridgewock and in the Centerville-Jonesboro area, the main losses in central and northern Maine were timber. This aerial view shows the fire that burned to within two miles of Norridgewock and here threatens a set of buildings on Route 201. The buildings were saved.

Gannett Publishing Company photo

Roy Paul, father of eight, began rebuilding the day after fire swept his Lyman home, declaring, "I've always stayed up this way, and I'd hate like blazes to get out now."

Ted Dyer photo

The same unwillingness to accept defeat was shown by the people of Brownfield in Oxford County, which was practically wiped out by a fire. With all the town's public buildings gone, the selectmen used a combination baggage car and smoker, loaned by the Maine Central Railroad, for a "town hall."

Gannett Publishing Company photo

After the fires, towns all over Maine held fund drives to buy equipment for their fire companies. In Kennebunkport the old 1850 hand pumper, still hung with leather fire buckets, was parked in Dock Square to call attention to the need for new equipment.

Photo author's collection

This picture of the flag flown by the Abbott family over the ruins of their Dayton home symbolized for many who saw it in the Portland Press Herald the determination of Maine people to rise above the worst disaster in the state's history.

Portland Press Herald photo

This former schoolhouse, now a private residence, survived the fire that threatened it in 1947. It still stands on the corner of Federal Street and West Avenue in South Waterboro.

Photo courtesy The Brick Store Museum, Kennebunk

Visitors to fire areas like Goose Rocks Beach likened what they saw to the ruins of war-torn Europe.

Portland Press Herald photo

Heroic efforts had saved houses in devastated fire areas, but often no one could explain why houses like this one at Goose Rocks Beach had survived.

Portland Press Herald photo

Aerial photographs like this one of the Waterboro fire, taken from 3,000 feet Wednesday morning, October 22, show the incredible scope of the fires that swept through Maine in 1947.

Portland Press Herald photo

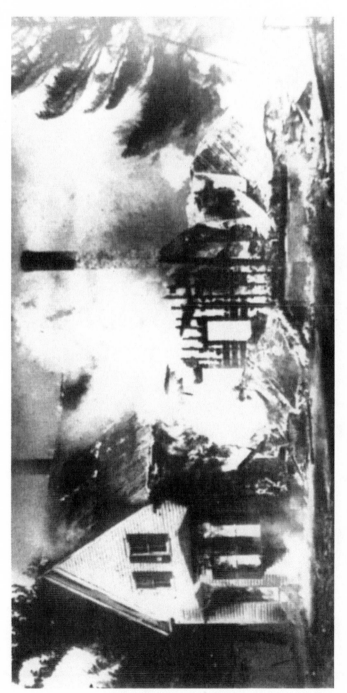

n every fire area families lost homes and possessions. Here a North Waterboro home is swept by the wind-lashed flames that roared out of the surrounding woodland and meadows on that terrible Thursday, October 23.

Gannett Publishing Company photo

Although animals, both wild and domestic, were lost to the fires, surprising numbers survived. This flock of poultry wanders around the ruins of a North Waterboro barn.

Portland Press Herald photo

Chapter VIII:
"We thought we were going to be comfortable."

To the southeast the industrial city of Biddeford had been almost encircled by fire. For three days and nights the North Kennebunkport fire had worked its way around Biddeford, eating toward the outskirts of the city on three sides. Only to the east, where the Saco River separates Biddeford from Saco, was there no fire.

Fire Chief Frank Cantara—weary, grimy, unshaven—had been juggling his firemen and volunteers for three days, trying to keep all the fire lines covered. On Thursday he had about a hundred men on the Newtown Road just above the summer settlement of Fortunes Rocks where the eastern front of the Kennebunkport fire was smoldering. He had men at Clifford Park and at other points along the Pool Road. Northwest of the city another finger of the Kennebunkport fire had crept along the Mountain Road, crossed Route 111, and was in the area between the new turnpike and the Boston and Maine railroad track. From there it could burn into Five Points, where Route 111, Route 1, and West Street came together; it could cross the railroad tracks to May Street; and it could reach South Street. Two hospitals, the Webber and the Trull, would be in its immediate path, and once it started burning houses it could sweep right through the city. Cantara knew he didn't have enough pumpers and hose to stop a fire that big, and men equipped with brooms and shovels couldn't fight house fires.

Officials of Biddeford, and Saco, which could burn if Biddeford did, already had an evacuation plan. If Route 1 south was cut off at Five Points, the escape route would be Route 1 north out of Saco. But that afternoon word came of a vicious woods fire to the north in Scarborough just off Route 1 on the Gorham Road. It had spread to the Gillies Lumber Company where a million board feet of dry lumber was stacked.

If Route 1 toward Portland was blocked, the evacuation route would be to Old Orchard Beach by way of Saco's Beach Street and the Ocean Park Road, but not along the Ferry Road through Kinney Shores where the bridge over Goose Fare Brook was temporarily down. National Guard troops were stationed along these streets to keep traffic moving and the curious away. If the fire crossed the Pool Road in Biddeford and jumped the Saco River, then it could burn along Ferry Road and into Ferry Beach, Kinney Shores, Ocean Park, and on into Old Orchard Beach.

At Old Orchard Beach the owners of the big wooden entertainment pier watched nervously as wind-borne embers from the fires to the northwest dropped from the sky.

The Waterboro fire, which had already cut off Route 5, was headed toward Route 112 to Gorham, and another fire off Saco's Smutty Lane Road could close Route 112 too.

The only other road out of Biddeford and Saco was the as-yet-unfinished turnpike. State Fire Inspector Lawrence Dolby, who lived in Saco, called the foreman of the Lane Construction Company, which was building the turnpike. "If we need to, can we evacuate our people into Portland via the turnpike?" he asked.

"We've got a bridge that's out, that hasn't been completed," the man told him. "The bridge is in, but you can't get to it. But we'll find a way. We'll make a way to get your convoys around there if you need to. . . ."

At the Emery School on Birch Street, Biddeford, during recess Dotty Butler watched the wind swirling dry leaves in the corner of the school yard. It was another warm day, and a strange yellow haze hung in the air, as it had all week, from the fires burning around the city. The sun was an odd color behind the smoke. Dotty's mother, Martina, home for the afternoon from the canteen at Christ Church where she had worked since the crisis had begun on Monday, had lain down on the couch to rest.

Biddeford had become a relief center for York County. Evacuees could rest at the Red Cross canteen at St. Joseph's Hall, get a cup of coffee and a sandwich, and call family and friends to let them know they were safe. Hot meals for firefighters were provided twenty-four hours a day at Christ Church and the White Church, where never-ending streams of tired red-eyed men came to eat the soups, chop suey, beans, macaroni and cheese, and the pies and doughnuts that the women of the churches had made. Sometimes Martina's sixteen-year-old son, Bob, came in, giving her a chance to see him, for when he wasn't out fighting the fire, she was at the canteen.

Her husband, George, was helping to evacuate families. Incredibly, hundreds of houses had burned in Kennebunkport. Even a few Biddeford families had lost their homes, and even she and George had made some preparations for evacuation. They had put a few important things in the car, which stood ready in the driveway for flight. She had heard that the fire was burning in close to the woods at Clifford Park on the Pool Road, less than a mile away.

Martina fell asleep. She was never sure just how long she slept, but she awoke with a start and jumped to her feet. The room was filled with a strange, orange light. Something had changed.

The wind had risen from the northwest, fanning the fire near Five Points into new activity, driving it toward May and South Streets. The call went out for more men and equipment. The men on the Newtown Road were ordered to Five Points, now the danger spot. Trucks with loudspeakers were sent through the city streets asking all able-bodied men to report with brooms and shovels. Workers at the Saco-Lowell shops and the Bates and Pepperell mills were released to go. The sprinkler systems on the roofs of the Pepperell buildings were turned on, and fire patrols were stationed on the roofs of the Saco-Lowell shops, for the air was filled with flying embers. There were rumors that money was being moved from the banks for safekeeping. All ambulatory patients were evacuated by ambulance and private car from the Webber Hospital on Elm Street and the Trull Hospital on South Street.

Mabel Emery, who had already been burned out of two previous homes, and had the day before evacuated her temporary home in an apartment near Five Points, was warned again to leave. "I'm not moving again," she said. Three times was enough. She stayed, and was watchful.

The fire had jumped the railroad tracks and was burning through a field toward May Street and the Webber Hospital beyond. Bob Butler was in the long line of men standing almost shoulder-to-shoulder along the edge of the field. Armed with shovels and brooms, with the wind blowing smoke and cinders in their faces, they stood their ground, stopping the fire at the edge of May Street just three hundred yards from the hospital and holding it there. Other men waited at South Street, but a wind shift kept it from reaching them. On the other side of the city, there was no one to stop the fire on the Newtown Road when the wind hit it and sent it racing to Fortunes Rocks.

At Biddeford Pool the people looked to the west and could see the fire coming toward the coast and Fortunes Rocks. The flames leapt in great arcs from tree to tree. Frank Handlen and Biddeford Pool Coast Guard Station Chief Dan Farnsworth headed for Fortunes Rocks. The fire was there before them, a vortex of wind, smoke, and flames among the houses. Handlen stood in the lee of a garage, buildings burning on every side, and marveled at the veritable snowstorm of sparks in the air around him.

About fifty men had gathered to try to save some of the houses, but with little equipment and no organization they were easily defeated. Burning houses set fire to neighboring buildings, and ground fire crept up on others. Most were summer homes, now closed for the winter, but John Kerr and his wife, of Marblehead, Massachusetts, were still at their cottage beside a freshwater pond. Mrs. Kerr fled to Biddeford, but her husband stayed to fight. Handlen and some of the other men tried to tell Kerr it would be dangerous to stay with his house; but, Handlen remembers, "He wasn't going to give up. Well, you don't just stop a fella. He was going to save his house. I remember seeing him disappear into the smoke . . . by gracious he did."

Later that night when she heard that Fortunes Rocks had been destroyed, Mrs. Kerr told reporters that she had left her husband "enveloped in an inferno of fire." Not until the next morning would she know that he was safe, and that their house, which he had kept wet with water from the pond, was one of only six still standing at Fortunes Rocks.

Juanita and Franklin Spofford lived on the Granite Point Road across Horseshoe Cove from Fortunes Rocks. Goose Rocks Beach was south of them on the other side of Little River. On Monday when the fire started down from North Kennebunkport, Juanita had been in Kennebunkport Village and had had to skirt the fire to get home. Tuesday, when it had burned into Goose Rocks Beach, she and Franklin had been afraid it might jump Little River and reach them. But it didn't. On Wednesday they relaxed. "We thought we were going to be comfortable," Juanita remembers. But on Thursday, when the wind swept the fire into Fortunes Rocks, it also brought it to them.

The Spoffords wet down their house with a garden hose until the pressure failed. Then they filled buckets and tubs and set them around the house. As burning debris carried by the wind fell in the grass, setting it afire, they wet brooms in the buckets and beat the flames out. Bushes beside the garage caught fire. The house across the street and others on the Granite Point Road burned, but the Spoffords' did not.

The wind blew such a gale that it seemed to Juanita she was between two iron walls. Smoke obscured the view across the cove to Fortunes Rocks, but she could hear a bang, and a bang, and a bang—like fireworks—across the water. It was, she thought, oil tanks exploding in the burning houses.

Marshall Goodwin was putting his father's lobster boat on a mooring for the night at The Pool. There hadn't been a sunset because of the smoke; the light on the water had just been a different—a strange—color. Now it was night. Looking across to Fortunes Rocks, he could see the outlines of houses against the fire. The roof timbers of one burning house were silhouetted against the red flames, and as he watched, an oil tank behind it exploded, sending a great spray of fire out over the water.

No one was sure whether or not the houses on The Pool were in danger. The community was surrounded by water, but The Stretch, a mile-long straight road that connects The Pool to the mainland and the eastern end of Fortunes Rocks, was lined with cottages. Most of the men were off fighting the fire, but Mitch Wilby, wearing his World War I helmet, and a few of the older fishermen had stationed themselves on The Stretch to keep watch.

Some families on The Pool were ready to evacuate in lobster boats if need be. Fritzie Handlen, Frank's wife, and some of her neighbors thought the Fortunes Rocks fire had a terrible look of closeness to it—they could actually see the fire in the houses. They decided they might be safer on the ocean side of The Pool's golf course. Fritzie tied herself and her three small children together with a clothesline and with her neighbors crossed the golf course to the rocky shore.

The wind held the fire at Fortunes Rocks where fifty houses, Tanner's Inn, the store, and the Casino (where Roy Emmons's furniture was stored for safekeeping) were destroyed. Gertie Graham, who owned a cottage at Fortunes Rocks, was in Yarmouth at her mother's house. That evening she heard on the radio that the settlement was gone. "I'm sure that's a mistake," she said. But it was not a mistake. Trapped by the ocean and held by the wind, the fire burned with such intensity that it left only chimneys, the black skeletons of trees, and a wasteland of rubble and thin gray ash.

The people of Kennebunkport would have said, that afternoon, that they had had their share of the fire. But they were not done with it. The wind that blew it in on Biddeford and carried it to Fortunes Rocks caught up the remains of the fire in Kennebunkport's Wildes District, which had been held down since Tuesday night, but never completely extinguished.

Marjorie Mosser, Kenneth Roberts's niece and secretary, had gone to Kennebunk at three o'clock Thursday afternoon to get her hair done. While at the beauty parlor, she heard that Biddeford was threatened and the hospitals were being evacuated. By the time she headed home to Rocky Pasture in Kennebunkport, she could see that the sky over Biddeford "looked very bad."[1]

Back home she found things were bad in Kennebunkport again. Kenneth Roberts and a friend, Arthur Gibbs, had gone down to the village fire station to find out what the situation was. The selectmen's office on the second floor was crowded with people, many of them panicky, some predicting that the whole town was doomed, that the roads were going to be jammed and impassable, that the people would "crowd down to the river and just burn there unless we get boats to take 'em across."[2] The fire above Wildes Town was burning hard again. More houses could go there, and a wind shift could bring it into Kennebunkport Village.

Roberts tried to tell them that a stand could be made in the open fields at Rocky Pasture, between the fire and the village. No one listened. Roberts went home feeling pessimistic, and said to Marjorie, who had packed up valuables on Tuesday when it had appeared that the fire would come into the village, "Well, aren't you going to pack up? This is the time to be doing it." So she gathered up the silver service again, taking the flatware and the butter plates off the table, already set for dinner. She collected her dressing table silver and her fur coat and all of Kenneth Roberts's diaries and loaded them into the station wagon.

In the village, families who had not left Tuesday did leave this time. They had heard stories from Goose Rocks and Cape Porpoise people of narrow escapes, of houses and trees exploding. No one could assure them that it was not going to happen in their part of town.

In the woods above the Wildes District Road the firefighters dug in again between the fire and Wildes Town, a cluster of houses between the burning woods and the ocean. Charlie Nedeau was there in charge of a pumper and its crew. He was a man everybody liked and everybody would work for, and, as one of his crew said later, "The night the fire went into Wildes Town he determined he was going to stop it there, and he did."

The Hutchins house and barn caught fire and burned, but it was the only house they lost, even though the wind scaled burning balls of hay from the barn all the way to Turbat's Creek. When the water mains went dry in one part of Wildes Town because of a pumper hooked to a hydrant back along the line, the men opened up an old well and bailed water out of it with buckets.

In the woods they used shovels and brooms, and then, through the influence of John Doherty, who ran the local hardware store, two bulldozers were brought in by Lane Construction Company workers to open a firebreak through the woods from the Wildes District Road to the Buttonwood Road (Route 9).

The bulldozers were huge: so wide that in places the drivers had to take them into the fields because the road was not wide enough, so high that they could just pass under the high tension wires. They cut a swath twenty feet wide through the woods. Their drivers raised their blades to topple large trees, pushing them over as if they were saplings, pushing everything—trees, boulders, and soil—away. The firefighters joked that now Kennebunkport had a superhighway, and they dubbed it "Doherty's Boulevard," but as one of the men said later, "No one will ever realize the extent of the contribution made by those bulldozers."[3]

Cliff Seavey and seven other men worked their way along the edge of this firebreak with a hose reeled out from the town's Mack pumper parked on the road, putting out ground fires along the edges of the trench. It was hard work, carrying the heavy hose as far as it would reach, then kinking it up to add on another piece, and pulling that along the rough trench, spraying the smoldering edges as they went. They had to climb over rocks and felled trees. Sometimes they stepped into piles of branches up to their hips.

Seavey was within a hundred yards of the Buttonwood Road when Bill Studley came up and told him that a new fire had started up, and was "all agoin' " in a patch of woods that had been fire free. Seavey was exhausted. He had hardly slept for seventy-two hours. Later he said, "I just didn't intend for that fire to go any farther." Seavey was not one of the fire chiefs. He was, as he himself would say, "just one of the Indians," but he had had enough of firefighting. He told Studley to go call the selectmen and tell them to send all the men and equipment they could to help put out the fire once and for all. He himself went back along the bulldozed line, climbed into his truck, and drove to the village to make sure the selectmen got the message. In the office over the fire station he told them, "They'd better be there." Then he headed back to the fire. The reinforcements were there. All through the night they sprayed water on the fire, tons of it. By morning it was out.

That night in Kennebunk, people who had fled there from their homes in Kennebunkport and Lyman discovered that they had simply walked into another threatened community. The Waterboro fire, which had burned down into Lyman, didn't stop there. It burned on across the line into Kennebunk at Day's Mills, broadening as it went. It came through Day's Mills at 5:30 P.M., burning two mills, a board yard, and the homes of Percy and Harold Day and their neighbors.

Some of the Kennebunk Fire Department's men and trucks were in Biddeford helping defend the hospitals, but about fifty hastily-gathered men went up from Kennebunk to meet the fire. They found that there was little they could do. The fire was racing before the wind, jumping from knoll to knoll in the rolling countryside.

South of Day's Mills on Route 35 toward Kennebunk, Roy and Lillian Taylor of Maple Top Farm sat down with their family for supper. Looking out of their dining room window toward Day's Mills they saw smoke in the sky. Minutes later, their meal hardly begun, they looked up to see the fire itself coming down across the open fields, a sheet of flame headed toward the Cole Road and West Kennebunk. They jumped up and fled, taking a few pieces of furniture and the kitchen stove with them. They moved so fast they didn't even stop to take the pans of vegetables and frying pan full of pork chops off the burners.

The fire missed Maple Top Farm but burned the Alewive Grange Hall and an old one-room schoolhouse. It swept the Cole Road, burning a dozen houses, before splitting around Alewife Pond and burning on toward West Kennebunk and Kennebunk.

One Kennebunk fireman with a home and business in town saw what was happening and went home to warn his wife. He found her getting supper for friends from Kennebunkport and Lyman, who had fled their homes. He took her aside and said, "Don't go to bed tonight. Pick up a few small things around here that you might want to save.

Put them in the car. Go down to the store and get the books out of the safe. Be ready to leave." He learned later that most of the Kennebunk firefighters found time to do the same.

The people of Kennebunk made ready to evacuate and waited. At midnight the wind dropped and in the woods off Route 35 the fire died down. Above West Kennebunk the fire was burning toward the Mousam River and the Wells line.

That afternoon the Kennebunk Fire Department had been asked to send help to Goodwin's Mills, a village of neat, white houses clustered around a pond and Swan Pond Creek on the line between Lyman and Dayton. Kennebunk had sent only its regrets. Some of its men and equipment had gone to Biddeford where the hospitals were threatened, and Kennebunk officials correctly thought the rest might be needed at home.

But Goodwin's Mills was in trouble too. It appeared that nothing could stop the fire, which had already swept Lyman, from going right on through the small village. Coyle Meserve was with a crew on the bridge over the Creek that afternoon. He could see the flames coming up over Grant's Hill three miles to the west. "I wouldn't have given three cents for the whole village," he remembers.

A wind shift and a wide bulldozed firebreak saved Goodwin's Mills. The wind turned the main fire south toward Kennebunk's Day's Mills, and the ground fire, which burned on toward Goodwin's Mills, was forced around the houses there by what Lloyd Davis remembers as "a hell of a firebreak completely around Goodwin's Mills. They saved Goodwin's Mills, but everything else around that went down."

Alfred, the York County seat, was also under siege. Many Waterboro and Lyman people had fled to Alfred. At the town hall refugees from South Waterboro could see the red glow in the sky to the north where the fire that had destroyed two-thirds of their village was moving toward them down Route 202. To the northwest the Waterboro fire had burned through Ross Corner and was headed toward North Alfred. To the northeast it had swept into Lyman and was burning in on that side toward Alfred village.

Lloyd Davis had raced the fire down from Waterboro. He wanted to get to his farm on Alfred's Back Road, a narrow road off Route 111 on the east side of the village that came out on Route 202 on the north. When Davis and a crew of about a dozen men reached the Route 111 entrance to the Back Road, they found two National Guardsmen posted there with orders to let no one through. The fire was coming down from Bunganut Pond, burning in the neighboring Massabesic Forest. It was going to sweep the Back Road. "This road is going to be closed in half an hour. You can't go in there because you couldn't get out," they told Davis.

"Who says I want to get out?" was Davis's reply. After a week of firefighting he was weary. It frustrated and angered him to be told he couldn't go in to his own property. He had, as he said later, "some strong words" with the guardsmen, and got his crew by.

At home he found that his wife had evacuated after arranging to have the cattle and furniture trucked to safety. The big, old, center-chimney house was empty—not even a chair had been left behind. In the barnyard were three or four hogs, half a dozen geese, and three or four goats. It was night and it was cold and the fire was coming. Davis let them all into the barn, shutting the windows and doors behind them, thinking they would be better off there when the fire came by than wandering loose. He didn't think about the barn burning. He didn't intend for that to happen.

Next morning, after fighting the fire up and down the Back Road all night, Davis returned to his barn and found it full of smoke. At the back, one small, bottom window had been left open, and the pigs, geese, and goats were crowded around it, every snout, bill, and nose reaching for air. Davis marveled that they had survived—had found a way to survive—in the smoke-filled barn.

One set of buildings on the Back Road burned, but with a backfire and just plain hard work Davis and the other men kept the fire from crossing the road into dried grass and bushes that grew right up into the back yards of the houses on the east side of Alfred's main street. "We figured," Davis explained later, "if we lost this road, we'd lost Alfred."

To the north on Route 202 a savage battle raged. The men there pumped water from Shaker Pond to save the Notre Dame Institute and stopped the fire from coming into Alfred village. To the west it would be another three days before firemen from Springvale and Sanford and hundreds of volunteers would stop the fire there. But Alfred would lose only four houses.

In Saco, Bessie and Ruel Ricker, reunited again, sat up all that night with her father, who could not lie down to sleep because of his asthma. They kept the radio on, and as they listened to the reports on the progress of the fire Bessie went over in her mind the harrowing details of the trip home from Waterboro.

After their rescue on the Lindsey Road by Cousin Oscar, they had reached Alfred and the county jail. Ivory Smith had been a trial justice for twenty-one years, and he had said, "Get us to the jail." There would be state police there who would know what roads were open to Saco.

Bessie was deeply moved when prisoner trustees, some of whom Ivory had sentenced, welcomed them kindly, saying, "Come right in, Ivory." They could see how ill he looked and what difficulty he was having breathing.

They stayed only long enough for Everett Smith to find them and long enough for Cousin Oscar to hear on the radio that a serious fire was burning in Rochester. He could take them no farther. The fire was near his house, and he and his wife had left their young son alone.

Miraculously, an uncle from Portland, who had come looking for them also, found them at the jail. Now there was transportation to Saco for Bessie, Esther and her two girls, and Ivory and Ruth Smith.

The state police advised them to take Route 111 through Lyman. The police did not know the fire had already reached Lyman. As the Smiths and Bessie headed down 111 they passed cars and trucks and even a man walking leading a pair of oxen, all going toward Alfred. "I don't understand why there's no one else going this way," Bessie kept saying. At last they had to stop for some men who were driving a herd of cows across the road. The men waved their arms and shouted, "Go back, go back. You're headed right into the fire." They turned back and went by way of Sanford to Wells and from there along Route 1 into Five Points, Biddeford, where the fields were still smoldering on both sides of the road, and so on to Saco.

At home Bessie found Ruel and his brother. Ruel's parents had gone to Sanford to stay with their daughter. "There were eleven of us here that night," Bessie remembers. "We bedded everyone down, everyone except my father who couldn't lie down to sleep. My husband's brother took me aside and said, 'Don't you know your father is dying?' I told him, 'I don't think he is. I've seen him like this so much with his asthma.'

"In those days I had a big, old coal range in the kitchen, and that night we took a big chair out by the stove and put comforters in it and tried to get my father comfortable. My husband and I sat up with him all night.

"Of course, the radio was on and reporting, 'Waterboro has burned. East Waterboro has burned. North Waterboro has burned.'

And my father would say, 'I think the old place is still standing.' And my husband and I would look at each other and think, 'Oh, it's impossible. . . .' "

The next day Ruel and Everett took the truck and went back to Waterboro to see what had happened to the Smiths' house, to Everett's parents' home in South Waterboro village, and what conditions were on Ricker Hill. They were gone all day. At last, late in the afternoon, they drove in. There in the back of the truck was Ivory's old pine desk. It had stood for years in the living room. When he was a trial justice and had tried cases at home at all hours of the day and night, he had always sat at that desk. "They've got Dad's desk. The house must be standing," cried Bessie. Ivory Smith wept. The fire had burned right up in back of the barn, and then apparently the wind had shifted. But everything was gone on Ricker Hill and two-thirds of the houses in South Waterboro village, including Everett Smith's parents' home.

Thursday night in Augusta, Forest Service Commissioner Rendall and Austin Wilkins tried to take stock of the disastrous day. Rendall had named Tuesday, when Kennebunkport had burned and fires had raged all over the state, the worst day in the history of Maine forest fires. Wednesday night Wilkins had told newspaper reporters, "We're making progress. We have [the fires] all surrounded. Things look much better." Now, twenty-four hours later, everything had changed.

Fire was sweeping York County, wiping out whole communities, threatening others. The Fryeburg fire had gotten away and leveled Brownfield. On Mount Desert Island, Acadia National Park was being scorched, and Bar Harbor was burning. A fire in Portland had destroyed half the Maine State Pier. A fire in the business district of Fort Fairfield had already done $60,000 worth of damage.

Fires were threatening the towns of Anson, Baldwin, Bingham, Hermon, and Wayne. Crossroads communities were still in danger from the fire near Centerville and at Norridgewock. These two fires and another at Jackman were burning thousands of acres of prime timber. Power lines and poles were down. The Maine Central Railroad's bridge between Whitneyville and Machias was damaged, and the line was closed.

A new fire had started that afternoon at Richmond when the wind blew a tree across a high tension wire. Wilkins had scribbled notes as the report came in: "Richmond. Bad. Notice of evacuation to all central points. Richmond village cut off completely. Smoke so heavy

Mount Ararat tower can't see, and wind so heavy can't hear. Red Cross alerted."

His phone had rung all day, as it had for three days now. Equipment and men were needed, advice was offered, men with forest fire training were anxious to help. Businesses had called to offer help, as well as individuals like J. D. Tarr of South Gardiner who said he had two trucks and a bulldozer that he would take "anywhere in the state."

That night Governor Hildreth declared a state of emergency. He gave the Forest Service responsibility for fire control all over Maine, not just in the District, and created a Fire Emergency and Information Office at the State House to coordinate the work of state relief agencies, the Red Cross, Salvation Army, service organizations like the American Legion, and local organizations.

Hildreth went on the radio Thursday night to tell Maine people what steps were being taken at the state level to deal with the disaster. He asked them to "organize on the basis [you] did in wartime through Civilian Defense" to fight the fires, control traffic, handle evacuation, and give aid to refugees. Much of what he asked for was already being done.

NOTES

1. Details of Marjorie Mosser's experience on Thursday are taken from a letter written by her to her mother, Mrs. Harris Mosser, Saturday, October 25, 1947.
2. Kenneth Roberts, *Diary,* October 23, 1947.
3. Waldo Pray, "Trucks Play Major Role in Fighting Fires," *Portland Sunday Telegram,* October 26, 1947.

Chapter IX:
"All safe. Home gone."

The relief effort began simply with friend helping friend and neighbor helping neighbor. It was natural for firemen from Kennebunk to help Kennebunkport fight the fire in North Kennebunkport. It was natural for Thelma Burrows to put on a pot of coffee and set out a plate of doughnuts for the firemen, and for Biddeford people who had worked on the Red Cross Canteen Corps during the war to provide food for families who were evacuated from their homes on West Street on Monday night. But before the crisis was over, help would be coming from strangers: from distant towns and cities, even from out of state. Local, state, and national organizations and state and federal agencies would be involved, as well as private businesses of all kinds, and individuals. They provided manpower and firefighting equipment, food, clothing, medical care, and shelter for firefighters, evacuees, and the homeless.

The first and greatest need was for men and equipment. Not one of the small towns involved had enough of either to deal with the major fires that were burning. At first only neighboring towns helped, but as the fires spread help came from more distant communities. When Kennebunkport's Chief John Eldridge knew what he faced, he telephoned Portland's Chief Oliver Sanborn, who arrived in forty minutes with men and equipment. Thirty-eight foresters and employees of the National Park Service were flown to Acadia National Park in army planes from New York, Florida, Virginia, Georgia, and Kentucky.

The United States Forest Service dispatched experts from its headquarters in Upper Darby, Pennsylvania, into York County to fight the fire in the Massabesic Experimental Forest in Lyman and later provided help to Commissioner Rendall in coordinating York County's firefighting force.

With World War II just ended, all branches of the armed services still had installations in Maine. These sent help as did units in Massachusetts and other nearby states. Soldiers from Portland's harbor defenses went to Kennebunkport and Waterboro. More than two thousand men from Bangor's Dow Field and two hundred more from New York's Mitchell Field were on Mount Desert Island. The navy sent men into York and Oxford Counties, and when the destroyer escort *Powell* arrived at Bar Harbor after midnight on the twenty-third to find that the people they had been sent to rescue from the town pier had been evacuated by land, crew members were sent ashore to help as firefighters.

Coast Guard stations all over Maine and in Boston sent ships to Kennebunkport, Saco, and Bar Harbor, which ran hose lines ashore. Reserves from the U.S. Marines' 18th Engineers Company in Portland fought in York County, and two marine doctors helped man a medical unit set up in Waterboro by Maine General Hospital staff. Maine National Guard units were called up and served on all fire fronts directing traffic, patrolling burned-out areas, setting up communications systems, and in some cases fighting fires.

Each military unit came with a commanding officer and its own equipment. Often the military men helped bring order out of chaos. Some of them were retired officers who knew how to give orders and organize crews. Reports of college freshmen leading firefighting details seemed surprising until it turned out that the "freshmen" were veterans, back in school under the G.I. Bill.

Kenneth Day of Parsonsfield knew a lot about fighting fire. He had been trained at a Civilian Conservation Corps camp in the White Mountains National Forest during the 1930s. In the spring of 1945, when he returned from a tour of overseas duty, he had been sent to serve with the U.S. Army's 3212 Engineers, a firefighting company stationed in Washington and Oregon where balloon-borne Japanese incendiary bombs were setting forest fires. On October 18, Day wrote to Commissioner Rendall in Augusta to "offer my help in York County during this crucial time." His knowledge of the use of backfire would keep the Newfield fire out of Parsonsfield.

The military training of Andrew Mavrakos of Sanford saved a Lyman family from disaster. Late Thursday night Mavrakos, a recently returned veteran, and his brother-in-law, Robert Lord, were sent in a truck to evacuate a family that lived on a remote, wooded road. The men found the French-speaking family, a father and three children, huddled in their dooryard. The father was pouring water over his children to offset the terrific heat of the fire, which was burning on all sides.

Realizing their escape route had been cut off, Mavrakos grabbed a shovel and began to dig furiously, carving a wide but shallow hole— a foxhole—in the ground. Luckily, the family, who did not understand English, did not have to be told the purpose of the foxhole. Without a word they dropped into it with Mavrakos and Lord and crouched there. The greedy flames destroyed the house and truck and encircled the foxhole before racing on. Mavrakos's war-time training and quick thinking had saved the lives of the little group.[1]

As important as the servicemen themselves was the equipment they brought with them. Their trucks, pumps, hose, radios, and in some cases planes, were a vital supplement to the skimpy, obsolete, often makeshift equipment of the small-town fire departments. The military equipped its own men, and, as hundreds of volunteers flooded the fire areas, arriving without even the most rudimentary tools, the military helped equip them, bringing supplies in from out of state when inventories at Maine bases were exhausted.

Besides the usual equipment, the military had fog pumps, portable lighting units, field kitchens, medical supplies, radio-equipped vehicles, and walkie-talkies. All were useful, but it was the radios that helped the most. Radios came to be considered one of the keys to successful fire control,[2] but in 1947 they were not part of the equipment of a small-town fire department. "We didn't own such a thing," Lloyd Davis remembers. The state police had radio-equipped cars, but even they did not have walkie-talkies—portable, battery-powered, two-way radio sets.

In every instance where radio equipment was available it was effective. In York county, state troopers in radio-equipped cars passed to firefighters valuable information supplied by their radio technician in the Ossipee Hill tower in Waterboro. The police barracks at Wells looked "like an army field operations office with maps marked with pins and red crayons showing fire districts, and tags with troopers' names on strategic locations."[3]

On Wednesday when the Waterboro fire swept over Ossipee Hill, driving the watchman and the technician out of the tower, the radio transmitter was knocked out of commission. For the next two or three days, until it could be repaired, radio communication was maintained with cars, one stationed on the hill, another beside an open window at the Wells barracks. Messages received from Ossipee could be relayed through the window to an operator inside, who transmitted them to patrol units throughout the county.

At Bar Harbor state police in radio-equipped cruisers patrolled the perimeter of the fire and maintained contact with their Bangor barracks. This system was knocked out Thursday night when the operator in the control tower on Cadillac Mountain was forced to flee, and the transmitter was damaged by the fire. By 9:30 the next morning an engineer from Bangor's radio station WJOR had the transmitter working again. In their official report on the week's events the Bar Harbor police would say, "The assistance rendered by the state police radio communication during [Thursday] and the next few days cannot be over-emphasized. . . ."[4]

One problem officials did not have was finding enough volunteers to fight the fires. As soon as the magnitude of the Kennebunkport blaze was evident, appeals were broadcast over the radio for help. Volunteers were told to report to Portland's police headquarters where trucks would take them to the fire area. The American Legion quickly responded by registering and transporting the hundreds of volunteers. The Portland Coach Company and Greyhound Bus Lines, local businesses, the military, and individuals provided buses and trucks. By the end of the week when it was estimated that twenty thousand men were fighting Maine's fires, volunteers were being turned away from registration centers. There was such a diversity of firefighters that one reporter from the *Sanford Tribune,* who saw a conventionally dressed fireman in raincoat and boots, commented on that rare sight.

There were no special qualifications for being a firefighter, just a willingness to go where you were sent and to work hard. Some volunteers did have special training—as veterans or as members of the Civilian Conservation Corps during the Depression. Some had simply fought fires before. When factories, stores, and businesses of all kinds began to release their employees for firefighting, some of the men had special skills to offer. Lane Construction Company workers came off the turnpike with their bulldozers, as did construction workers from the Saco River's Skelton Dam at Union Falls. The Saco-Lowell Shops in Biddeford and the New England Shipbuilding Company at South Portland sent their own plant firefighting crews. The Maine Central

Railroad sent a thirty-five-man section gang to North Kennebunkport when the fire threatened the railroad track there. Guards from the mills in Biddeford were assigned to guard duty and traffic control.

But employees of the Bath Iron Works, who fought the fire at Brunswick, were just able-bodied men willing to work. If a factory was near a fire, it released its employees. Workers from the Machiasport Canning Company and American Sardine Company fought the Centerville-Whitneyville-Jonesboro fire, as did men from the Crane Lumber Company and officials of the St. Regis Paper Company. Workers from the Saco-Lowell Shops, Bates, and Pepperell mills fought the Biddeford fires. One hundred men from the Norwalk Shoe Company fought the fire at Norridgewock. On October 24, the day after York County was swept by the Waterboro and Newfield fires, the Goodall-Sanford mills in Sanford closed "for the duration" to release employees for fire duty. By the end of the week even retail stores like A. H. Benoit in Portland were organizing employees into crews.

Wherever men were part of a group, crews were organized. Forty men from the Junior Chamber of Commerce in Bangor fought at Bar Harbor. Native Americans from the reservation at Pleasant Point fought a bad blaze at Dennysville. In Windham seventy-five cottage owners at Duck Pond held a fire in check until the fire department arrived. Football coaches led their squads to fight, and the Brothers from St. Louis High School in Biddeford joined the battle to save the Notre Dame Institute in Alfred.

Plaid-shirted fishermen, farmers, and businessmen volunteered too. Men came from out of state. A Michigan man, visiting in Portsmouth, who had experience fighting forest fires, came with his four sons to help fight the Kennebunkport fire. Aurele Cote, crew member of an army transport docked in Boston, got leave to come to Maine to fight the fires. "I'm here because I know how it is," he explained. "My dad had a good farm stand at Van Buren until a fire got loose up there two years ago."[5]

Among the most enthusiastic volunteers were the high-school and college students. They came from Bates, Colby, Bowdoin, and the University of Maine. The entire student body of the Bangor Theological Seminary went to Bar Harbor. Young men from the University of New Hampshire were bused to Kennebunkport and Waterboro.

For Forestry Department students at the University of Maine the fires offered experience as well as an opportunity for service. University crews were organized under the direction of fifty forestry students. By the end of the disaster the university estimated that twelve hundred of its students had put in twenty-four thousand man-hours as firefighters.

High-school boys were encouraged to collect brooms, work on canteens, or serve as messengers, but many went out on the fire lines. It was an experience they never forgot. They relished being on their own, sharing the experience with buddies, coming home at dawn along familiar streets—unfamiliar in the early-morning light when the people in all the houses were still asleep. Kid-like they horsed around: it was fun to ride in the back of a truck with an Indian pump and squirt water on all the passing cars. But they worked hard too and learned lessons that would stay with them all their lives.

One middle-aged man, looking back on his experience as a sixteen-year-old, has said, "I had a lot of interesting experiences during that two-week period, but there were lessons that I learned about myself, and other people, and life in general. I remember on several occasions I would be out in the woods, quite a ways back in the woods, and it would be dark, and the flames would be roaring up through, and the sky would be brilliant red, full of flame and smoke and embers. And the noise was fantastic. And I can remember being back away from the flames, and looking at them a half a mile or more away, and it looked like the whole world was on fire.

"The flames and the heat and the red would be so high, and to know that we would have to be going up to that fire in order to fight it was frightening. I would think, 'This is crazy. There is no way a person can survive up that close to those flames.' But we had to do it. Someone had to do it, and we were there, and that's what we were trying to do.

"So we would just grit our teeth and grab our tools, and with our weary arms and legs either walk or bum a ride on a running board, or on the back of a truck, and go right up to that big, red, fiery monster, and jump out and go to work. And it was interesting—once you got up close to the flames, the situation seemed to be something that you could handle. You were so close that you couldn't see the massive effect, the massive scope of the fire. What you did see was a set of flames or a wall of fire no more than three or four feet high. Every once in a while a tree nearby would go up—the fire would crown momentarily in one of those trees and it would explode just like a Roman candle going off; but, most of the time the fire would be only three or four feet high, and there would be gaps in the fire line . . . it wouldn't be one solid wall of fire. And as you got close to it you'd think, 'Well, this is something I can handle. I just won't worry about what's on either side of me. I'll just take care of what's right straight in front of me, and this I can handle.'

"As I've lived these next thirty years it has seemed as though a lot of life's problems are that way. As you look at the total complexity and scope of the problem, whatever it is, it seems to be so massive that you wonder, 'How can I ever cope with it.' But once you decide that you've got to do something about it, grab the bull by the horns, and step right up to it, you find that on close examination it's something you can handle."

These young men found it hard work to carry the heavy back pumps full of water. It was a strain for them to keep up with the men they fought beside. Occasionally their youth and agility gave them the advantage. Allen Salisbury of Bar Harbor remembers being given a group of high-school boys to help him move a line of hose through the woods. "I would say, 'Ahead,' and they was supposed to drag the hose along. Kids, you know, they was young and full of pep. I came home and my clothes was practically in rags—almost not decent to go around. . . ." The boys had moved so fast through the underbrush and brambles that Salisbury had all he could do to keep up with them, let alone to avoid getting his clothes torn.

The large number and diversity of firefighters presented grave problems. When busloads of men arrived in a small town, someone had to find equipment for them and send them out on the lines. On the lines someone had to tell them what to do; show them how to clear a firebreak down to mineral soil; dig out a smoldering root system; use an Indian pump; tell them that they were not in danger from a roaring wall of fire, which more experienced men knew would pass overhead.

Someone had to be sure they did what they were told to do. Sometimes inexperienced men, left to patrol a fire line, would decide things were under control and simply walk away. In one case a group of college boys was left to patrol a fire that was burning on one side of a road. Their job was to see that it did not cross the road. It was night and cold. When their fire boss came back two hours later, he found the boys asleep around campfires they had started on the fire-free side of the road.

Many volunteers did not even have proper clothing. They would leave home dressed for the heat of the day. At night, out in the woods, it was cold. Someone had to provide them with warm clothing. One firefighter remembers how quickly he discovered that he needed "to get a pair of boot shoes because low shoes just filled up with hot ashes."

Small-town firemen found they not only had to tell inexperienced volunteers what to do, they had to try to re-educate big-city firemen, who were trained to fight house fires. The rural firefighters were on home ground and had fought woods fires, but the city firemen with their elaborate equipment did not always listen to them. One volunteer remembers an incident that happened in York County when a group of professional city firemen came to relieve a bad situation on a country road. "They drove up in a big white truck with all the latest equipment. Most of us were standing along the road waiting for the fire to come to us. After a week of firefighting we thought we'd become kind of professionals. They were told not to move their equipment into the woods, but they insisted. It wasn't long before they came out again . . . without the equipment. They found they couldn't fight the fire in the woods with hoses."

The influx of firefighters into unfamiliar territory led to comical situations. Liz Gould overheard a group of Portsmouth high-school boys speculating about the absence of sidewalks in rural Waterboro. And Allen Salisbury tells the following story: "They sent Park Service men here, you know. And this one from out in the middle states . . . he was never near the ocean. And they gave him a group of men to go down by Otter Creek and put a pump in the creek there and pump salt water to try to wet down the ground and try to keep the fire from crossing there. The tide happened to be going out. He went back up to the park office, and he says, 'Say, we ought to have more pumps like the one I got. That thing's lowering the creek to beat the band.'" Salisbury laughs, and adds, "You know, that really shook the whole outfit!"

Leadership was a problem. Natural leaders came to the fore—men who knew how to get along with their peers and to get them to work together, but there were not enough leaders. Sometimes there were too many: selectmen, wardens, fire chiefs. It was not easy to know who had authority or who was best qualified to take charge. In some instances volunteer firemen from a small town would take orders only from their own chief. Usually when a military unit came in, this problem would be overcome, for the officer in charge would extend his command to non-military personnel and would coordinate the whole force.

But for all the problems of inexperience, poor leadership, and inadequate equipment, the dedication, unselfishness, and willing spirit of the firefighters was universally praised. They left their jobs, which meant sacrificing personal income; they went without sleep and proper food; they endured miserable conditions and even danger. And many would say afterward, "I never worked so hard in my life."

"We worked twenty-five hours a day," Arnold Stinson of Cape Porpoise said, and then told the story of the man who once worked on a forest fire "and put his time in for twenty-five hours. The selectmen called him on the carpet and said, 'How is it . . . there's only twenty-four hours in a day and you fought twenty-five?'

" 'Well,' he says, 'I fought my noon hour.' "

Paying the firefighters was one of the problems. It was customary for towns, with state help, to pay men who fought forest fires within their borders. At the beginning of that week when Maine burned, when fires were still small and easily contained, although not put out, firefighters were sent home by some officials who wanted to limit the expense to their town. In one or two instances where this was done, the fires later destroyed thousands of acres of timber and homes. But as the week went on, paying the hundreds of firefighters seemed less and less possible and even unimportant.

Alfred's fire chief had been keeping a careful record of his crew's hours on the Waterboro blaze. Finally, one of his men said to him, "Why don't you throw that book on the fire. This bill is never goin' to get paid. How they goin' to pay with half the state of Maine burnin'?"

Pay was not on most men's minds. They had come to help because it did seem that half the state was on fire. They went unselfishly where they were needed. Sometimes this meant that a man was not home to save his own house when the fire came. Lawrence Ireland was fighting the fire at the western end of Goose Rocks Beach when his home on the eastern end burned. Men from Lyman lost their homes to the fire while they were on the lines in Waterboro.

The work was dirty, hazardous, even dangerous. Few firefighters escaped without minor burns, cuts and bruises, and eyes that bulged and smarted from the smoke. Smoke-filled lungs caused problems during the winter of 1948 when men who had fought the fires seemed especially prone to chest colds and coughs. Fumes from burning poison ivy caused skin poisoning. Men were carried off the lines prostrate from heat or shortage of oxygen. There were more serious injuries too, some caused by related traffic accidents; but not one firefighter lost his life, even though there was real danger.

Nine men were almost trapped near Fryeburg. Surrounded by fire, eight of them crawled a quarter of a mile to safety, dragging the ninth, who was overcome by smoke. In Jonesboro Allan Brown and two other students were reported missing. When they turned up, they had a frightening story to tell. Trapped in the woods by the fire, they remembered a large, steel culvert under a nearby road. They raced to the road and crawled into the culvert after first burning back a patch of ground on each of its open ends. They waited, sharing their refuge with a porcupine, a skunk, and several rabbits, for the fire to pass. It took twenty minutes and sounded like a freight train overhead.[6]

Sometimes a crew went from one dangerous situation to another. John Kelley, whose experiences fighting in the Waterboro area have remained vivid to him after thirty years, tells what happened after he and a crew of men escaped from the burning hilltop above what was probably the tiny settlement of North Waterboro. "It was a real shake, rattle, and roll type of ride down that steep mountainside in that old dump truck, but we finally got down into the main settlement from which we had started. We no sooner got into the town, and it was late afternoon now, than we were told the fire was building up all around this particular settlement. It was like in a little valley, kind of flat. I remember there was a sawmill and a pond across the road from the mill, and dwellings in a little village complex. The place was just filled with firetrucks and dump trucks and bulldozers and Merrill Transport trucks that were hauling water. Night was coming on and the fire situation was worsening. It was getting dark, and the whole town was under a rain of burning embers, smoke, and sparks, and the word was around that the town was completely encircled. They were afraid that the whole town was going to go, and there was no way that we could get out or additional equipment could get in.

"The fire was so close now that buildings around the edge of the town—I'm speaking of a town maybe a mile in diameter—were burning. Our main effort was to try to keep the roofs of the houses in the town wet down because there were so many large embers that would fall and ignite whatever they landed on.

"I spent most of my time near the sawmill. Stacks of lumber that were piled up to dry were burning furiously, and sparks from this were blowing all over the area. We really had our hands full trying to keep the roofs wet so they wouldn't ignite.

"Then finally the situation deteriorated so that everyone was forced to the center of town near the pond. Well, all afternoon the firetrucks had been pumping water out of it, so it was practically nonexistent. There was maybe a foot of muddy, sloppy water left in it. All the people left in town gathered near the pond, and most of us went out and scootched down in the mud and water. We were afraid the fire was going to consume the entire town, and we figured our best chance to pull through was to get out in that pond.

"The smoke was so thick that you couldn't breathe if you stood up. This thick, heavy, acrid smoke hung like a curtain of fog over the whole town. Three feet from the ground it was still fairly open so you either had to lie down or crouch down to get under the smoke so you could breathe.

"We spent a good part of the night there, until just before dawn the fire quieted down and some additional tank trucks and equipment were able to get through the fire and get in to us."

Although all the firefighters did not experience danger, the hard work and long hours were universally shared. Kelley has said that one of the things he learned was that "a human being can stand a lot more physical exertion than he thinks he can. The excitement and the glamour, if you will, in any disaster situation wears off pretty fast. Ninety percent of forest firefighting is just plain old back-breaking, stomach-wrenching, hand-blistering hard work.

"One of the biggest problems in fighting a forest fire in natural areas like Maine's forests is that the duff and litter and all the organic material in the upper few feet of the forest floor—and sometimes quite deep—is flammable. And you'll get an old tree stump system that will smolder and smolder for days and weeks, even months, unless it's dug out and wet down and put out. And that means someone has to go in there and dig those persistent fires out. What a miserable, rotten job that is!"

The firefighters learned that they could go on a long time with little sleep. One Kennebunk fireman who went ten days with only two or three half-hour naps said, "I didn't believe I could do it." Some went home to rest, others just slept where they could—at one of the canteen centers where cots were set up, or in the firehouses on the floor or sitting up in chairs, on the ground, or in their trucks.

In Waterboro on Friday, the twenty-fourth, Malcolm Barter of the *Boston Globe* asked a fireman how long he'd been fighting the fires. "How long?" answered the man. "I started Tuesday. That's last Tuesday. Last week. We started up in Shapleigh, and here we are."[7]

Getting proper food was a problem too. The relief effort to supply food for the firefighters was stupendous. If a man could get to a canteen in a church, Grange hall, or somebody's home, he would find plenty of hot, nourishing, homecooked food. But on the lines he was apt to get sandwiches and coffee. Allen Salisbury remembers, "Everywhere I was stationed a canteen would show up with Spam sandwiches. I got so I was throwin' the Spam away and eatin' the bread. . . . Took a year and a half before I could eat Spam."

One canteen worker who carried food into the woods to firefighters waited patiently while a small crew of men finished filling a cracker barrel from a water truck and then came over to eat. They were dirty, red-eyed, unshaven, rumpled, and hungry. One was delighted with the contents of his sandwich. "No jelly in this, George," he said to a companion."[8]

Clayton Weymouth went eight days and nights without sleeping in a bed or eating a proper meal. He never forgot that he got his first hot meal at a church in Kezar Falls, and said, "After that week I didn't like sandwiches for a long time."

There was plenty of food. It was distributing it that posed the problem. As soon as firefighting crews were organized, there were people working to feed them. Even before the Red Cross and Salvation Army were mobilized, individuals were busy making sandwiches and coffee. From modest beginnings grew full-fledged canteens. In Kennebunkport Thelma Burrows progressed from supplying coffee and doughnuts to running a twenty-four-hour-a-day canteen in her home. She did not work alone. Her first helpers were Arundel Engine Company wives, but neighbors and friends joined in. "Even people on the outside realized that we needed things," Thelma explains. "I can't tell you the amount of sandwiches that came in. Well, of course, that was wonderful only they made them in a hurry, and the men needed something to drink with them besides coffee."

The men also needed more than sandwiches to eat. By the second day of the fire the women had borrowed chairs and long tables from the hall upstairs over the fire station, where potluck suppers were usually held, and set them up in Thelma's large dining room. "We could seat forty," she remembers.

In an effort to provide hot food the women took some of the sandwiches apart and fried the cold meat and toasted the bread, but soon regular meals were being cooked. The kitchen at the Burrows house did not have the facilities for cooking large amounts of food so Adelaide Day, Eleanor Clough, and Louise Swain opened the kitchen at the Sea Side House, a hotel at Kennebunk Beach, and the main dishes were prepared there.

Each morning the women met to decide what the hearty meal of the day was going to be—meat and vegetables, creamed chicken or turkey, spaghetti, chop suey, or baked beans. It would be cooked at the Sea Side House and delivered by 11:30 to the canteen where all morning eggs, cereal, doughnuts, toast, fruit, and coffee had been served. The mid-day meal was served until it was gone. During the afternoons and evenings there would be chowders and stews. A hot meal was available no matter what time of day a firefighter arrived at the canteen.

The food came from many sources. Supplies at the Sea Side House were used, and other local hotels like Breakwater Court and the Narragansett, which had been closed for the winter, contributed what they had on hand. The selectmen told the canteen women to buy what they needed and send the bill to the town. Women brought jars of vegetables from their own cellars and cooked and sent food to the canteen. The owner of the Star Dust Inn in York heard about the canteen and sent up two milk cans full of turkey stew.

One day a man came into the canteen and asked, "What do you need most?" The answer was milk. They needed it to make chowder, but they also had discovered that the first thing men just in from the fire should put into their stomachs was milk. It seemed to settle the smoke they had swallowed. If they ate a solid meal first, they would be sick. The stranger, who turned out to be the owner of the Merrill Transport Company in Portland, made arrangements with Hood's Dairy to supply the canteen.

The women learned what was needed as they went along. One experienced firefighter took Thelma aside and suggested that she would be doing the men a real service by providing prunes. After that, prunes and applesauce were kept on the tables at all times.

The canteen in Thelma Burrows's home was not the only one in Kennebunkport. The Red Cross arrived with mobile canteens, and meals were available at the Grange hall where 1,500 loaves of bread were made into sandwiches in one day, and stews, chowders, cake and doughnuts were served. But even so, and despite the fact that food was taken to the firefighters on the lines, it was estimated that during the ten days the Burrows canteen was open about 1,000 firefighters a day consumed 210 gallons of milk; 107 pounds of cold meat; 130 pounds of beef; 15 gallons of creamed turkey and chicken; 130 gallons of fish and corn chowder; 500 gallons of soup; 3 cases of dried spaghetti; 5,000 doughnuts; 60 dozen eggs; 25 pounds of dried beans; quantities of potato salad, scalloped potatoes, chop suey, and spaghetti sauce; thousands of sandwiches; and about 60 gallons of coffee a day.

The canteen stayed open even when it appeared that Kennebunkport Village itself was in danger of being swept by the fire. On Thursday, when they needed more silverware, one of the women brought in her best sterling flatware and laid it on the table. "Why that's your best silver," Thelma said. "You don't want to use that."

"The way things look it might just as well be used here. We aren't going to have anything anyway."

"Oh, it can't be that bad," Thelma said.

"I guess you haven't heard," the woman replied. The fire was headed into Buttonwood at the other end of School Street.

The women stayed on duty, feeding the men, opening their homes so they could sleep and wash, relaying telephone messages to the fire station across the street when that line was busy. Everyone helped: cooking, serving, washing dishes, making toast under the broiler to keep up with the demand for large quantities.

This kind of effort was put forth by people all over the state. A *Portland Press Herald* columnist described a canteen at Richmond.

> The women of the town, the Grange, and the Red Cross had those big tables set up covered with clean, white paper, and loaded with baked beans, bread, cake, cookies, fresh doughnuts and butter. The ladies cruised up and down behind the eaters, never allowing a coffee cup to be emptied. In the kitchen a crew kept the big coffee urns bubbling, the beans heating in the oven, and the pitchers filled. A huge vat of pea soup for the field crews steamed on the stove. Volunteers filled milk cans and Red Cross thermos jugs with coffee and soup.[9]

Church women, sewing circles, home economics classes, restaurants, and individuals channeled their contributions through the Red Cross and the Salvation Army. Everyone wanted to help. At Christ Church in Biddeford, every morning without fail a small, old, French man would appear with a pot full of savory tomato-rice soup.

On Tuesday the National Red Cross alerted all its southwestern Maine chapters to feed firefighters and assist the homeless and sent its disaster chief to direct relief activities in York County. In Biddeford, the churches opened canteens to supplement the work of the Red

Cross. The Red Cross also sent out mobile canteens, but most men re-member that it was the Salvation Army who sought them out on the fire lines.

It seemed to some that the more remote their position, the more apt they were to see the Salvation Army. One man remembers that he was one of about two dozen men who had gone way back in the woods, up on a hill, somewhere near Kezar Falls, to set a backfire. It was about two o'clock in the morning, and they had been hard at it for some hours digging out a fire line. They were tired, hungry, thirsty, and cold. Suddenly, way off down the rough, rutted, narrow old log-ging road that led up the hill, they could hear "a vehicle coming. It was grinding and groaning, and every once in a while we could hear gears clash." The men wondered who would be coming up that road in the middle of the night.

Soon a pair of headlights appeared, and the car came right up to the top of the hill where the men were working. It was a black 1938 Oldsmobile sedan. The driver was a man in his fifties wearing a Sal-vation Army uniform. With him was a woman. "She must have been in her sixties, a white-haired grandmother type. And she was wearing a Salvation Army uniform too . . . bonnet and the whole thing."

On the back seat of the car they had a cardboard box full of sand-wiches and two big thermos jugs, one of coffee, one of soup. They had heard about the crew working up on the mountain and thought they might be hungry. The man who remembered this incident added, "I tell you, we were mighty pleased and mighty grateful. We were so tickled that we could almost cry for the sheer happiness of it."

The Salvation Army wanted to be where the trouble was. Perhaps it was this same couple—an elderly man and woman, wearing Salva-tion Army uniforms, and driving an old black sedan—who pulled up to Warren Walker, who was directing traffic at Clark's Mills, leaned out the window of their car, and asked, "Where's the hottest place."

But if firefighters were often touched by the actions of canteen workers, in at least one instance it was the other way around. A man from the Red Cross canteen in Kennebunk told of going out with sandwiches and coffee to men in the field. "Only by shouting could he locate the men, who then came out of the woods to receive the food. It was so dark it was impossible to identify the firefighters. After delivery of the packages there came a deep voice from the fog and smoke, saying, 'I have been in the habit of saying grace before eat-ing.' " The firefighter offered a prayer, which the man from the canteen said was "one of the most impressive petitions he had ever heard considering the unusual conditions."[10]

No one organization was responsible for any one phase of relief. Resources were channeled through the most effective agency. In Biddeford the Masons offered the use of their well-stocked kitchen to the Salvation Army. Grange halls were opened up to the Red Cross. In Sanford four businesses and two private citizens loaned Salvation Army workers three jeeps, a truck, and two cars for mobile canteens. The American Legion provided transportation and food for the firefighters and collected clothing for burned-out families. Andrews Post in Portland sent out seven hundred of its members as firefighters in three days, and on Saturday, the twenty-fifth, when stubborn fires were still burning, all twenty-three thousand Legionnaires in Maine were placed on a twenty-four-hour, standby alert as a ready source of manpower for the Forest Commissioner.

Everyone found some way to help. Members of the Fraternal Order of Eagles, Casco Aerie, in Portland, too old to fight forest fires, made fifteen gallons of lobster stew for men on the lines. In Anson a farmer's wife supplied food to firefighters until the Red Cross stepped in to help.

In Newfield Marion Moulton and her sister and mother-in-law fed firefighters until they themselves were evacuated. When their own supplies of food ran out, they called a Saco Red Cross Canteen that sent up bread and tuna fish. A local poultryman contributed eggs. Carpenter's Dairy in Springvale provided milk, free of charge, throughout the week. When the women heard that the local store had some beef, they bought it. One had a large pressure cooker and cooked it. Another cooked potatoes, carrots, and onions that she had stored away in her cellar for the winter. "We sent out stew to the men that noon," Marion remembers.

Marjorie Walker of Clark's Mills remembers that she learned not to put mayonnaise on the sandwiches she made. No one knew just where they were going or how long it would be before they were eaten, and they didn't spoil as fast without the mayonnaise.

The Coca Cola Company in Sanford contributed 5,794 bottles of Coke. When the Red Cross in Portland put out a special plea for old-fashioned molasses cookies, the women of the Clark Memorial Church supplied them. The Maine Extension Service contacted the chairman of one of their women's groups in a town near Bar Harbor one morning, asking for food. By noon, seventy-five freshly-baked pies had been delivered to the fire front. At Ellsworth, ministers of the Baptist and Congregational Churches and from the Seminary in Bangor teamed up to make coffee and were dubbed "The Coffee-Making Ministers."

Food was not, of course, the only need. In Biddeford teenage girls and Boy Scouts canvassed the city for brooms for the firefighters, who used them to literally sweep out ground fire. So many were collected that the stack in front of the White Church was, according to one observer, "as high as a room." Student Donald Dubois carried messages for the Red Cross from their center at St. Joseph's Hall to the Western Union Office. Joe Audie, who had had some experience in handling horses, was sent on a truck into the countryside to help move livestock from threatened farms.

Filene's Department Store in Boston sent its transportation manager with ten trucks, drivers, and mechanics to help evacuate families and their furniture. When the fires were out and supplies for burned-out families were pouring into relief centers, these trucks were used to carry food, clothing, and bedding, gathered by the Legion in Cumberland County, to Bar Harbor.

In the aftermath of the fires, relief work on behalf of the fire's victims reached new heights of effectiveness, generosity, and ingenuity, with the Red Cross playing the major roll. But during the fires perhaps the greatest contribution made by the Red Cross was registering displaced people and helping them to make contact with family and friends near and far.

On Wednesday morning after Goose Rocks Beach and Cape Porpoise had burned, notes were pinned to the door of the Arundel Grange Hall by people who had been evacuated before they could make contact with other members of their family.

"Mrs. Frank Holbrook. Two children and mother at Peggy Littlefield's Green Heron."

"Frank Montgomery. Wife at Narragansett."

"Two Black boys. Call home."

But people from other towns and states, who had family or property in the fire areas, called the Red Cross. Red Cross workers all over the country were deluged with telephone calls asking for information. The Red Cross in St. Louis and Kansas City, Missouri, reported that phone calls about Maine had become their "biggest burden."

In every fire area evacuees were asked to register with the Red Cross. Their temporary location, the health of family members, the fate of homes was recorded, so that when inquiries came in they could be answered. The message, "All safe. Home gone."[11] went out from Red Cross centers in Maine to chapters all over the country, and even to servicemen and -women still stationed abroad who had heard about the fires back home.

The Red Cross helped fire victims to find temporary housing, matching up homeless families with people who called in to say they had extra rooms or even houses to offer. Eight hundred Bangor families contacted the Red Cross offering shelter. Ellsworth families housed evacuees from Bar Harbor. Lady Harry Oakes, whose mansion at Bar Harbor did not burn, telephoned the Bar Harbor police Friday morning to say that she had instructed her gardener to make it available to people who had been burned out.

Fryeburg opened its doors to people from Brownfield. In Portland the Red Cross soon had a list of 200 householders with one or two rooms to offer refugees, 35 who would take in complete families, 25 with houses, and 30 halls where beds could be set up. Many offers included food as well as lodging.

But in noting this generous eagerness to help, the Red Cross also noted the lack of response from fire victims. On Wednesday in Kennebunkport, Red Cross workers talked to a reporter from the *Press Herald* about the "curious hesitation among refugees to ask for aid." Only a handful of the estimated eight hundred homeless in the town had asked for shelter and none at all had asked for clothing or other assistance. They wondered if the people were "too upset or if their reticence was merely another example of Yankee independence."

The answer was partly that in a small town like Kennebunkport everyone knew or was related to everyone else. Most evacuees had more fortunate friends or relatives nearby. But there were also people like the Wallers of Lyman.

Eighty-one-year-old Herbert Waller, who was blind, and his sixty-eight-year-old wife, Abbie, were burned out of their home on Meetinghouse Road in Lyman. At Pepperell Hall in Biddeford on Friday Mr. Waller told their story.

> I had thirty-five cords of wood and all my winter's food in. The Missus wanted me to go out yesterday morning, but I felt as though we was safe. My eyes ain't your eyes and the fire deceived me. I'd have bet $5, $10, even $100 that the fire was seven to ten miles away.

I had all the plans in the world. I was going to put my things in a trunk and put my trunk on a rock for safe keeping, but the fire came up so fast I couldn't.

I started out with three little grips, but I got played out before I got a quarter of a mile, and I got fretty and threw them over a wall. I thought the fire would never get them there.

Then we walked three miles to the state road, and flames were all around us. I fell down two or three times, but the Missus helped me up again.

Burning leaves was blowing around and landing on my shirt and back. Jack rabbits were a runnin' through our legs as we were walkin'.

Just when I thought we were surrounded and gone, a fella came along in a truck that was out just lookin' to see if he could help somebody. He put us in a car and we went to Selectman Ray Taylor's. They let us sit in a chair there all night. We all had what I should call a good social time, under the sorrowful condition of affairs.

When I went back about six this morning . . . the fire had cleaned us all out clean. All we had left was ashes. You couldn't find a stitch to make a fire. My poor little cat. I had to leave him, and I loved him too. I had a shed like a dog-house to keep the leaves out of the well. There was only about a foot of water in the well. I had it in mind to get down in there. When I came back today, there wasn't even a little corner left of that shed. I'd sure been a goner if my wife hadn't talked me out of staying in that well. I never saw such a plucky woman. There ain't a braver woman in the world.

We can't build up again. I'm not going to attempt it. I ain't got a thing. I ain't got a home. I ain't got a blanket, and I'm blind. If I wasn't blind, I'd try it, but I can't do nothing now.

Waller and his wife admitted that they had spent part of their meager savings for clean clothing when they got to Biddeford, despite big Red Cross supplies. "We've never accepted anything before," explained Mrs. Waller.[12]

On Friday morning, the day after the big wind, Henry Baker, the disaster chief who had been sent from the National Red Cross office in Washington, D.C., said that in his thirty years of dealing with flood, tornado, and fire disasters he had never seen such "extraordinary self-reliance" and such a "superb attitude of helpfulness" as he had seen in Maine. "There is more neighborliness in Maine," he concluded.[13]

Neighbors were helping neighbors, friends were helping friends, families were caring for their own. In Brownfield Charlie Harmon was one of the few whose home survived the fire. He took in family members and less fortunate neighbors until eighteen were living in the one-family house. It was a joke among them that "the first one in at night gets the best bed."

The fires that swept Maine in 1947 were the greatest disaster in the state's 127-year history, and as one native said in retrospect, "Everybody knew somebody who knew somebody else. It was a family affair."

NOTES

1. "Sanford Man's Experience Digging Foxholes Saves 5 Trapped by Fire," *Portland Press Herald,* October 27, 1947.
2. "Forest Interpreter's Primer on Fire Management," U.S. Department of Agriculture, Forest Service, 1976.
3. *Biddeford Daily Journal,* October 24, 1947.
4. "The Bar Harbor Fire: Record of Law Enforcement," Prepared for the Record by Members of the Bar Harbor Police Department, 1947.
5. *Portland Press Herald,* October 25, 1947.
6. *Bangor Daily News,* October 27, 1947.
7. Barter, "Inferno in Maine."
8. Richard G. Kendall, "Journal of a Journeyman," *Portland Press Herald,* October 27, 1947.
9. *Ibid.*
10. *Kennebunk Star,* October 31, 1947.
11. *Biddeford Daily Journal,* October 27, 1947.
12. "Future Black for Blind Man, 81, and Wife, 68, after Losing Home," *Portland Press Herald,* October 25, 1947.
13. *Portland Press Herald,* October 25 and 26, 1947.

Chapter X:
"Rumor has a thousand tongues."

On Friday morning, October 24, the people of Maine woke to find their state in crisis. The forest fires, which had begun slowly, had grown in size and number. Towns had burned, lives had been lost, thousands of acres of valuable timber and some of the most beautiful parts of Maine had been ravaged. The money value of lost property had not been assessed, but it would be in the millions of dollars. The loss of tax dollars to the towns and the state would be enormous. Hundreds were homeless and displaced, and pictures of them at the Red Cross centers looked like pictures coming out of war-torn Europe. "This," one woman wrote to relatives, "was what we feared during the war, you know."

Most of the biggest fires were still not out, and new fires were still being reported. There was talk of arson. It seemed possible: there were so many fires and strangers were everywhere. There had been looting, and someone said an elderly woman at Goose Rocks Beach had lost all of her valuable antiques to two men driving a truck with out-of-state license plates who had come to her door offering to move her furniture to safety. A man in Waterboro lost his herd of cows the same way.

Everyone seemed to have a story about the fire: about people narrowly escaping with their lives; of children separated from parents; of pets lost; of furniture moved to safety and burned, while the house from which it had been taken did not. The newspapers and radio were filled with terrible reports and warnings.

On Friday morning the front page of the *Portland Press Herald* carried only the huge banner headline "Fires Wipe Out 6 Towns" and pictures of the devastation. Inside the paper were stories written by reporters who had been shocked by the destruction caused by the fires. They had written dramatically about events that were already dramatic. They had found facts hard to get from people who hardly knew themselves what had happened. They had arrived on the scene "at the worst possible time. Those who knew what had happened were too busy and dog tired. Only the uninformed had time to talk."[1] As a result their articles were mixtures of fact, misinformation, and rumor.

Of Bar Harbor, Friday's *Press Herald* said, "more than half of the resort town, hotels, and palatial cottages have been destroyed." Half the business district was destroyed or in "imminent danger" of it. At Hulls Cove the flames had been "stopped . . . by the sea," and the "shore from Hulls Cove to Bar Harbor [was] one continuous sheet of flame." On the western side of Mount Desert Island the fire "was in Seal Cove and menacing Northeast Harbor" and "residents of these communities had evacuated with Bar Harbor residents." At Bar Harbor "3,500 people [had been] trapped on the piers." "More than 700" of these people had been evacuated by sea before a "heroic army crew" had used bulldozers to push aside "a fire barrier across Route 3" to open an escape route by land.

Other articles reported that at Brownfield 250 homes had been lost and the little town looked "as if it had been hit by an atomic bomb." In Biddeford a "fire which acted with almost human strategy" had in two hours "razed 150 of 156 cottages and four hotels" at Fortunes Rocks. In Portland the "smoking State Pier ruins" had been "guarded far into the night." Fort Fairfield was "ablaze" and "all Main Street was seen in danger." In Scarborough a "vicious woods fire" had burned 500,000 feet of lumber at the Gillies Lumber Company and residents in the area "reported seeing a black sedan with New York license plates pass slowly through the area two minutes before the fire broke out." At Richmond "nearly a score of farm houses and 25 frame dwellings" had been destroyed Thursday night before the changing wind took the fire away from the town. The Augusta National Guard had been ordered out to help people evacuate along the River Road that was "choked with children leading cattle, and trucks loaded with furniture." At Jackman a "raging timber fire" had downed telephone lines so there was "no communication" with the area.

At Newfield seventy-five-year-old Fred Sprague had died of injuries received when he jumped from a horse-drawn carriage set afire by flames that "leaped" from the woods while he was fleeing the fire.

In Bar Harbor three were dead, and in Ellsworth a woman had been "struck by an army truck" and died.

Hiram, East Hiram, and Denmark were "threatened with destruction," and residents in "all towns in Southern York County" were warned to be "on the lookout" for a fire in the Alewive section of Kennebunk that was "traveling toward the sea unabated."

All of these stories appeared in the *Press Herald* Friday morning. Similar stories appeared in newspapers all over the state, New England, the country, and the world. Beyond Maine, the Bar Harbor fire received the most coverage because of the town's international fame and because the burning of mansions, the loss of the famous Jackson Laboratory, and the evacuation of the townspeople from the Municipal Pier best captured the imagination of editors. As one York County man said bitterly, "The newspapermen down country didn't know York County existed."

On Friday the office of the *Bangor Daily Commercial* was in chaos. The fire was big news. At 2 A.M. photographer Warren Roll returned from a foray into Bar Harbor with incredible pictures. Reporter Miriam Pottle appeared at eight, wearing an army coat, to write an eyewitness account of the fire. She'd been up all night. By 9:30 she was on her way back to Bar Harbor in a *New York Herald Tribune* plane. During the morning men from the Boston bureau of the Acme News Service, which supplied all the Scripps-Howard papers, arrived and set up their telephoto machine. Photographers for International News Pictures arrived at noon, and late in the afternoon two reporters for *Life* appeared. Before the day was over the *Commercial* would play host to reporters from newspapers in Hartford, New York, and Washington, D.C.

On Friday in a dramatic, often inaccurate front-page article, the *New York Times* reported that ships were speeding to Bar Harbor to evacuate four thousand people who had "fled to the sea to await rescue by the Coast Guard as the worst forest fire in Maine's history roared through the town." The article, based on information gathered Thursday night by Associated Press reporters, said much of the resort town was "declared completely destroyed," that "the entire town faced destruction before morning unless the gale winds abated," that "all communications were cut off," and the people who were "crowded on Bar Harbor's docks and shorelines as flames raged through the town" were being taken off in fishing boats and other small craft in a "Dunkirk-like evacuation."

In Paris *Le Figaro,* in a front-page story about the Bar Harbor fire, reported that it was believed to have been set by "dissatisfied farmers" protesting the "attitude" of the "great landowners."[2]

Richard Hale and Cleveland Amory, who wrote histories of Bar Harbor in the years following the fire, pointed out the ridiculousness of *Le Figaro*'s story, and Hale rejected the comparison of the World War II evacuation of British soldiers from Dunkirk with the evacuation of four hundred people from Bar Harbor's Municipal Pier.

In the weeks and months immediately after the Bar Harbor fire, well-informed officials and private citizens would attempt to correct the misinformation spread about it. Dynamite was not used to stop the fire. All the patients were not evacuated from the Bar Harbor hospital. Three men in a rowboat were not run down by a larger boat during the evacuation. Communications were not cut off completely at any time. First reports that two-thirds of Bar Harbor was destroyed were erroneous, as were later reports that half the town was gone. Every newspaper list of homes lost in the fire was inaccurate, including corrected lists. The Atwater Kent estate did not burn—only one small building on the grounds was lost—and the Rockefeller estate at Seal Harbor was not touched.

Richard Hale, who so conscientiously wrote about the fire, cautioning readers about particularly sensationalized accounts, was himself a victim of careless reporting. One newspaper printed a picture of him sitting in the rubble of his grandparents' home on Schooner Head with a caption explaining that he was disconsolately staring at the ruins. A close look at the picture reveals that Hale is writing on a pad of paper propped on his knee. He was, perhaps, taking notes for his book, *The Story of Bar Harbor,* which was published in 1949 and contains one of the best accounts of the fire ever written.

On November 16 John Heath, co-author of the Bar Harbor Fire Department's official report of the fire, wrote the editor of the *Boston Sunday Herald:*

> It is with a great deal of amazement that we, the citizens of Bar Harbor, discover via Paul Stevens' article in last Sunday's *Herald* that the navy was the agency that saved us from total destruction. . . . It is preposterous for any one group to claim the role of hero. . . . Without attempting to minimize the "gallant and well-placed efforts of the navy" it is ridiculous to claim the fire was brought under control only by their efforts.

The battle of Bar Harbor was fought the night of October 23 in the teeth of a howling northwest gale, and by the time the *Powell, Perry* and other naval craft arrived on the morning of the twenty-fourth the battle had been won by representatives of fourteen eastern Maine fire departments, soldiers from Dow Field, and members of the National Parks firefighting service. When the navy arrived, the worst was over.

[It is] totally untrue that confusion and chaos reigned. It is also untrue to imply Bar Harbor had an inadequate pumping station. We are blessed with a natural gravity feed pump system which is more than adequate to our needs, and this is the prime reason we were able to save the majority of the town.

The Reverend Russell Hubbard of Bar Harbor's St. Saviour's Church wrote a letter, which was sent to all his summer parishioners, giving details of what had happened, and including a list of cottages that had burned and those that had not. He explained that he had been prompted to send the letter because "there has been so much inaccurate information on the radio and in the press about the situation here."

During the crisis and the busy months of rebuilding, no one had time to set the facts straight for the people of Bar Harbor. At last in July 1948, a meeting was held at Bar Harbor's Jessup Memorial Library to give people who had experienced the fire an opportunity to tell what had happened. Officials were there to answer questions, and people had been invited to bring their scrapbooks to share with others. In reporting this meeting the *Bar Harbor Times* commented that people appreciated "this opportunity to learn the actual facts regarding many aspects of the fire."

Radio appears to have been the worst offender in spreading misinformation. Evacuees from almost every threatened town would hear over the radio that their town had burned flat, only to discover that in many cases this was not true. Kennebunkport Village did not burn. All of Waterboro was not destroyed. Biddeford and Saco were not swept by fire.

Radio reporters at the fire lines tape-recorded reports to be played over the air. Stories that were told later about their methods may be apocryphal, but at least indicate the distrust people came to feel toward radio reports. One reporter, in Kennebunk at a moment when the fire was being well controlled, described into his recorder the desperate plight in which he found himself ". . . surrounded by the conflagration. . . ." A firefighter, standing nearby listening, leaned over the recorder and said, "Bull." Another reporter in another location, who was making a similar tape, was seen to be manipulating a piece of cellophane in his hand in order to simulate crackling flames.

People were dependent on radio and newspapers for most of their fire information. By the end of the week, travel in fire areas was restricted to those with official business or property owners. A system of passes was devised and strictly enforced. Telephone lines were either down or overloaded. Day and night operators handled emergency calls for firefighters and relief agencies, as well as hundreds of calls from people trying to locate family or to learn the fate of their property. Records for toll calls for every exchange were broken, exceeding even those made on V-J Day, when the war had ended.

Charlotte Stuart manned the Bar Harbor telephone exchange from four o'clock Thursday afternoon until seven the next morning. From the windows of the telephone office she had been able to watch the fire's progress along Eden Street. As it advanced, telephone lines went dead. She worked with the wire chief to locate and disconnect damaged circuits. "Each time a light would come on, I'd go in on it," she explains, "to see if it was a call or if I could just hear a noise." If the line was out of order, she gave the number to the wire chief, and "he'd pull the coils to save the juice for whatever telephones were still working." When at last the only line out of Bar Harbor still open was to Southwest Harbor, Charlotte and Lillian Ingalls took turns manning it through the night. "Lillian and I talked to Southwest Harbor all night long," Charlotte remembers. "We were never cut off at any time."

In other Mount Desert Island communities, switchboards were manned by faithful operators. At night they worked by the light of kerosene lamps and battery operated lights. Boats stood by in nearby harbors to evacuate them if necessary. Food was brought to them, and they took turns "catching a bit of sleep when it was impossible to go on without it."[3] At Seal Harbor Ada Bowden, Ruth Donnell, and two other women were on duty for almost a week. "On a small table behind [them] was a lonely and bedraggled bouquet of flowers, snatched from a roadside garden by the fire chief of Seal Harbor, who took time off during the height of the firefight to present them to the operators with the remark, 'We would be lost without you. Please keep going.' "[4]

At the Bar Mills telephone exchange in York County, Violetta Wallace stayed on duty for five days and nights, occasionally napping on a cot, having her meals brought in from the village restaurant. She remembers it as the "worst time I ever worked. Just one madhouse. And I've worked through flood—two floods, in '36 and '52, and they bothered me, but nothing like the fire did. It was just one nerve-racking time."

The Bar Mills exchange served Waterboro, Hollis, Buxton, Groveville, Clark's Mills, parts of Lyman and Dayton—all the neighboring towns. It was a magneto system. When someone placed a call a lever would drop on the board and it would buzz until the operator answered the call. Each telephone was crank-operated. There were very few private lines; most were "party" lines with 15, 20, 25, even 30 telephones on a line. Every call rang on every telephone. Every call on every line buzzed at the central exchange. If a man whose number was 13 wanted to call his neighbor whose number was 12 and who was on the same line, he would crank one long and two short rings. The telephone next door and all the other phones on that line would ring, and at the exchange the line would buzz.

The system fostered neighborliness (some would say nosiness). If the operator placed a call to a number that didn't answer, it was not unusual for a neighbor to pick up the phone and say, "I saw them drive out a few minutes ago. There's no one home there." People who were going to be away from home might call the operator saying, "We're going down street for a bit. If anybody calls tell 'em we'll be back in an hour." If someone needed the doctor, he might call the operator at the exchange to ask where the doctor was, figuring she'd know if anyone did. If the whistle blew for the fire department, the operator would be flooded with calls wanting to know where the fire was.

The system worked well enough under normal conditions, but during the emergency it served to compound the confusion. Two women, who worked part-time for the Bar Mills exchange, came in to help, but found they could not take the confusion.

Although radio messages asked people in the fire areas to use their telephones only when absolutely necessary, freeing the lines for emergency calls, even these calls were so numerous they could not be handled. People who needed transportation for themselves, cattle, or furniture, called the exchange. Official calls came in steadily for more men, equipment, or medical aid. People from away called to ask about friends, family, and property. Many of these toll calls were never charged. "We never even attempted to make a record of them," Vi Wallace remembers. "We just pushed them through as fast as we could."

One of the calls she took was from her brother in Lowell, Massachusetts. He had heard over the radio that Bar Mills was burning. Bar Mills was not burning, but towns all around it were. Vi could look out the window and see burning leaves and fine, wind-blown ash, falling in the village. An armed National Guardsman stood at the bridge leading in and out of town, and at night he came into the exchange for a cup of coffee. A family from a wooded area on the outskirts of the village had brought its heavy, old-fashioned furniture and stacked it in the next room. Her brother Linwood, a nurse, was working at the first-aid station in the Parish House. Her mother was home alone in their little brick house on the other side of the bridge. Before her the switchboard buzzed and buzzed. It was, she thought, like being in the middle of a war. "It's awful, you know," she said later. "You take all that ringin' in your ears, all that confusion . . . your head gets mighty tired when you've worked like that twelve hours right at a stretch."

The inaccuracy of fire information itself created problems. Rumors about damage to Maine's utilities and industries caused a panic on the New York Stock Exchange on Friday. For a few hours "the New York financial district . . . lost its head . . . and tossed stocks of a few Maine corporations on the market at prices several dollars a share below their Thursday levels."[5] Frightened stockholders in Maine corporations tried to sell their holdings at almost any price. In all but one case these stocks involved companies that were not even near the fires.

Ironically it was the headlines in New York papers about the Bar Harbor fire that caused the value of stock in the Central Maine Power Company, Maine's largest utility, to tumble. Bar Harbor was not even in the company's territory. Friday afternoon Central Maine issued a public statement saying that it had lost only about 50 miles of wire in its entire 7,119-mile system. Damage to transmission lines was negligible and no generating or substation facilities were affected.[6]

It was surprising how slight the damage was to utilities in general. The New England Telephone and Telegraph Company lost only 1,183 telephone poles and 65 circuit miles of wire.[7]

Small sawmill and wood lot owners in southwestern Maine suffered crippling losses, but none of the large companies like Great Northern Paper sustained appreciable damage to their holdings and no textile mills were touched.[8]

There were inaccurate reports of deaths. When the mother of Dow Field soldier Paul Morris of Dorchester, Massachusetts, was notified that her son had been killed in a motor convoy accident at Bar Harbor Thursday night, she hurried to Bangor and found him with only a broken leg and arm.

An unidentified body was found in Lyman and assumed to be that of missing William Bodycott, whose home had burned. When Bodycott heard over the radio that he was dead, he reported to the York County Sheriff's office that he was "very much alive." The "body" turned out to be the carcass of a cow.

But the most serious problem created by inaccurate reporting and rumor-mongering was the rise of vigilante groups to deal with arsonists. The newspapers were full of stories of suspected arson. By the end of the week everyone was suspect, and "men went armed and talked darkly of arson."

Friday was Malcolm Barter's third day in Maine gathering news about the fires for the *Boston Globe.* He had hardly found time to eat and sleep, let alone to shave, shower or change his clothes. He laughs now remembering that after "two or three days we looked like tramps, you know. I smelled like a rubber boot. Of course, they began to get suspicious of people driving around with no identification. So I got identification from the Mayor of Biddeford, a fellow named Lausier."

Barter also went to Sheriff Knight of York County for a pass to get through the fire lines. "His house was in Alfred adjoining the jail. I remember going up there, and Mrs. Knight set up a typewriter on the oil cloth on the kitchen table and on official stationery she typed me out a pass. We were getting stopped, you know. Two or three times I showed it, and they would let us through. Course a lot of nuts began to get loose. You're bound to flush some of these out every time you have a disaster."

State Fire Inspector Lawrence Dolby's principal involvement toward the end of the week was "to run around chasing people that were reported to be setting fires, because a situation like this brings on an epidemic of fire setting. It brings in people from all over the country—and when I say 'the country' I really mean it. There were people came here from far and abroad to witness this or to be a part of it. They came as firefighters—or fire setters.

"People were finding gadgets in the woods that other people had set fires with. People were bringing in items that they said they'd found. I'm convinced a lot of them they'd made up themselves and brought them in to be heroes. Others were sincere: they had found something."

At Gorham four matches tied by a string to a package of cigarettes were found near a portable sawmill on Fort Hill Road. The matches had gone out before they set the cigarette package on fire. In Standish a pile of burning wood shavings was discovered near a wood lot. In West Falmouth two young girls found a partly burned candle near the scene of a brush fire. They reported it, and the fire chief called it a "clear cut case of the work of a firebug." In Scarborough a burning candle was found in a pile of pine needles. At Durham, near Auburn, a crude, partially burned firebomb was found near an old barn filled with hay.

Other towns escaped serious fires, but experienced a rash of small fires of suspicious origin, one at China, another at Bucksport. Nine hundred men turned out to fight the Bucksport blaze. At Lincolnville an arson probe was begun when a "mysterious broken bottle" was found near a small fire. At Winterport a deputy sheriff found "cotton cloth and a forked stick, soaked in kerosene, [which had] evidently been thrown from a passing car."

At Camden, in Knox County, a woman saw an object thrown from a "black sedan towing an aluminum trailer." Upon investigating she found it was a book of matches with a burning cigarette attached. On the cover of the matchbook was written, "From one friend to another."

Not all the arson attempts failed. At Palermo the state police said a fire that burned ten acres in an "inaccessible area" was definitely set. They were looking for a black car observed just before the fire was spotted. Skowhegan police were searching the woods and fields between Skowhegan and East Madison for a man "wearing a red hat and plaid coat" after a series of woods fires were extinguished, and a farmhouse, barn, seventeen cows, and three pigs were destroyed.

At Bar Harbor, Biddeford, Centerville, and Waterboro arson was suspected, but although people were questioned, nothing was proved.

Once or twice arsonists were seen at work. In Brunswick two boys were seen setting a fire near the high school, but escaped in a "green coupe." The most chilling incident occurred at South Windham. Fireman Albert White and a companion were wetting down a fire that had been brought under control in the woods near the Haven Road when White heard someone shout in the woods about a hundred yards away. When he went to investigate he saw a man standing beside a small fire. "Let's see you put this out," the man shouted, and turned and ran. White chased him, but encumbered by the rubber boots and raincoat he was wearing, lost the man. state police rushed to the scene. That night all area roads were blocked off as grim-faced residents led by special deputy sheriffs and town constables sought the firebug. He was never found, but someone who had seen him reported that he was accompanied by a little white dog.[9]

Towns that experienced unexplained fires shut themselves off to outsiders. At Cape Elizabeth, where two attempts were made to start fires, residents patrolled all roads into the town allowing only fellow townsmen through. St. George didn't wait for trouble to begin. Residents there called a special town meeting to make emergency plans to patrol the nine square miles of their tiny town.

Everywhere aroused citizens took matters into their own hands and patrolled with guns, stopping cars, and sending scores of people to officials for questioning. The numbers of at least a thousand license plates from "suspicious" vehicles were circulated.

In this atmosphere of hysteria, innocent people like Arthur Roberts of Lyman sometimes found themselves in trouble. On Thursday Roberts almost lost his house to the fire. On Friday he drove to Clark's Mills, now threatened, to offer his help. He started home at approximately 12:30 that night. "On the way home about right where the Central Maine Power sand pit was, this side of Clough's Corner toward Goodwin's Mills, I saw a flicker of flame down over the bank. I pulled into a little side road there, and I heard a pumper going. I went down and found Fred Elwell and Harry Mullet operating the pumper spraying a small fire with water, so I helped them for ten or fifteen minutes. But I had left my car out by Route 35 with the dimmers on. Central Maine Power trucks hauling sand to the Skelton Station construction site on the Saco River reported in that they'd seen a car there, but it was smoky and they didn't see the firetruck.

"Well, the next day I left Goodwin's Mills around noontime heading for Clark's Mills, and I got to Clough's Corner and I got stopped. The National Guard wanted to know how, why, and what. Fortunately a good friend, Hugh Googins of Kennebunk, and a couple of other fellows ranged up beside me, and some Legionnaires who thought they were going to rough me up a little bit didn't."

Roberts's friends vouched for him, and a National Guard officer rode with him to Clark's Mills to be sure he would get safely through and to check him out with local officials. Roberts waited at Clark's Mills to be cleared. Within an hour he was told that his license plate number had been taken from the guard's list of those in question. "How about the state police," Roberts asked.

"I don't know," the guardsman answered.

"You FIND out," demanded Roberts, a mild-mannered man who was at last angry. "I was *burned*," he remembers. "And I was so pooped that the tears came right down over my face."

Two arsonists were caught and convicted, both young boys. One of them had set three fires, one of which destroyed a farm. He directed firefighters to the fires and worked frantically to help put them out. Asked why he had done it, he said it was because he enjoyed the excitement.

On Friday two Newfield men were arrested for spreading false alarms about the fire that was still burning in their town. They drove through areas in Newfield and Parsonsfield that were not immediately threatened, and warned terrified home owners to evacuate.

But despite these arrests, and firm evidence that fires were being set, despite Senator Owen Brewster's call for an F.B.I. investigation to "look for evidence of deliberate destruction,"[10] state and national officials ruled out arson as a major cause of the disaster. A report filed by personnel of the National Forest Service concluded, "Despite newspaper rumors, it seems that incendiarism played little or no part."[11]

Although newspapers did report case after case of suspected arson, they also conscientiously urged the public to guard against idle talk. An editorial in the *Press Herald* warned, "Rumor has a thousand tongues. It can spring up like fire itself." Newspapers all over the state called on self-appointed vigilantes to lay down their guns.

No doubt some did so reluctantly, for many people still did not understand why there were so many widespread fires, or that, due to the drought, the slightest spark, the slightest careless use of fire, could start a blaze.

On the twenty-fifth the following letter appeared in the Letters to the Editor column in the *Press Herald*.

A large part of Greater Portland last night was viewing the awesome red glow on the horizon from the heights of the Western Promenade. People stood silent and awed and looked away in the distance thinking how grateful and fortunate we were to be some thirty miles away perched on a hill, nearly surrounded by water.

Suddenly there appeared directly below us an eerie orange glow, a glow that almost immediately changed to an angry red glare. There on the banks of the Promenade was a fast spreading brush fire that even as you looked to make sure your eyes weren't deceiving you, leaped to the tops of the small trees. In less than three minutes the flames could be seen some blocks away.

Someone, viewing the distant devastation from their impenetrable perch on the hill, probably flipped a still glowing cigarette down among the tinder-dry grasses and bushes. . . .

Don't kid yourself. It can happen to you.

NOTES

1. Hale, *The Story of Bar Harbor*, p. 229.
2. "La Ville De Bar-Harbor est à demi détruite par un incendie que l'an croit criminel," *Le Figaro*, October 25, 1947.
3. *Telephone Topics.* Special Edition. "The Maine Fire Story," n.d.
4. *Ibid.*
5. Harold J. Boyle, "How Maine Industry Fared in Fire," *Portland Press Herald*, October 26, 1947.
6. Annual Report, Central Maine Power Company, 1947.
7 *Telephone Topics.*
8. Annual Report, Central Maine Power Company.
9. *Portland Press Herald*, October 28, 1947.
10. *Bangor Daily News*, October 28, 1947.
11. Crosby Hoar and Ed Ritter, "Report on Forest Fires in Maine, Fall of 1947," Forest Service, Eastern Division, United States Department of Agriculture, December 1947.

Chapter XI:
The Battle of the Bulldozers

Governor Hildreth's order Thursday night placing all fire control responsibility in the hands of the Forest Service in Augusta gave Maine what it needed most: a central authority. For four days the department had been on an around-the-clock schedule, its personnel sleeping on cots at the office, having their food brought in. As the department's supervisor of the forests in the organized territory, Austin Wilkins had charge of coordinating the state effort. He had tried to find out where equipment was needed and to supply it. He had done what he could to coordinate the firefighting effort, but without overall authority his job had been difficult. Now he had that authority. Now all federal, state, municipal, and private firefighters would work through his office. All requests for men and equipment, all offers of assistance, would come to him. He would place all orders for extra equipment.

Wilkins worked from lists of available trained personnel and equipment on hand or ordered. Providing firefighters was easy. The public was so aroused that hundreds of volunteers were being turned away from registration centers in the cities. Before the crisis was over, Wilkins would hear of one instance of more than two hundred men with every conceivable firefighting tool converging on a two-and-a-half-acre fire and surrounding it. The flames would have had to go through their legs to escape.

But there simply wasn't enough equipment. Pumps and hose were needed desperately. There were not enough shovels, brooms, and rakes for all the firefighters. Jonesboro needed equipment for between five hundred and a thousand men who had come out to fight the fire there. At the height of the desperate battle at Bar Harbor, equipment was taken from one spot to another where it was needed more.

Great ingenuity had been shown in devising tank trucks out of old trucks, barrels, tubs, and portable pumps. In Alfred one crew hauled water in a septic tank.

Dairies and oil companies had loaned their tank trucks and drivers. Seven Randall and McAllister Company trucks were used, and the Merrill Transport Company put all of its twenty-three trucks into the field. On Friday morning Wilkins received word that eight milk tank trucks were en route to Maine from Somerville, Massachusetts, with twenty-four thousand gallons of water, and the Maine Central Railroad was sending three tank cars loaded with water to drought-stricken West Baldwin.

Everyone was anxious to help end Maine's ordeal. New Hampshire had had its own spate of fires, but announced Friday morning that all were under control. Governor Dole had wired Governor Hildreth extending the sympathy of his state to the "people of Maine in the great loss they have suffered by destructive fires," adding, "If New Hampshire can assist in any manner, please call on us."[1]

Equipment that was in short supply was ordered. Twelve small, gas-driven water pumps were due to arrive from Seattle, Washington, by plane Friday morning, and Wilkins had received a telegram from the D. B. Smith Company in Utica, New York, confirming an order for a hundred Indian pumps, advising that they had been "expressed" for Augusta at 8:45 Thursday night on Train #56, Car B. Wilkins had ordered hose, nozzles, and Drench, a chemical that when added to water caused it to penetrate deep into the ground to put out deep-burning fires.

Wilkins had also asked the National Forest Service people how they could help. They promised to send personnel and to get the army and navy to send equipment. Thousands of feet of hose were drawn from surplus army and navy stores and rushed to Maine, then immediately trucked to the fire lines. There firefighters discovered that the army and navy used two different kinds of hose. Adaptors were needed for joining them. Wilkins called the War Assets Administration's machine shop in South Portland pleading, "Make us some adaptors." Three men worked around the clock to make the hundred that were needed.

At 11:30 Friday morning Wilkins issued what was to be the first in a series of twice-daily fire reports. The Brownfield fire was burning in West Brownfield and was still a threat to Denmark, Hiram, and Porter. No report had come in that morning from the Centerville-Jonesboro area where the last word had been that fifteen to twenty homes had been lost in Machias and Jonesboro was in imminent danger. The fire on Mount Desert Island was spreading toward the western half of the island. In York County many separate prongs were reaching out from the main fire, threatening Hollis, Clark's Mills, Dayton, Alfred, Kennebunk, and Wells.

Friday was another Class 5 fire day. Only a good drenching rain would relieve conditions. On Thursday afternoon, with the humidity registering at 15 percent of saturation, one of the lowest readings ever recorded, an attempt had been made to make rain with dry ice. Publisher Guy Gannett had loaned his plane to Ernest Kliemann of the Portland Weather Bureau and Portland Airport Manager Milton Smith. They dropped 150 pounds of dry ice, which had been donated by the General Ice Cream Corporation of Portland, into a high cumulous cloud formation over Fryeburg. "Anything is worth an attempt," the would-be rainmakers had said, even though they knew the temperature was three to eight degrees above the thirty-two degrees considered necessary for the experiment to succeed. No rain fell, and none was forecast. The drought would continue.

Since June less rain had fallen in New England than in a comparable period for sixty years, and temperatures had been above normal.[2] In Portland the rainfall for August had been .27 of an inch, as opposed to a normal fall of over 3 inches. In September only 1.73 inches fell, about half the normal rainfall. So far in October precipitation had been unmeasurable. Some areas of the state had not had rain for 108 consecutive days.

Friday morning dawned on Mount Desert Island "beautifully clear and quiet as though Nature was seeking to make up for the terrible things she had done the night before."[3] In Bar Harbor piles of household goods were scattered over the Athletic Field, and cars still stood where they had been left when the people had evacuated to the pier.

On the hills above the village and out along Bay Drive smoke curled from blackened ruins. Half-burned garden hoses stretched beside smoldering cellar holes, and lines of hose snaked up steep driveways. Chimneys stood like gravestones over the ruins of once fine houses, fireplace flues exposed, wooden mantles burned away, a marble carapace, still intact, hinting at the elegance of a vanished room.

Granite steps led to nowhere. Stone cupids, which had stood in gardens, danced through desolation. Granite lions guarded rubble.

Inexplicably, here and there the fire had left a magnificent pine tree or a house, although everything around it was in ruins. The summer home of Mildred McCormick still stood, white and clean, in an area of great devastation. The fire had not swept across Bay Drive to the shore of Frenchman Bay, and the great mansions there, among them Wingwood House, had survived. Above them on the hills, where the view out over the bay was so magnificent, all the houses were gone.

Crews of firefighters patrolled the boundaries of the fire, wetting down smoking ruins and hot spots. Although the worst seemed to be over for Bar Harbor, a strong reversing wind could turn the fire and bring it back on the village. The wind had swung from the northwest to the northeast. After a two-hour early morning lull, it had sprung up again, rekindling fire lines on the western slope of Cadillac Mountain. Now the fire was burning toward Otter Creek, Seal Harbor, and Northeast Harbor. Orders were given for their people to evacuate, and before the sun was up, bulldozers and crews of men were at work cutting a firebreak, fifty to a hundred feet wide, from Somes Sound to Town Hill. It was a desperate attempt to keep the fire from spreading from the east side of the island to the west.

Traffic onto the island was restricted. National Guardsmen were posted at the Trenton bridge to keep everyone without a pass off the island. Bar Harbor home owners were told they would not be allowed to return until it was judged safe and some kind of order had been restored. There was still no electricity, and Bar Harbor was virtually an armed camp.

Members of the Bangor Humane Society were allowed on the island to care for pets that had been left behind. For the next three days they went from house to house, peeking in windows, checking barns and hen houses. They left a three-day supply of food for the animals they found. Three badly burned cats were put to sleep. One small dog with severely burned feet attracted the attention of firefighters and led them to a patch of woods where a large dog lay unconscious. Humane Society workers took both dogs to a Bangor veterinarian. A German shepherd, fiercely guarding the front door of a house, was tamed with food, and he too was taken to Bangor to be cared for until claimed. Pigs appeared out of the woods where they had wandered and were fed by the Humane Society workers, who also made arrangements for two thousand hens to be fed and watered by firefighters.

Allen Salisbury and a student who had worked at the Jackson Laboratory that summer thought they might be needed at the lab, and drove to the Trenton bridge where they were stopped by guardsmen who did not want to let them through without a pass. "Why do you need to go on the island?" they asked. The student thought fast. "I work at the Jackson Lab, and I've got some mice that I injected with typhoid. I want to make sure they don't get loose."

"We weren't held up at all," Salisbury remembers with a chuckle.

They were shocked by the destruction they found at the lab. Unit 1 was completely destroyed, its ruins still smoking. The walls of Unit 2 were still standing, but the shell was too hot to be entered. Dr. Clarence Little, director and founder of the lab, who had been out of town the day before, had already arrived. Before the end of the day every staff member and every assistant had returned to the lab to help even though no effort had been made to find or assemble them.[4]

The walls of Unit 2 were still hot to the touch when Dr. Little, Salisbury, and other staff members went inside to see if anything could be salvaged. Dr. Little's first concern was for the 60,000 specially bred mice. Most were dead. Some were just barely alive, but it was clear they had survived only to die slowly. Dr. Little, a humane man, told Salisbury, "Let's get these killed." They dropped the mice into large glass jars with balls of cotton soaked in chloroform. Once dead these mice and the thousands of others who had died from the heat and smoke, and their blackened bedding, were literally shoveled out the windows. The use of gas masks was necessary before the operation was completed, and the great piles of removed material were finally soaked with kerosene and burned.[5]

Still useable equipment was taken to Hamilton Station at Salisbury Cove, a facility where a small colony of mice was kept and some of the lab's work was conducted. There a business office was set up, for although the laboratory had suffered a seemingly insurmountable blow, Dr. Little, sustained in those early hours by the "magnificent loyalty and high morale"[6] of his staff, believed its work could go on. When asked if the lab would be rebuilt, he exploded, "Rebuild? Of course we'll rebuild!"[7]

All over Maine that day, while small towns still battled for survival, those which had already lost everything displayed the same tough optimism. In Brownfield bulldozers were pushing over burned trees. As their roots hit the air they burst into flame, a reminder that the danger was not over. The selectmen opened the new "town hall," an old-fashioned combination baggage car and smoker that the Maine Central Railroad had brought to an East Brownfield siding.

Central Maine Power Company linesmen already were hanging wires on half-burned poles, on trees, even on bushes—anywhere they could—to get the power going again. Postmistress Julia Wells was one of the first to return to Brownfield Friday morning. The post office was gone, but she drove to what had been the railroad station at East Brownfield, parked beside the track, and waited for the morning train to pick up the mail bag. On Saturday Brownfield's regular mail delivery was made. Later she would say with pride, "We lost just one day."

That afternoon on the green near the soldiers' monument, a writer for *Collier's* magazine interviewed a young man who told him, "The fire came too fast. There was nothing we could do."

"Where will you live now?" the writer asked. The Brownfield man looked at him in surprise.

"Where? Why here. Only the houses are gone. Brownfield's still here."[8]

At eight o'clock Friday morning Roy Paul of Lyman came back to see what had happened to the house he and his pregnant wife and eight children had fled the night before when the wind had swept the fire through Lyman at what some said was a mile-a-minute speed. All that was left of the house and the barn he and his wife had almost finished paying for was "smoking ashes, . . . the steel of the stoves and beds twisted and rusty in the cellar, and his new brooder only a formless heap of sheet steel.

"There wasn't a feather left of the three-week-old chicks, five hundred of which he had bought only three days before. His two pigs, six months old and each weighing more than a hundred pounds, he found dead in the ashes of the woods nearby, their snouts probing for good air they never found. Three pet dogs were gone.

"Big areas in and around Lyman were still afire. But Paul got his brother's truck and drove over to Lavallee's lumber mill at Whicher's Mills, five miles east.

"Lavallee, hard pressed by fire, was turning up fresh sod around his mill and stacked lumber. He laid aside the plow for a few minutes, however, and sold his last four thousand feet of rough, second-grade stock to Paul."[9]

Four days later, *Portland Press Herald* reporter Harry Foote stopped to talk when he saw Paul at work building his house beside the cellar hole of his old one. Paul hoped to move his family into the new house in two days. His two brothers and a brother-in-law were helping him, working even by moonlight. When Foote commented on his speed, Paul said, "They tell me I'm the first one round to start rebuilding. Well, I've got to. I've got eight kids, with another one coming in December. And winter's not far off. We've got to have a roof over our heads. As soon as I get this place finished up so we can move in, I'm going to start right in putting a wing on it for another bedroom. That'll be this weekend."

Paul told the reporter how friends had thought him foolish to buy lumber and start putting up a new house with the fire still burning in Lyman. "Are you crazy, do you want to lose that too?" they asked.

"But I told them, 'It can't burn me out again, because everything's burned around me four inches into the ground.' " Paul looked around at the charred waste in which his new house was rising. "I've always stayed up this way and I'd hate like blazes to get out now. I'm not going to get out either. I own this land and I'm not going to buy someplace else."[10]

Malcolm Barter asked Percy Day of Day's Mills if people who were burned out there would move away. Day answered, "Lord no! You couldn't shake 'em out of here."[11]

On Friday morning the fire was burning in Kennebunk and, on another front, was moving toward Hollis and Dayton. At 5 A.M. one of Kennebunk's volunteer firemen drove up Route 35 to Curt Coombs's house to check on the fire. It had split around Alewife Pond the night before, one tongue of it burning off toward the Mousam River and Wells, the other toward the fields and woods west of Route 35. The fireman parked his truck in Coombs's yard and walked out to the woods behind the house. There he found the fire, spread out in both directions, just mulling along under the trees. He hurried back to the house, where he had to step over people who had spent the night sleeping on the floor after evacuating their own homes, to use the telephone. He called the firehouse in Kennebunk and told the men there to "get ready for one hell of a combustion." Every man, truck, and bit of equipment Kennebunk had was sent up Route 35. When the fire began to move they were ready for it.

Carl and Louise Russell lived in one of the oldest houses in Kennebunk. It was one of three eighteenth-century farm houses grouped where Route 35 curved west toward Kennebunk center. Big elm trees grew in the dooryard and near the road stood a one-room schoolhouse.

Across Route 35 a magnificent stand of pine trees grew right up to the edge of the road.

On Thursday Carl had telephoned his brother Raymond in Massachusetts, advising him, "I think you'd better get down here right away. We have been told we probably should move everything out of the buildings." By the time Raymond arrived, everything had been moved out except the stoves. The furniture had been hastily loaded on trucks and taken to the Rogers Fibre warehouse on Water Street. Carl had turned his cattle out into the back pasture, and he and Louise had sent their children to stay with his mother.

The Russell brothers joined the firefighters in the woods off Route 35. All day Friday the fire burned toward Kennebunk. There was little wind so its progress was slow.

At the crossroads community of Clark's Mills in Hollis, Cecil Clark had turned over the sprawling Victorian house where he and his wife and their daughter, Marjorie Walker, and her husband Warren and their children lived, to the National Guard for a headquarters. The guard had been brought in to prevent looting in the burned towns. The Clark place could house a lot of men and had a deep, rotary drilled well with plenty of water. There was a cupola on the house and another on the connecting barn. The guardsmen strung an antenna between the two towers and posted a man in the cupola on the house, which had windows that provided a wide view of the surrounding countryside. The lookout could keep track of the fire and radio instructions to men on the ground.

The house was stripped of its furniture. People from Biddeford and Saco came with trucks and took it all away. (When the Clarks and Walkers went looking for their furniture a week later, they found it had been taken all the way to South Windham.) The only piece that was not moved was the grand piano in the front room. The guardsmen used the room for a first-aid center and found the piano, with its cover flat, a suitable place to spread out their bandages and supplies.

Mrs. Clark and Marjorie Walker and her children had been sent to Saco by their husbands to stay with friends. Clark's Mills was in the direct path of the fire. The fine old house, which had been built in 1894 by Mr. Clark's father; the fifteen to twenty other houses in the settlement; the church; the community house; and the Clarks' mill could all go down to the fire.

To the north the Newfield fire had become a threat to Parsonsfield. Kenneth Day of East Parsonsfield had had a lot of experience fighting forest fires and had written to Commissioner Rendall at Augusta offering his services. But he was in West Newfield fighting the Province Lake blaze before Rendall could get back to him. On the day the Fryeburg and Newfield fires blew up, Day had been in Porter "up on this mountain pickin' Northern Spy apples. It was so damned hot we had to cover the boxes to keep 'em from blisterin'. It was way up in the eighties. We saw the fire break loose in Fryeburg. And then as we were comin' out, she began to boil up in the southwest. That night I went over to West Newfield. On Red Thursday I was on the Lost Mile Road. Harry Boothby had brought in a bunch of seniors from Porter High School, and we just barely made it out of there when the wind started up. I know the firetrucks—what they had for firetrucks—they took off out of there with their hose draggin' and the bulldozers just opened her up and took off. I was concerned about those kids—one of 'em was my kid brother. So Boothby rounded them up, and I took those school kids and headed to Maplewood, and we were the last through to Maplewood before she jumped and went acrost."

The next morning, Friday, the fire was working in toward Parsonsfield. The main fire had gone through Newfield and on toward Waterboro, but on the north it had just touched on Parsonsfield's Benson Brook. Day went to Fred Leavitt, who was a selectman. "Fred, we got to do something," he said. "A shift in the wind and it's going to be right into Parsonsfield." Day wanted to backfire along the Mountain Road. Leavitt told him, "You take over and do as you see fit. I'll back you."

Day remembers, "There was quite a lot of hollerin' about it, but I said it was either that or nothin' and Fred had given me the go-ahead and I figured I knew what the hell I was doing, so I started backfirin'. I had . . . I think it was a gasoline truck that they'd converted over with a hose, just a sprinkler hose on it. And Everett Moulton over here to South Parsonsfield had an apple spray rig. So I had a bunch of those high-school boys, kids, and we worked and we backfired all day and all that night. Went clean around to Province Lake and back around to the Lost Mile Road, that whole corner . . . probably four miles."

Day showed the boys how to burn a small area at a time. Wind conditions were right for controlling the fire, and they guided it carefully around the few houses in the area. The backfire just crept along the ground until it began to get near the big fire, then the draft from the big fire sucked it up. The two fires came together with a bang. "That lit up the sky when they got together," Day remembers. "It scared some of 'em. But after Friday I didn't have to worry about Parsonsfield."

In Newfield on Friday, Arthur Moulton had set up in a new headquarters in an unused room at the back of Boozer's store in Lower Village, one of the few buildings that hadn't burned. "I got hold of a piece of plywood, a couple of orange crates and set up a table in there. There was a telephone man outside up on a telephone pole. I went out and said, 'We've got kind of hard straits here. We're going to set up our headquarters in here. How about putting in a telephone?'

" 'Sure, where do you want it?'

"Once we got in there with the telephone set up we'd say, 'I want to call Augusta.' They'd just give you an operator in Augusta—put it right through. We had that telephone in there two weeks I guess, and I don't think we paid a dime for it."

Some of the villagers had taken security into their own hands and, carrying their hunting rifles and shotguns, were on guard against looters and arsonists. "I could see right there that we had problems," says Moulton. He didn't like the idea of "folks parading up and down with guns." And he knew the curious would flock into Newfield to see the ruins, hampering relief workers and mop-up crews, if the roads were not closed off. One of the first calls he made was to get the National Guard to take over security. The guard arrived within a couple of hours.

Newfield still had a problem with fire. Eighty percent of the town's area had been burned over. In the woods trees still smoldered, and roots burned deep underground. Patrols and mop-up crews had to be organized, and many of these were led by men who were not familiar with the town. Topographical maps were needed. With Arthur Baker's help a source of supply was located in Boston. Maps were put on a small plane that flew to Newfield. There a sheet was spread out in the town cemetery, which was about the only landmark left in town. The pilot of the plane spotted the white sheet in the black wasteland and dropped the maps.

Governor Hildreth had announced Friday night that federal aid to fire-ravaged communities would start the next day. At Hildreth's request, and the urging of Maine's congressional delegation, on Saturday President Truman authorized the Federal Works Agency to extend federal aid to Maine. This action cut red tape and made surplus personal property available free of charge to the state and local government of Maine.[12]

H. J. Eberley of the U.S. Forest Service had arrived in Maine on

Friday with orders to do anything he could to help Commissioner Rendall. Major General Frank Keating, commanding general of the army's First Service Command, and his staff had flown from Boston to Portland on Friday to put into operation the army's Master Plan for Disaster Relief. The plan had been devised in the spring when the army had been called in to help with a flood in Rutland, Vermont. Keating's staff had records of every source of supply in New England for cots, blankets, clothing, and medical supplies.

The army plane had encountered a haze of smoke over Boston at four thousand feet, and, twenty minutes later, a solid wall of smoke from Maine's fires. The crew of a Norwegian tanker six hundred miles at sea had radioed that it smelled the smoke from the mainland.

Wilkins was encouraged: everyone was cooperating magnificently. The governor had ordered all state parks closed and guards posted at their entrances. Travel on many secondary roads was restricted, and sightseers were urged to stay away. College students were asked to stay on their campuses that weekend, and football games and many public events were canceled. It was the first time in the history of Maine's college grid series that the games had been postponed. Racing at the New Gloucester fair grounds had been canceled. Army-Navy Day celebrations scheduled for Sunday were called off, not only in Maine but in Boston. (The navy's light cruiser *Little Rock,* in Boston for the occasion, headed to Maine with a thousand men to offer their services as firefighters.) Services to honor Maine's war dead on October 30 were postponed, and the governor even asked children to give up their normal observance of Halloween.

The Coast Guard had gathered radio equipment from Boston, New York, Cleveland, and Norfolk, Virginia, and had set up a communications system for the Red Cross in York County to help them locate missing persons and gather information on burned-out families. Twenty-five "ham" radio operators were doing the same thing for the Red Cross in Portland. The Extension Service, a state and federal agency with particular interest in farmers, had announced that it had trucks available to move poultry and cattle. Many towns re-activated their Civilian Defense units as the governor had requested.

But a sense of normalcy was returning. The Freedom Train reached Augusta after being forced by the Richmond fire to make a detour through Lewiston and Waterville, and people in Maine's capital city would see the historic documents over the weekend.

All the news was not good. There had been two more fire-related deaths, bringing the total to fifteen. Early Friday morning four Bowdoin College students were returning to school by car from Biddeford. The night before they had been in the Waterboros fighting the fire there. The young men had harrowing stories to carry back to campus, for they had been among a group of ten firefighters caught in a ring of fire. They had escaped by pulling their jackets up around their heads and sprinting through the flames. They had seen Lower Main Street in South Waterboro after the fire swept through, leaving behind burning utility poles—each a flaming cross—and only a string of smoking foundations and bare, jutting chimneys to mark where houses had stood.

But their frightening foray out of their protected college environment was not over. The home of one of their number, Constantine Karvonides, was in Biddeford. Leaving South Waterboro at 11 P.M. on Thursday, they had driven to Biddeford. Before daybreak they were on their way back to Brunswick in Ainsley "Lee" Drummond's 1946 Crosley. Karvonides shared the front seat with Drummond. Ed Herlihy and Jim Wyman were asleep in the back seat. With the road through Falmouth under construction, drain pipes and other equipment lining its shoulders, Drummond was driving a careful twenty-five miles per hour behind a tractor-trailer truck. There was no escape when suddenly a car coming from the other direction sideswiped the cab of the truck and rebounded into the Crosley. Herlihy was killed instantly, Wyman died soon after. Drummond and Karvonides were lucky to escape with serious injuries.[13]

There were increased reports of arson and of phony house-to-house solicitations in the name of the Red Cross, and firefighters were being asked to pay for donated food. The Biddeford and Portland papers warned their readers and asked them to report such abuses.

The news from the fires on Saturday morning was mixed. Richmond and Jonesboro had escaped destruction, and officials were cautiously reporting both fires under control. The Mount Desert Island fire still burned savagely, but heroic efforts had kept it out of Otter Creek, Seal Harbor, and Northeast Harbor. Late Friday night one official said, "Barring a bad break in the wind, we've got it sealed off for the night. But the situation is still fluid."

The most alarming news was that a fire was burning at Duck Cove on the east side of Moosehead Lake, the first reported in the state's Forestry District. It posed a major threat to Maine's vast woodlands. The Moosehead fire could be reached only by water, and thirty-mile-an-hour winds were delaying travel across the lake.

But Saturday morning the worst news was from York County. Tongues of the fires that had already swept Brownfield, Newfield, Waterboro, and Lyman were now threatening Kezar Falls, Alfred, Hollis, and Kennebunk. Goodwin's Mills and other tiny communities that had already come close to destruction were still threatened. In Wells and Dayton, not yet touched by fire, men were anxiously keeping watch. Fires were still burning within the city limits of Biddeford, and the whole York County situation was further complicated by the serious fire just across the county's southwestern border in Rochester, New Hampshire. If that blaze jumped the Salmon Falls River, Berwick would be in trouble.

The Cape Elizabeth Fire Department and students from Bates College were among those who responded to radio appeals for help in Hollis Center, Clark's Mills, and Union Falls. Twenty-four navy firefighters, arriving in Portland at noon, were rushed to Hollis with portable pumps and radio equipment. The construction crew that was working on the Saco River's Skelton Dam at Union Falls used bulldozers to dig firebreaks. At Clark's Mills a line was cut between the mill's lumberyard and the woods. This, and another firebreak at Hollis Center, was backfired. At Union Falls a fleet of dump trucks piled sand around houses and along roads and evacuated families. The only escape route was across the cofferdam. Trucks loaded with furniture and livestock parked on the earthen dam, which seemed one of the safest places since all of its sod had been plowed up during construction work.[14]

Saturday's wind did not blow a gale like Thursday's, but it was strong enough by mid-day to turn manageable ground fires into roaring, leaping crown fires. In Kennebunk the fire, which all day Friday had slowly burned its way through the fields and woods west of Route 35, was swept into the tops of the trees. It was headed out of the northwest along Ward Brook toward Route 35 where it turned west toward Kennebunk center and joined the Thompson Road where five houses had recently been built. If the fire crossed Route 35, other houses would be in its path, and it could broaden out and burn into the outskirts of the center itself.

Firefighters from Kennebunk, Kennebunkport, Ogunquit, York, Pease Air Force Base in New Hampshire, and Auburn had been fighting in Alewive. Now they pulled back along Route 35 before the wind-driven flames, looking for a chance to stand and meet the fire again, to stop it, to hold it, to put it out. Raymond Russell remembers how they pulled back along Route 35. "It was like a retreating army. They streamed down this road in groups of a dozen or more. They kept coming and coming."

The men regrouped along Route 35 from the Russells' house to the Thompson Road, determined to stop the fire there. They backfired and bulldozed and pumped water on houses and surrounding land. A bulldozer operator, defying the fast approaching fire, drove his machine into the beautiful pine growth opposite the Russell farm, leveling large trees, throwing up walls of dirt to reduce the height of the blaze. Men went up and down along the road with apple sprayers, spraying a fine mist of water on trees, houses, and fields; passing again and again until everything was soaked.

Raymond Russell, who was on the roof of his brother's house wetting it down with a hose, could hear the fire coming. Then he saw it, rolling through the tops of the pine trees across the road. When it came into the open space above the road, it exploded "like a bursting shell . . . with flames and sparks and debris." Balls of fire flew through the air and landed in a field and in a growth of hardwood trees on the other side of the road.

Louise Russell was in her dooryard with a broom putting out small fires set by falling embers. She had stayed calm even when she had heard the terrible roaring, even when her face had been burned as she beat out flames in the grass, but when she saw the fire jump Route 35, she lost her courage. "When I saw it go across the road down there and go into the trees, I went to pieces. My children were downtown, and I thought I was trapped. I just couldn't take any more."

But although it would be another twenty-four hours before the fire was completely out, the stand at Route 35 was successful. The jump fires were quickly extinguished. In Kennebunk the fire had been defeated.

Biddeford fought its last battle on Saturday too. A general alarm rang Saturday morning for a rekindled blaze on the Pool Road, and once again a truck with a loudspeaker drove through the streets calling for firefighters. One Pool Road house was lost, but with the help of a Coast Guard tug that steamed up the Saco River, tied up near the bank, and ran a hose half a mile to the fire, the flames were kept from jumping the road. If they had, the fire could have burned to the river, jumped it, and set Camp Ellis on the other side ablaze. But only fly-

ing embers reached Camp Ellis, setting grass fires that watchful home
owners stamped out.

The town of Dayton, northwest of Biddeford, doesn't show on
most maps. Its center is not a village, like Goodwin's Mills, but just a
crossroads—Clough's Corner—where Route 35 and Route 5 come together. In 1947 the town hall and garage were there, and a filling station and a small cluster of houses. Most of the people lived on farms
scattered along Route 5 and through the surrounding countryside.

The people of Dayton had been watching the fire that had burned
most of East Waterboro and now was threatening their neighbor, Hollis. On Saturday a twenty- to twenty-five-mile-an-hour wind picked it
up three miles south of Clark's Mills in Hollis and swept it toward
Dayton.

Arthur Roberts was with about a hundred men, "milling around at
Clough's Corner. The fire was coming toward us, and there was nobody to take charge. One of the National Guardsmen came to me and
said, 'Mr. Roberts, will you handle these men and set a backfire? *Can
you* set a backfire?' I said, 'I can, but I have no right. I'm outside my
territory.'

" 'If I back you up, assume the responsibility, will you set a line
of men out here and set a backfire?'

" 'If you say so,' I said. We set a backfire. But it didn't do any
good. The big fire just overrode it." The fire came through Clough's
Corner at twenty minutes to four that Saturday afternoon.

About six miles away Roy Meserve had watched the sky grow
dark. A bulldozer from the dam at Union Falls had bulldozed a line
between the woods and Meserve's farmhouse and barn. Rabbi Cohen,
a friend from Biddeford, had come up with a small truck and taken
some of the furniture out of the house. It was a nice old house, at least
150 years old, with a center chimney and an ell. It sat on a hill with
the wide sky behind it, looking down over a sweep of pastures and
small woods. Fine old elm trees grew in the front yard. Meserve's
grandfather had bought it in 1880, but Meserve had a deed for the
property that was dated 1776. Dayton had been called Freetown then.

Next to the ell was a stable, and next to that a big barn. Meserve
was a dairy farmer. There were two horses and thirty-two cows in the
barn, half of them his, half belonging to Clement Meserve, a nephew.
Two of the cows had been bought the week before for $300, and that
summer Meserve had put in a new $1,500 tie-up. He had ninety tons
of hay in the barn.

Meserve had not turned his cattle out to pasture. If the fire came close, he thought they would be safer in the barn, for his pasture ran into woods. One fourteen-acre field hadn't been used as a pasture that year and had grown up to grass, dry now and about a foot high. It would be a dangerous place for the animals if the fire came. He would have moved the herd out altogether if he'd had the trucks and a place to send them. Everyone had agreed there was little chance the fire would come, but Meserve had prepared for it anyway.

The fire swept through Clough's Corner, burning five houses, the town hall, and the filling station. Someone had taken the new snow-plow out of the town garage, which was surrounded by trees, and parked it in front of the filling station, thinking it would be safer in the open. The garage escaped, while the plow was reduced to a twisted heap of metal.

From Clough's Corner the fire swept into an area of almost solid pine growth, some of it virgin timber—trees that had been there as long as anyone knew. The trees, dry and highly flammable, fed the flames, hurrying the fire and increasing its heat. An eighth of a mile from the corner Paul Johnson stayed with the farm he had worked for sixty-two years until the buildings were enveloped in flames, then fled. All the small homes and farms dotted along Route 5 burned. The fire raced through the woods and fields, heading unchecked for the Saco River.

At his farm on the hill above Route 5, Roy Meserve watched until the sky began to show red over the edge of a hill about a half mile away. Then he ran to the stable for a tool kit he wanted to save and then to the barn to loose his horses and cattle. He had turned out twenty of the cows, most of them his nephew's, when he heard some-one shout from the barnyard. He ran to the door and had to drop to his hands and knees and crawl to safety. The barn was on fire. The sky was raining sparks. At twenty minutes past four, less than an hour after the fire had reached Clough's Corner, the roof of Roy Meserve's barn was on the floor. The animals he had not had time to loosen died in the flames, the flesh burned away from their bones. His house—everything he had worked for all his life—was gone.

From the hill the fire went on down through the fields like a race-horse. It did not burn the house of Lesley Meserve, another of Roy's nephews, which stood almost directly across the road. Lesley's house had asphalt shingles, and he stayed with it, dousing flames as they caught on the porches, with water, and new cider when he ran out of water. The fire burned one more set of buildings before it reached the Saco River and leaped it. It had traveled six miles in six hours. In one afternoon Dayton had lost its town hall, a school, twenty-nine houses, and twenty-seven barns. Dayton was a town that would consider it important to include barns in an accounting of its losses.

On Sunday roving *Press Herald* reporter Franklin Wright drove through Dayton. He stopped at Roy Meserve's farm. Meserve led him slowly up the driveway. "His feet were heavy as he stepped to the side of the barn and gazed down at the charred carcasses of twelve cows. A few feet away lay two old horses on which Meserve had bestowed much affection. Meserve spoke slowly.

" 'I was born in this house just sixty-three years ago next Thursday. It has always been my home. My brother and I farmed it together. I guess between us we have some 450 acres here. Now it's gone—all gone.' " He paused for a moment and his fingers wiped at tired eyes.

" 'We were watching, of course, all day yesterday. At noontime the fire was about six miles away across Route 5. Then it began to get dark. Some men came with bulldozers and cut wide swaths all around the buildings. Those swaths would have stopped an ordinary fire. They didn't mean a thing to those flames.' "[15]

Meserve described what had happened, then said, " 'It's been a hard year for me. Last May my wife became ill and died. . . .' His voice broke." He walked away from the reporter to regain his composure, and then, his shoulders straightened, said apologetically, "I'm sorry, but I guess our nervous system can stand only so much. But I'm not as bad off as thousands of people in this state. I have no little children. My family is all grown up. I'm still able to earn my own living. But I'm not going to do anything this fall, perhaps not next spring. . . ."

Meserve's only definite plans were to move what stock he had left to his nephew Clement's farm on Route 5, which had not burned. All but three of the cows he had been able to turn loose had survived. Those three had such badly burned nostrils that they had had to be destroyed.

Meserve talked about the house still standing across the road. "That's my nephew's farm, and he saved it with a barrel of cider. He had used two or three cans of water and the porch ignited for the third or fourth time. Nothing was left but the barrel of cider. He dumped it on the fire and saved his farm. I never had much respect for cider before." He managed a weak grin, but the smile was brief.

"It burned about half of our town. There must be forty farms destroyed. It burned all the biggest and best farms too. Even the town hall is gone. Even our snowplow. I don't know what these small towns will do. Probably not more than one-half of the people have paid their taxes this year."

Meserve looked again at the ruins of his own farm. "The house was at least 150 years old, but it was in good repair. Those old elm trees there made the place in the summer. Now they're both gone—everything's gone. It's just a barren hill now." But it was the fate of his horses that moved him to tears again. "Those poor horses," he said huskily. "Those poor horses. Tied by the neck, and I couldn't get them out. If they had been free and had been caught by the fire, it wouldn't have been as bad. But tied by the neck, unable to go anywhere—if only I could have helped them." Roy Meserve's story was one of the most moving to come out of the fires.

For two more days the newspapers were filled with stories of desperate battles to save threatened towns, but Dayton was the last community to be devastated by fire. When the radio reported that Clark's Mills had been overrun by the fire, friends of Marjorie Walker in Saco tried to keep the news from her, not wanting her to know until she had to that her lovely big home and the little village where she had lived all her life were gone. Marjorie could sense that something was wrong. "What is it?" she asked. When she was told, she called Vi Wallace at the Bar Mills telephone exchange. "Is Clark's Mills gone?" Vi assured her that it was not and put her through to her house. Marjorie talked with someone—not her husband, not her father, who were out fighting the fire—but someone who said everything was still all right.

For three hard days and nights men battled to save Clark's Mills, Hollis Center, and Union Falls. At 9 P.M. Sunday night a prong of the fire that had burned northwest from Union Falls was within half a mile of Clark's Mills. Flames were within a mile and a half of Hollis Center. But on Monday all that was left of the fire was a patch of flames not more than a mile square in the woods between Clark's Mills and Hollis Center. There was no wind to help it, "and the fire shrank like a cornered, dying beast as men equipped with hose, pumps, and bulldozers closed in on it from every side."[16]

When Marjorie Walker and her mother finally went home, they found the floors scratched and scarred by the boots of the soldiers who had been quartered there. Wallpaper was torn and walls gouged by guns that had been propped up against them. The soldiers had used the bathtub for a wastebasket, and it was overflowing with paper towels.

The Red Cross had dispensed hundreds of meals out of the kitchen. The house was a shambles, but it was standing.

One of the toughest battles fought that weekend was to subdue the last of the Brownfield fire that was threatening Porter and Kezar Falls. Officials would dub it "the battle of the bulldozers."[17] The fire was burning on the side of Little Sugarloaf Mountain and deep in woods where there were no roads. Bulldozers cut great swaths six miles into the woods, giving firefighters access to the fire, and pushed a heavy gasoline truck loaded with water halfway up the mountain where there was no natural source of water. A few farms were lost in Porter and Kezar Falls, but the main villages were saved. Fifty sailors from Newport, Rhode Island, who had been sent to this fire, were reluctant to leave when the worst of the battle was over. They felt they had an investment in the little towns and considered themselves practically citizens.[18]

At six o'clock Sunday night the Topsham-Brunswick fire was finally reported out, and on Mount Desert Island, where Hulls Cove had been threatened again on Saturday, the fire was brought under control on all fronts. The Rochester, New Hampshire, fire did not gain a foothold in Maine: it jumped the Salmon Falls River on Saturday but was quickly put out, and on Sunday firemen patrolled the river in boats.

In Saco firemen fought for forty-eight hours to subdue the fire that had jumped the Saco River from Dayton. Not a single Saco building was lost. With phone lines down, the alarm was spread to nearby home owners by Richard Stickney, racing from house to house in his jeep. Saco's Mayor, Myron Savage, who rode with him, said afterward, "I can testify that a jeep can travel to almost any place in the world."[19] The firefighters hauled water from Sandy Brook three miles from the fire, pouring so many gallons on the boundaries of the blaze that they created a sea of mud three to four inches deep.

The only uncontrolled fire in Maine Sunday night was in Washington County. In Township 19 between Wesley and Crawford a fire was burning unchecked, but it was in an area where there were few houses. The Moosehead Lake fire was under control, no longer a threat to the vast timber tracts in northern Maine. The Centerville-Jonesboro-Whitneyville fire had been fought to a standstill after burning almost twenty thousand acres, seventeen thousand of them forested. Bulldozers had opened up miles of fire lines through heavy forest growth.

Both Governor Hildreth and Commissioner Rendall went on the radio Sunday night, Hildreth to give the first official estimates of Maine's losses and to outline the state's rehabilitation plans for fire victims, Rendall to urge continued vigilance. He reminded the people that until a soaking rain came, continued control depended on the strength and direction of the wind.

In southwestern Maine, where the largest number of communities had been lost and were still threatened, Rendall gave U.S. Forest Service Ranger H. J. Eberly responsibility for directing fire control. Eberly set up headquarters at the Wells state police barracks on Monday. With efficiency and tact he appointed key men in each fire area, advising them that to avoid confusion and duplication of effort, all requests for assistance should be made through his headquarters. For the next three days, every request for men or equipment, every offer of help, problems of any kind, and news releases about the fire situation in southwestern Maine were handled by Eberley. It was the kind of system that had been needed from the beginning.

It had been just a week since the fire had broken loose in North Kennebunkport. In just a week nine communities had been practically wiped out, four more had suffered severe damage, and scores of others had lost buildings. Property damage was estimated at $30 million. Fifteen had died. Many thousands of acres of trees were blackened stubble, and three million feet of cut lumber had been destroyed. In many sections the earth itself had been consumed. Maine had become an armed camp, her roads patrolled by the National Guard, Legionnaires, the police, and self-appointed vigilantes. Firefighting equipment and relief supplies were pouring into the state, much of it being brought in by C-47s, C-45s, and a huge C-82 "Flying Boxcar," which put down gingerly on the short runway at the Augusta airport. Travel was restricted even in areas that had not been swept by fire. Communication lines were down, and most public gatherings had been postponed or canceled.

Organized as they had been during the war to respond to Civilian Defense guidelines, the people felt they had been at war. The enemy had been fire. Their burned-out towns were being compared to bombed-out cities in Europe. The men who had fought the fires talked of "battles," "front lines," "retreats," and "victories." Their "ally" had been the bulldozer. The "armistice" would come when rain fell—a good soaking rain—and then the task of rehabilitation could begin.

NOTES

1. *Biddeford Daily Journal,* October 24, 1947.
2. W. H. Tracy, "Climatological Data," New England Section, U.S. Department of Commerce, Weather Bureau, Vol. LIX, No. 10, Boston, Massachusetts, October 1947.
3. Sleeper, *The Bar Harbor Fire.*
4. "19th Annual Report of the Roscoe B. Jackson Memorial Laboratory, 1947–48."
5. *Ibid.*
6. *Ibid.*
7. Spiker, "Like a Giant Blowtorch."
8. Corey Ford, "Brownfield's Still Here," *Collier's,* February 21, 1948.
9. Harry T. Foote, "Lyman Father of Eight Plans to Have New Home by Friday," *Portland Press Herald,* October 29, 1947.
10. *Ibid.*
11. J. Malcolm Barter, "York County Men Return to Survey Ruins of Homes," *Boston Globe,* October 25, 1947.
12. Letter from President Harry S. Truman to Major General Philip B. Fleming, Administrator, Federal Works Agency, October 25, 1947.
13. Correspondence, A. H. Drummond, Jr., with Joyce Butler, February 13, 1989.
14. "Company's Fire Losses Comparatively Slight As Some Areas in Maine Suffer Severe Setbacks," *The Exciter,* Vol. 29, No. 10, Central Maine Power Company, Augusta, Maine, November 1947.
15. The details of Roy Meserve's story are taken from a front-page story by Franklin Wright, which appeared in the *Portland Press Herald* on October 27, 1947, and was reprinted with "Man's Generosity to Man Helped Him Back Along the Fire-Blackened Road," by Wright, *Portland Sunday Telegram,* November 13, 1949.
16. *Portland Press Herald,* October 28, 1947.
17. Wilkins, "The 1947 Forest Fire Disaster," p. 78.
18. *Biddeford Daily Journal,* October 28, 1947.
19. *Biddeford Daily Journal,* October 31, 1947.

Chapter XII:
Rain, Beautiful Rain

"Can't the Associated Press make it rain?" joked firefighters in Waterboro,[1] reflecting not only their awareness of the ubiquitous reporters and their own sense of humor in the face of disaster, but everyone's desperate wish. It rained in York County on Sunday, but just a little, enough to make the people of Dayton feel that they had come tragically close to being spared their disaster, but not enough to relieve the drought conditions.

The Weather Bureau forecast twenty-five-mile-an-hour winds for Monday, and in Boston the temperature hit eighty-one degrees at midday. The Boston Weather Bureau advised Austin Wilkins that there would be a "good dew" all over the fire area Monday night. The need for moisture was so desperate that even a good dew was significant.

Now even the northern part of Maine was withering in the drought. After the potato harvest, the drought had intensified, and most wells were dry. Many streams and rivers had all but disappeared. Springs that had never failed were dust holes. Farmers had no water for livestock, let alone to fight fire, and they worried that the long dry spell would affect the next year's apple and hay crops, for hay roots were being burned right in the ground, and apple tree roots would soon wither and die.

Before winter brought rain and snow to northern Maine, electricity would be rationed, Daylight Saving Time would be resumed, and a naval vessel would be requested by Governor Hildreth to anchor offshore to generate electricity that was transmitted overland to Aroostook County.

On Wednesday, the twenty-ninth, with forty fires still burning, a second attempt was made to produce rain artificially. The army, the navy, and the General Electric Company joined forces in "Project Cirrus." Two B-17s were to take off from Schenectady, New York, and drop dry ice into clouds over Maine. The ice would reduce the temperature in the clouds until ice crystals formed. These would reach earth in the form of rain. But at 8 A.M., when the two planes left Schenectady, rain was already falling in York County.

In his office at the State House in Augusta, visibly weary from his long duty at the capital and his travels to fire-stricken areas, Governor Hildreth was told that it was raining in York County. He sank back in his chair, saying, "Thank God."[2] Commissioner Rendall said, "It's a godsend and a blessing, but we need a lot of it." Central Maine Power Company officials in Biddeford carefully measured the rainfall at 11:45 Wednesday morning: 25/100ths of an inch had fallen.

When it began to rain in Portland, people there telephoned ahead to friends in Bar Harbor to tell them that rain was coming. When it reached Bar Harbor people went out into the streets and held up their hands to the beautiful rain. Rain fell through the night and into Thursday, reaching as far north as Greenville at the southern tip of Moosehead Lake. Some credited Project Cirrus with the good fall, but whether the rain was man-made or natural, what mattered was that it was raining.

The rain wet down but did not extinguish the fires burning deep in the ground. Word went out along the smoldering fire lines that the vigil must not be relaxed. A downpour of long duration was needed. In Township 19 and near Whitneyville and Machias men were still working to contain fires. A group of New Jersey Christmas tree buyers who arrived in Township 19 found the residents, weary from fighting fire, were not pleased to see them. For the first time since coming to Maine to buy trees they found the "welcome mat rolled up and taken in."[3] Near Whitneyville winter would set in before the fire was out. Hose lines froze on the ground and were buried under snow.

While these weary battles were being fought, men and equipment were gradually being recalled from the southern Maine fire lines. On Thursday Eberley was able to advise twelve trained, fully-equipped men from Boston that their services would not be needed. The peak of the trouble had passed, and he was closing down the Wells control center and heading to Washington where he was overdue for another assignment. One hundred and twenty-five men from the U.S. Navy's cruiser *Little Rock* were recalled from Hollis to their ship in Portland harbor, already two days late in sailing for overseas duty. National Guard units and Coast Guardsmen from Norfolk, Virginia, and New York were recalled from York County, and the Red Cross closed down its special communications system in Biddeford. Many firefighters had gone home, taking equipment with them, and an appeal was made for its return. Boy Scouts in Biddeford went looking for $1,000 worth of cots, blankets, and lights that had not been returned to them.

By Wednesday the Maine Forest Service had begun to estimate the extent of the fires and losses in terms of timber. Approximately 200,000 acres had burned, most of it forested. In York County alone more than 131,000 acres, 80 percent of it woodland, were black. More than 150 separate fires had been burning at one time or another during the week of October 20.[4]

Still, despite the widespread fires, only about 1 percent of Maine's 16,783,000 acres of forest land had been involved. In his final report Austin Wilkins would write, "Geographically a straight line 313 miles long and one mile wide . . . would be the equivalent of the burned area."

Millions of trees had been killed, millions were severely burned. Others, whose root systems were destroyed, would fall in the first good wind or heavy snow, if not before. Sunday night at the Brunswick burn, before firemen had put out the last smoldering snags, trees around them, their prop roots burned, began to topple. Some of them were thirty-six inches in diameter. The firemen pulled out to wait for daylight when they would have a better chance to dodge the falling trees.

Much of this timber was salvageable, but it would have to be cut before the following summer when insects and fungi would attack the damaged trees. Money would be lost because of the glut of lumber on the market, for 110 million board feet of softwoods and 10 million board feet of hardwoods were involved; but, thousands of dollars more would be lost if useable timber was not salvaged.

There were losses that couldn't be measured in terms of dollars. Wildlife cover and feed had been destroyed. Water tables would be altered where there were no longer trees, undergrowth, and moss to catch the rain and hold it. It would take fifty to a hundred years for the forests to grow back; longer where the fire had burned away the soil in which new seed could sprout.

And there was no way to measure or compensate for the lost aesthetic value of venerable old trees that had been regarded with pride and awe. In towns like South Waterboro, houses could be rebuilt, but there was no quick way to replace the handsome elm trees that had lined the main street.

One of the important questions to be answered after the fires was how much wildlife had been killed and how much had survived. As soon as fires were out in York County, Fish and Game Commissioner George Stobie called on sportsmen's organizations to conduct a survey of fire-devastated areas. Their members were to count all wildlife they saw, alive or dead. Stobie could not wait for the careful, time-consuming surveys of his wardens. He needed to know the figures quickly to make his recommendation to Governor Hildreth for winter hunting.

An estimated five hundred members of fish and game associations and rod and gun clubs spent the weekend of November 1 and 2 combing the woods and fields of York County looking for animals. Surprisingly few dead animals were found, and many deer, partridge, porcupine, and rabbits had already returned to their former haunts, Reports of great losses of wildlife, circulated before the fires were out, could not be substantiated. These initial findings were confirmed by a five-month study begun by the Fish and Game Department in late November.

This was not to say that animals hadn't died in the fires. Wardens found deer suffocated in fields where they had taken refuge. One deer, evidently fleeing the fire, running and leaping through the smoky woods, had impaled himself on a snag.[5]

Small game had raced before the flames, fleeing with evacuating people down highways. The morning after Lyman was swept by fire, Route 111 was strewn with rabbits and other small animals, dead of asphyxiation.

Dead trout were found in a North Kennebunkport brook. Reports that birds had been seen flying with their wings on fire were never substantiated, but firefighters saw confused grouse flying into the fire. There was no question that large numbers of game birds died, but a good breeding stock was left.

Slow-moving porcupine were an easy prey of the flames, but some escaped ground fires by climbing trees, as did raccoon. The day after the fire had been put out in Kennebunk, "Warren Wyman spotted a porcupine crouched in the top of a high pine tree on his lot. At the suggestion that he kill it he said any animal that could weather such a terrific fire deserved to die only from natural causes."[6]

Stories were circulated that small animals running with their fur aflame helped to spread the fires. Firefighters came out of the burning woods and fields to tell that burning rabbits looked like "little balls of flame rolling along the ground." One firefighter, patrolling the edges of a burn, came upon several small fires all in a straight line leading away from the fire line. They led him to a dried up mudhole where a raccoon lay dead and almost completely singed. But, the extent to which fleeing animals spread the fires was negligible compared to jump fires and wind-blown embers.

Wildlife that escaped, particularly deer, faced starvation in the long winter ahead, for the fire had destroyed their natural feed and cover. When hunting was allowed in November in order to lower the deer population, hunters found many of the deer they killed had severely burned feet.

The main concern of state officials and relief organizations was the rehabilitation of homeless families. The Red Cross estimated that 3,500 people had been displaced and 2,500 were homeless. In 35 communities 109 houses had been damaged, and 851 permanent homes, 397 summer homes, and an undetermined number of barns and garages had been destroyed.

There were other losses. Furniture, dishes, clothes, fishing gear, tools, farm machinery, and automobiles could be replaced, but not antiques, art objects, the record books of towns and organizations, or personal papers, pictures, and possessions of sentimental value. Lawrence Ireland, who lost everything he owned at Goose Rocks Beach, said, thirty years later, in describing what it meant to be burned out, "Everything connecting you with the past is cut off right there."

An all-out rehabilitation effort was begun on behalf of the victims of the disaster. Again Governor Hildreth went on the radio, this time to outline the kind of aid that was available from the Red Cross and to explain what help the state could provide to towns whose tax revenues had been severely cut by extensive property losses.

Before the Red Cross shut down its rehabilitation offices the following July, it had spent almost $2,000,000 helping the people of Maine, about $639,500 during the fires, the rest for rehabilitation. It had supplied food, clothing, household furnishings, medical care, farm equipment, livestock, and occupational rehabilitation. It had paid for repairs on 480 buildings and helped in the replacement of 376 houses, 75 barns, and 194 other buildings.[7]

Some of the supplies distributed by the Red Cross came from the

War Assets Administration, a federal agency that controlled surplus war materials, whose resources were available because of President Truman's action in recognizing that an emergency existed in Maine. This agency provided firefighting equipment during and after the fire. To stricken families it gave lumber, shingles, cement, wiring, roofing, windows, heating units, toilets, beds, bedsheets, pillowcases, towels, stoves, cooking utensils, and refrigerators. Its most important contribution was 150 prefabricated metal houses. With winter just around the corner, the building of conventional houses would be delayed until spring. Housing was made available to homeless families at various institutions all over the state, but most people wanted to stay in their hometown. The "tin houses," as they came to be called, made this possible. In Brownfield and Newfield they were even used as schools.

For families with resources or those who did not wish to accept Red Cross help, loans were available at an interest rate of only 3 percent from the Reconstruction Finance Corporation, a federal agency created during the Depression to maintain the country's economic stability. To cut red tape, the RFC announced it was prepared to give home-building loans based simply on character references.

General Omar Bradley, head of the Veterans Administration, announced that a GI loan on a burned house could be continued on a new home even if it was not built on the same site. Ordinarily the GI Bill allowed each veteran only one loan. A veteran whose house had burned would have been required to pay his mortgage on it with money collected from fire insurance and then would have had no money to rebuild. Under Bradley's ruling a veteran could put his fire insurance money in the bank and use it for rebuilding, and replace the mortgage on the burned house with a mortgage on the new one.

Although officials estimated that only about 35 percent of the value of lost property was covered by insurance, insurance companies sent teams of adjusters to Maine's fire areas. The state waived the forty-five-day waiting period on insurance claims. The Mutual Insurance Company of New York granted a thirty-day extension of the grace period for paying policy premiums and authorized its Portland office to make emergency $500 loans on life insurance policies.

The Maine Unemployment Commission set up contact stations to expedite the payment of unemployment compensation. The Maine Chapter of the American Institute of Architects met to see what they could do to help, as did the Farm Home Association.

The Federal Reserve Bank of Boston sent telegrams to Governor

Hildreth, Maine's Banking Commissioner, and the secretary of the State Banking Association suggesting that Maine's banking community organize to provide credit where it was needed for rebuilding, offering to assist banks by extending advances to them "to the fullest extent of the law."

The Home Builders Association of Maine called a special meeting at the Falmouth Hotel in Portland on October 30 to discuss the rebuilding of an estimated one thousand houses. Forty builders and representatives of the Red Cross and state and federal agencies assured selectmen from badly damaged towns that "the rule book [would] be tossed out the window"[8] to expedite rebuilding in York and Oxford Counties.

Materials were scarce, and costs were high. "There are not normally enough nails in Maine to build fifty homes or enough toilets for a hundred," said Hamilton Shields, president of the Builders Association, but he expressed the belief that builders and suppliers working together could solve this problem. Suppliers reported that they had received "scores of calls" from manufacturers all over the country offering materials, no matter how scarce, so long as they were for fire areas.

A Federal Housing Administration official pointed out that a man whose family was homeless could not be told "this isn't an opportune time to rebuild." He estimated that a very simple house with a floor area as small as 360 square feet could be built for $3,000. He also said his agency's normal requirement that borrowers be employed would be waived, considering that many farmers who needed loans were technically out of work until they could replace their machinery and herds.

The carpenters' union offered to build schoolhouses for nothing, provided materials were supplied, and to help all they could on reconstruction of town halls and churches.

The Maine Extension Service provided special advice and help to farmers. Those whose cattle had survived but whose barns and feed supplies were gone were urged not to sell their animals. This warning came in the wake of reports that cattle buyers had come into burned areas and were trying to buy herds for cut-rates from farmers who had lost their barns. One farmer was offered $800 for a herd worth $3,000. Farmers were reminded that "livestock economy" was the key to restoration of many areas. By selling, they would be sacrificing not only their own economic future but the futures of their towns.

The Extension Service did not just offer advice. Transportation to shelter and feed for six hundred head of livestock had already been arranged, and the Extension guaranteed delivery of hay within a day or two to farmers who still had their cows and barn but no feed. Farmers who felt they must sell their livestock were asked to talk with the Red Cross or their county Farm Bureau first.

Farmers outside the fire areas were quick to offer help. A farmer in Lee, Maine, two hundred miles from York County, told the Red Cross he had a barn full of hay he would give. The Red Cross in Biddeford received a check for $100 "for a farmer."

Another group with special problems was the lumbermen who faced the enormous job of tree salvage. The fire-killed or -weakened trees had to be cut by July 1 if they were to be saved from warm-weather insects and fungi. Trees that could not be sold outright could be stored in ponds and lakes, where the water would preserve them. Saving the lumber would be a race against time because of the millions of board feet involved.

In York County on November 2 representatives of all the largest lumber companies in southwestern Maine and many of the smaller companies met with wood-lot owners, farmers, and bankers in the Community House at Clark's Mills to form a county-wide organization to get the job done. Maine Forest Service representative Robert Dineen and Arthur Roberts of Lyman had already begun a survey of part of the destroyed woodlands and advised the group that while it would be obvious to them that trees whose crowns were burned away and whose bark was badly blackened would have to be cut, trees whose root systems were gone would also have to come down.

The lumbermen felt that if extra equipment was brought in from other parts of the state to supplement what was still available in York County, most if not all of the lumber could be salvaged for commercial use by July 1. One sawmill was already operating in Waterboro.

All that winter and into the spring York County, Oxford County, Mount Desert Island, Washington County—wherever the fire had left dead and dying trees—rang to the sound of sawmills. Men who had lost everything welcomed the chance to work, but even as they raced to harvest the trees, they knew that once the job was done there would be no more lumbering in some areas for another generation. Many landholders, seeing no hope for rejuvenation of their land in their own lifetime, sold it off for a dollar an acre.

For burned-out families help came from organizations, companies, and individuals who had looked for ways to help the firefighters during the fires and now found ways to help fire victims. A "Rehabilitate a Maine Family" fund drive was begun by the Rotary Club in Bath. The Maine State Society in Washington, D.C., launched a drive to raise money for fire victims. Higgins Classical Institute offered scholarships for all expenses to ten boys from families who had been burned out at Bar Harbor. The Maine Central Institute offered free board and tuition to two students. The Portland School Committee offered to turn over extra books and equipment to towns that had lost their schools.

Portland's Independent Retail Grocers Association voted to give $250 to the Salvation Army and the Red Cross for their relief work. The Bangor Elks pledged $1,000 to buy clothes for homeless children in Bar Harbor. Employees of the Veterans Administration at Togus raised $3,700 for fire relief.

The Windham Lake Shore Lodge, IOOF, planned an "old-fashioned dance," the proceeds to be turned over to the Salvation Army for the benefit of Kennebunkport and Waterboro families. The Kiwanis Club in Biddeford canceled a dance and turned its efforts to collecting money for relief. The Elks in Portland held a dance, and the price of admission was one item of clothing for a fire victim.

Everyone collected used clothing, including summer residents of Maine who sent it from their homes in Massachusetts. The Sanford-Springvale Hairdressers Association, which had been collecting clothing for a rulmage sale, gave it to the Salvation Army and the Elks for distribution. Newspapers carried notices of where clothing could be left, and it was taken by the truckload to Brownfield, Bar Harbor, and all the other stricken towns.

Many stores gave discounts to fire victims. The Philco Dealers of Maine secured an extra allotment of two hundred refrigerators and freezers, scarce during those post-war years, and reserved them for sale at a 10 percent discount to burned-out families.

In Biddeford a hundred teenage girls canvassed local businessmen for donations of articles, but many businesses came up with offers of assistance without being asked. Chapman's Clothing Store advertised that it would cancel out and mark as paid outstanding bills owed by families who had suffered total loss. Maxie Tetreault, a Brunswick dealer, said he would give a $2,700 trailer free to a burned-out family whose name could, he suggested, be pulled in a drawing.

The Mack Truck Company of New York sent $6,000 to the Red

Cross for fire relief. The C. H. Sprague Company of Boston and Searsport, Maine, gave a thousand tons of coal. William Hobbs of Kennebunk placed an ad in the *Kennebunk Star* offering his services "free of charge to all fire victims who have oil-burning stoves needing to be reset." And newspapers in Biddeford and Bangor carried a modest little advertisement from the Massachusetts Envelope and Drinking Cup Company that said: "We will replace—absolutely free—all drinking cups destroyed or damaged by the fire that were purchased from us." Everyone wanted to do something.

Some of the most meaningful help was that given person-to-person. One afternoon soon after she had returned to her home in Lyman, Lorraine Roberts went out to the barn chamber and saw Claude Emmons, the hired man who had lost his own home and had helped to save hers, standing by the open drawer of a bureau. "What are you doing, Claude?" she asked.

Emmons took a pair of pants out of the drawer and held them up. "Just think, Mrs. Roberts," he said. "This is all I've got left in the world." She wept for him. Later the Robertses built him a small house and helped him to get started again.

Governor Hildreth appointed a Fire Emergency and Information Committee to cope with the needs of the fire victims, but towns that had lost large percentages of taxable property as well as tax income from damaged farm and woodland, needed special help. In his October 29 radio address the governor outlined three possible solutions for towns in financial difficulty: abatement of state taxes, due on December 1, "at least in part"; turning over control of their finances to the state Emergency Municipal Finance Board, which would administer town affairs until financial stability was regained; or "deorganization," meaning becoming part of the state's unorganized territory whose affairs were administered by the state.

A fourth solution—allowing towns to increase their debt limits—would require action by the state legislature. The legislature would not convene again until 1949, and with the three alternatives already available, a special session was deemed unnecessary.

"There are a thousand complicated details—physical, legal, and financial to be worked out," warned Hildreth, "but red tape has been cut from beginning to end, and you can be assured that the solution of the problem facing our unfortunate citizens is being made as rapidly as possible."

Before the winter was over the selectmen of many of the towns with financial problems would show themselves dissatisfied with the decision not to call a special session of the legislature on their behalf,[9] but at the same time they had not waited for help from the state, but had gone ahead on their own to deal with their problems.

At Bar Harbor all men who had been evacuated and could serve on fire patrols, and mop-up crews were allowed to return on Monday, October 27. On Wednesday, at noon, even though the fire still had not yet been officially declared out, the selectmen and emergency officials decided to let all evacuees whose homes were still standing return, but a 6 P.M. curfew was imposed for women and children. Those who had lost their homes were allowed back to look at the ruins of their property, but then were required to return to their temporary housing. When the Red Cross had arranged emergency housing for them in Bar Harbor at the Shore Club, they were brought back in groups of fifty.

When Bernie Hawkes's wife got home, she plugged in her washing machine and finished the washing she had left the Thursday before. Some families had to go to the Athletic Field to get property still stacked there and guarded by soldiers. Owners of some of the large estates found that the police had dug in the ruins of their houses to find salvageable valuables—safes, statuary—and had taken them to the police station for safekeeping.

Chester Wescott searched in the ruins of the Malvern Hotel until he found a small safe. When he opened it, the contents were still so hot they burst into flame when exposed to the air. But he got what he wanted: the key to the hotel's large, concrete vault.[10] When he opened the vault, after waiting another week to be sure that it had cooled sufficiently, he found Oriental rugs and silver, stored there for the winter, intact. Some of the hotel's linen had been sent to a local laundry at the close of the season and that had survived, but all the antique furniture in the hotel and cottages was gone. Irreplaceable valuables such as Wedgewood pitchers and bowls, used in the hotel before bathrooms were installed, and stored in the attic, were gone.

Returning evacuees were surprised to find that the damage done by the fire was not as extensive as they had been led to believe, although, as one man said, "It's bad enough." Bar Harbor's leading citizens were already talking about rebuilding and expressing hope that even summer homes would be rebuilt, although recognizing that they would probably be less lavish. Sheldon Goldthwaite, president of the Bar Harbor Banking and Trust Company, had already told reporters,

"We all feel the town will be reconstructed. The enthusiastic younger generation will rebuild."[11] Bar Harbor would continue to be an important vacation retreat. "We still have our nineteen mountains, twenty-two lakes and ponds, and the Atlantic Ocean," said Chester Wescott.

"After all," said Joseph Pulitzer, who had flown in to view the ruins of his sister's home, "Nothing can destroy Bar Harbor's climate."[12]

Dr. Marion Bradshaw of the Bangor Theological Seminary, a photographer familiar with Mount Desert Island, was asked by the *Bangor Daily News* to visit the island and comment on what he found. "I would not willingly minimize the tremendous damage to beauty spots," he said, "but my strongest impression is that Bar Harbor is still a place of tremendous beauty."[13] Bradshaw was most moved by the ruins of Bar Harbor's "modest homes."

Everyone's first concern was for "the small home owner, the permanent resident of Bar Harbor. People seemed to feel that the loss to the owners of fabulous mansions was a financial one and one that they could probably bear, but to the 'little fellow,' everything he had saved, everything he had, everything he had created was gone in the fire. [But these people] appeared to be more disconsolate over the destruction of the mansions than over their own personal loss. For it was on these mansions and the commerce that resulted from their being there that the so-called little fellow depended for his livelihood."[14]

The people of Bar Harbor regretted the loss of the mansions not just for economic reasons. They had looked on them with pride. They embodied the history of the town as a famous resort. Everyone had enjoyed their grace and dignity. Morris Gilley, who had left Bar Harbor on foot along Bay Drive at the height of the fire, told United Press reporters, "It almost makes you cry to see those big houses come down."[15]

Year-round residents were encouraged when they read in the paper that Mrs. Potter Palmer was planning to rebuild her cottage, Havre Forest, and that Dr. J. Austin Furfey of Boston had vowed, "I shall rebuild my home. I shall replace every blade of grass."[16] Dr. Furfey was as good as his word: he had an exact replica of his cottage built.

The summer people expressed concern for rehabilitation of the year-round residents and for the future of Bar Harbor. On Monday, the twenty-seventh, the Bar Harbor Citizens' Committee, which had been formed quickly to receive donations for fire victims, received a

telegram from the four daughters of Walter and Margaret Blaine Damrosch, which said in part, "We . . . want to pledge $5,000 to be used
to help those who have suffered most and who have lost all they hold
most dear. As our father has not yet recovered from his recent illness,
upon his doctor's advice, we have not told him or our lother of the loss
of their home or of the disaster that has befallen their beloved Bar
Harbor."

On October 28, even before all of Bar Harbor's refugees had returned, the selectmen and the planning board, recognizing the danger
of reckless rebuilding, announced a moratorium on building permits.
With financial help from summer residents, the firm of Harland
Bartholomew Associates of St. Louis was hired to study Bar Harbor's
problems and make recommendations. One of the first made by the
firm was that a zoning ordinance should be adopted at once. By the
end of November a hard-working committee of townspeople had prepared a preliminary draft.

Bar Harbor took advantage of the tin houses being offered by the
Red Cross. Some were put up on land loaned by the Bar Harbor Land
Company that had been, someone noted, the site of the 1867 Alpheus
Hardy Cottage, the first summer cottage in Bar Harbor. The tin houses
were considered a temporary expedient and were removed as soon as
proper houses were built.

Almost as important to the people of Bar Harbor as the attitude
and intent of the wealthy summer people was the fate of the Jackson
Laboratory, which employed 190 people. Dr. Little had said it would
be rebuilt, but where?

Bar Harbor was uneasy when it was reported on October 30 that
seventy-five members of the staff, among them some of the nation's
best cancer research scientists, had temporarily moved their work to
the Memorial Hospital in New York City, and that the Atomic Energy
Commission had offered to provide a site, building funds, and equipment to the lab at the Brookhaven National Laboratory on Long Island
in New York. But on November 1, Dr. Little announced that the lab
would be rebuilt at Bar Harbor. The trustees felt that Bar Harbor offered a "distinct advantage in the environment it provided for workers and experimental animals alike."[17]

Significant amounts of money for building the new lab had already been pledged—$10,000 from the Maine Chapter of the Ameri-
can Cancer Society, $50,000 from the Damon Runyan Fund, but small
gifts began to come in too, donations from institutions and people all

over the world who believed in the lab's work. When a drive was begun the following May to raise $1,500,000 for the lab, the money came flooding in.

Another kind of help was given. Almost immediately messages had poured in from scientific and medical institutions and societies all over the United States, Canada, and the British Isles offering vital breeding colonies of basic genetic stocks of mice. Many of these institutions had developed their colonies with Jackson Laboratory mice, and therefore were returning to the lab's scientists strains they themselves had developed. "We got our mouse back," says Allen Salisbury.

This outpouring of support gave Dr. Little and his staff a sense of the respect with which their work was viewed by the scientific community. None of the staff had guessed the extent of this feeling. They resolved to rebuild.[18]

On May 7, 1948, ground was broken for the new laboratory. The first spadeful of earth was turned by Frank Clark, who had worked on the first building twenty-nine years before and was the lab's oldest employee. In his remarks, Dr. Little said, "This simple ceremony is a pledge to more than 150 research laboratories here and abroad, which use various strains raised here, that the function of this lab will be continued."[19]

In the following years several additions were made to the laboratory, and its programs were all expanded. By 1977 the Jackson Lab had 38 staff scientists and 440 employees.

All Bar Harbor's hotels had been destroyed. A group of the townspeople pooled their resources, bought the Shore Club, and converted it into a hotel.[20] Mary Roberts Rinehart, whose cottage had burned, rented one of the suites, unwittingly setting the pattern for the "new" post-fire Bar Harbor as a town with more hotels (and motels) than elaborate vacation homes.

Acadia National Park was to continue to be one of the reasons for coming to Bar Harbor. Its ten thousand burned acres were quickly cleaned up with funds provided by a special appropriation from the United States Congress and were by 1954 showing such a luxuriant new growth of young birch, aspen, oak, cherry, pine, and spruce that one official of the National Park Service asked rhetorically, "Has nature performed a miracle in Acadia National Park?"[21] By November 13 when the first snow of the winter fell over Mount Desert Island and the fire was finally officially declared out, the pattern for Bar Harbor's future was set.

But what of the crossroads communities and small towns of southwestern Maine that had lost more than Bar Harbor but had no wealthy "summer folks" to look to and no international fame to call attention to their plight? What of Brownfield, of whom Franklin Wright of the *Portland Press Herald* had written:

> We had seen Bar Harbor Friday and it had seemed as horrible as could be imagined. Yet it did not make the profound impression that we carried away from Brownfield. These had been no stately mansions. These were homes of little people, men and women who had worked with their hands. These were homes of men whose daily bread came from the timberlands that bordered their town on every quarter.
>
> Now the timberlands were ravaged. Their homes were gone. At least at Bar Harbor enough remained to make the village recognizable. Here there was nothing. What would they do? Would they rebuild or turn to greener fields for their livelihood?[22]

At Brownfield in the new "town hall," a boxcar loaned by the railroad, the selectmen were dealing with some of the problems facing their town. One of their first concerns was to knock down all the chimneys standing on the sites of burned houses before they fell on people. They borrowed pickpoles from Central Maine Power Company linesmen and knocked the chimneys over. Another concern was wells whose covers had burned off. These were found and covered again.

Donations of used clothing had begun to come in and were piling up at one end of the boxcar. People who came looking for something to wear found the contributions included high-heeled slippers, evening clothes, feathered straw hats, and an impressive heap of men's suit coats. "Mebbe they figured we only got burnt out from the waist up," someone said.[23]

On Wednesday, October 29, a special town meeting was held in a garage. The moderator used the back of a pickup truck for a rostrum, and the two hundred people stood. They eagerly asked questions and made plans for the town. They were able to laugh when Esther Boynton, with obvious good humor, asked how people whose furniture had been trucked to safety could find it, adding, "I'm not asking for myself. All I've got left is a cellar hole."[24]

Committees were appointed to find temporary employment for men out of work and to salvage partly burned trees. It was agreed that the first public building raised should be a church that could double as school, town hall, and assembly hall. Leon Brooks urged the appointment of a committee to plan the location of public buildings instead of "just letting them grow like daisies."

It was announced that the School Committee was going to meet with state Department of Education officials on Friday. Fifty prefabricated metal houses would begin arriving in town on Saturday. Mail was being delivered from a bed in one of Charlie Harmon's bedrooms. By Saturday postmistress Julia Wells had three cases of post office boxes, given to her by the postmaster at West Paris, and had put up a crayoned sign, "Brownfield Post Office."

Mrs. Harry Durgin had turned her West Brownfield home, Shepard's River Farm, over to the Red Cross, and food and clothing for fire victims was being left there. Another Red Cross center was to open in Perley Walker's garage in East Brownfield. The meeting lasted about an hour. All the town's problems were not solved, but it was a beginning.

The next day the selectmen drove to Augusta to look at a prefab house that had been set up at the Augusta airport. These all new, two-family houses, with wooden floors, measured twenty by forty-eight feet and came with bathroom fixtures and septic tanks.

Guy and Esther Boynton would spend the winter in one of these houses, but not before they had spent a week in a fully furnished house loaned to them by the Earlan Jones family of North Fryeburg, and not before they had lived for two months in a tiny house trailer that a friend loaned them and which they parked beside the cellar hole of their burned house.

The Boyntons' decision to stay in Brownfield was not an easy one. It would take hard work to make something out of the blackened ruin of their farm. Guy Boynton had lived all his life in Brownfield, and Esther felt he would not be truly happy living anywhere else. But she remembered that one day, after he had been "trying to pick up, trying to decide what to do with nothing to do with" he came to her and sat down with his head in his hands and cried. "I don't know what to do," he said. "I don't know where to turn." It was the only time Esther ever saw him shed a tear.

"I don't either," she told him. "But we've got to do something. We can't sit still. If you want to go back, we'll go back. We've got running water," she said, alluding to the horse trough in the barnyard that was filled by a pipe running from a deep, sweet spring in the hills above where their house had stood. "We've got a driveway," said Esther, her spirit and humor and strength shining through.

They stayed. Guy traded in his oxen, which had survived, for a pair of work horses and went to work in the woods hauling timber from one of the seven portable sawmills that came into Brownfield that winter. In the spring when the snow had gone, Guy would come home black with soot and marveling that the horses did not break their legs because they had nothing to walk on but rock, cobble rock, where the humus on the forest floor had been burned away.

One of the first things Esther did was register with the Red Cross. They asked her, "What do you need?" The Boyntons needed just about everything. They needed clothes. Esther was a big woman. "I'm sorry; I don't think I've got anything that will fit you," said the young worker. "But I know where I can get some things. I'll have them here tomorrow." When Esther went back she was given "two nice dresses, slips, underclothes, stockings, two pairs of Energetic shoes—they hadn't seen but very little wear, jackets; just about everything I would need." There were clothes for Guy too.

"Now what do you need for food?" Esther was asked.

"Well, I haven't got anything."

"Well, now, let's see." A good-sized box came out. It was packed: oatmeal, soda, cream of tartar, a box or two of cereal, some potatoes, toilet paper. This was only the beginning of the help the Red Cross provided.

During the following weeks and months the Boyntons and other Brownfield families would receive word that a load of supplies was coming in from Portland. Truck drivers from Portland firms like the Milliken-Tomlinson Company and Cole's Express would load up their trucks after a day's work and drive to Fryeburg or Brownfield where the things they brought would be distributed on a first-come-first-served basis to the families who had registered with the Red Cross. The trucks brought electrical wire, lightbulbs, cases of macaroni or spaghetti, twin beds, bureaus with mirrors, boudoir chairs, kitchen tables, hardwood chairs, footstools, arm chairs, and end tables.

What you got depended on how fast you got to the Red Cross center. Once Esther heard they had bedding, but when she arrived at the center the man in charge said, "I'm awfully sorry, but all the good sheets are gone. I've got some that are stained and there are one or two that are torn."

"I've still got soap and water. I still know how to mend," said Esther. The man gave her a dozen sheets.

The bedding and linen was army and navy surplus. Thirty years later Esther still had towels stamped "U.S. Navy—Dental" and army blankets and pillows. Most of the things were used, but useable. Esther made do. "Day in, day out you tried to find a way to get around, get by, and that's what we did," she remembered.

Early in December the American Legion and the *Portland Press Herald* began a drive to raise enough money to buy a Christmas box for every burned-out family registered with the Red Cross. In a little more than two weeks $28,771.69 was collected. The name of every donor was printed in the newspaper. Many had simply signed themselves as "A Friend" or "A Helper."

The Boyntons received one of the boxes. Esther remembered that it was about a yard long and a foot wide. "In it were potatoes, canned squash, two or three kinds of vegetables, canned mincemeat, about a five-pound bag of onions, cranberries, nuts, turkey—a whole Christmas dinner was in that box. They were marvelous boxes, and there was one for everyone."

In January Guy and Esther moved into their tin house. By October 1948, with the help of the Red Cross, they had built themselves a small house on the site of their old one. No one would mistake it for an old house although it is a Cape with four lights in the front door, but Esther had the old house in mind when she planned the new one with the Red Cross. "There's just one thing in this place that was in the old place," she would point out. "The step at the front door is a split stone step and it was the lower step into our other house. I informed the builders that they were going to put it there."

As the Boyntons, and others like them, made do and survived, so did the town. Everyone who could paid his taxes, even if his house was gone. This support and a tax rebate from the state were needed, for Brownfield had lost two-thirds of its taxable property. It took a long time before the town had a church again, and a town hall, and a library, and ten years before the two tin houses that had been used for a school were replaced with a proper building. A great deal of help came from "outside," but it is because of the unwillingness of the people to abandon their town that there is still a Brownfield in the valley where the Shepard's River runs to the Saco.

On November 4 the *Biddeford Daily Journal* reported a storm was surging up the Atlantic coast from Virginia. On November 8 it rained in Maine. Two days later Governor Hildreth lifted the ban on hunting in all counties but York. On the twelfth the closure was lifted in York County. On the thirteenth more than an inch of heavy, wet snow fell in Bangor. The drought was over. Winter had begun, and although here and there fires still smoldered deep underground and would burn up through the snow in December, the danger was past.

The people of Maine began to turn their attention to other news. Although state-wide services for Maine's three thousand war dead had been postponed, the first bodies had arrived home. On October 30, families from Turner, North New Portland, Portland, and Auburn had gathered at their railroad stations to receive the flag-draped coffins of sons, brothers, and fathers who had been killed in the Pacific.

In Rockport a bronze plaque had been mounted on the birthplace of Captain Hanson Gregory, the man who, in 1847, put the hole in the doughnut. In Hollywood the House Committee on Un-American Activities was investigating Communism among film writers. Truman was asking Congress to make an outright gift of 3 billion dollars to Europe under the Marshall Plan. The U.N. General Assembly's special Palestine subcommittee was meeting at Lake Success, New York, and the American delegate, Herschel Johnson, had suggested that sovereign Arab and Jewish nations be established through partition by July 1 and that British troops withdraw completely. Although most of the news was grim, it was a relief to read about something besides fire.

There was little in the newspapers now about the fires. Articles about the work of a canteen appeared here and there. Letters to the Editor praised firefighting groups, there were still Cards of Thanks from families whose homes had been saved. Banks inserted notices that they had been "advised in writing as required by Revised Statutes, Chapter 57, Section 26 that Deposit Book No. xxx is lost and that a duplicate is desired." Reading such notices everyone understood that "lost" meant burned.

When the Guy Gannett newspapers published a special pictorial review of the fire disaster, people bought it, glad to have a record of what had happened in their state during the week of October 20, 1947. They laid the review carefully away, knowing that as the years went by they would want to look at it again, and that children and grandchildren would be interested.

People continued to talk about the fires, especially those who had lost the most, but they looked to the future. Most would have agreed with Esther Boynton who said, "If you look backward, you're dead." But they knew they would never forget.

NOTES

1. Crocker, "Limerick Countryside."
2. *Biddeford Daily Journal,* October 29, 1947.
3. *Bangor Daily News,* October 28, 1947.
4. Wilkins, "The 1947 Forest Fire Disaster," p. 82.
5. Marion A. Marston, "Game and Fire," Department of Inland Game and Fisheries, State of Maine, n.d.
6. *Kennebunk Star,* October 31, 1947.
7. "Expenditures in Connection with the Maine Forest Fires, 1947," American National Red Cross, Eastern Area, January 25, 1950.
8 "Rebuilding Program Cleared Here," *Portland Press Herald,* October 31, 1947.
9. Edward D. Talberth, "Fire Swept Towns to Stage March on Augusta for Aid," *Portland Press Herald,* February 16, 1948.
10. Chester Wescott, Owner and Manager, Malvern Hotel and Cottages, Letter to the Editor, *Hotel and Restaurant News,* Boston, November 8, 1947.
11. "Leading Citizens Say Bar Harbor Will Build Again," *Bangor Daily News,* October 27, 1947.
12. "Bar Harbor Hopefully Begins $8,000,000 Restoration Job," *Boston Herald,* November 2, 1947.
13. Dr. Marion J. Bradshaw, "Bar Harbor Still Has Abundance of Beauty," *Bangor Daily News,* October 30, 1947.
14. *Telephone Topics.*
15. "Eye-witness Tells of Maine Disaster," *New York Journal-American,* October 24, 1947.
16. "Bar Harbor Hopefully Begins $8,000,000 Restoration Job."
17. "Fire Ravaged Towns to Be Favored in Establishment of New Industries," *Biddeford Daily Journal,* November 1, 1947.
18 "Annual Report of the Roscoe B. Jackson Memorial Laboratory: 1947–48."
19. *Bangor Daily News,* May 7, 1948.
20. Today the Shore Club is called the Bar Harbor Motor Inn.
21. Huston Thompson, "Has Nature Performed a Miracle in Acadia National Park?" *National Parks Magazine,* July-September 1955.
22. Wright, "Scorched Ruins All That Remain of Brownfield."
23. Ford, "Brownfield's Still Here."
24. "Brownfield Residents Hold Town Meeting to Plot Future," *Portland Press Herald,* October 30, 1947.

Chapter XIII:
"I wouldn't want to see it repeat."

Everyone wasn't ready to let what had happened slip quietly into history. There were those who wanted to know how forest fires could have gotten loose to burn 205,678 acres, to practically wipe out nine Maine communities and severely damage others, to cause millions of dollars worth of damage. The U.S. Forest Service, the Maine Forest Service, politicians, and newspapermen wanted to know why, and how, and what could be done to prevent a recurrence.

What factors had created the conditions that had led to the disaster? Careful analysts looked back to the 1938 hurricane that had swept through the Northeast. It came after heavy rains had so softened the ground that even large trees were easily blown down. The hurricane had left a great swath of downed trees and branches in its wake. Some of the debris had been cleaned up by CCC workers and lumbermen. In York County, the removal and salvage of toppled trees had actually revived the sawmill industry in small towns like Newfield. But most of the branches and slash had remained on the ground to weather and dry, and slash from accelerated lumbering operations during the war years had made things worse. A severe snowstorm during the winter of 1945 also contributed to the accumulation of slash in the woods. Trees were bent, and tops and branches were broken by the heavy snow.

State law required lumbermen to clear slash back fifty feet from roads and twenty-five feet from lot lines, because most fires are started by the carelessness of passersby. But the law said nothing about slash in the woods.

The snowfall of the winter of 1946–7 was normal, but the lack of rain, high temperature, and low humidity of the summer months dried out not only the slash in the woods, but the living growth of the forest. Juniper bushes and pine, hemlock, and spruce trees grow abundantly in Maine. When dry these resinous evergreens burn readily and with tremendous heat. The year 1947 was a "cone year," a year when evergreens produced an abundant supply of seed. The treetops were filled with cone clusters, all bone-dry like the natural accumulation of old moss, dried leaves, and pine spills, sometimes a foot deep, on the forest floor. The drought had turned Maine into a tinderbox.

Another factor that had contributed to the disaster was the wind, particularly the wind of October 23. Fire is a thermochemical reaction. In order to have fire, or combustion, three things are needed: fuel, heat, and oxygen. Abundant fuel—dried grass, bushes, trees, slash, even houses—had been provided by the drought. Heat—small fires—had been started by carelessly dropped cigarettes, burning dumps, downed power lines, and other agents. Air provides the oxygen, but wind supplies larger amounts and determines a fire's direction and speed. Gusty winds, which change direction unpredictably, make fire suppression more difficult.[1] Unpredictable, moderate to strong winds had blown all during the week of October 20.

Although state officials generally believed that it was not the wind but the unusually dry conditions that had been the main factor in the scope of the disaster, at least one study of meteorological conditions on October 23, the day Maine's largest losses occurred, disclosed that a cold front moving in from Canada early in the day had been preceded by winds of 59 miles per hour blowing at 2,000 feet, which had gradually increased to 87 miles per hour and lowered to 100 feet because of unstable conditions. These in turn affected surface winds. The strong winds and the front itself moved over the fire area in the afternoon, and the "increase in wind speed caused the fires to sweep southeastward down to the coast."[2] The study concluded that these conditions were unusual only in the strength of the winds—such wind speeds in a frontal system are rare. Certainly the winds that had erupted that day, whipping fires in all parts of the state into a fury, creating walls of flame that moved faster than a man could run, had never been seen by native firefighters before.

But Maine was not the only state in the Northeast to experience the drought, an unusual number of forest fires, and the wind on the twenty-third. Yet Maine's losses had been significantly higher—why?[3]

There were those who thought they knew the answer. There was criticism, and it was specific. An editorial in the *Bangor Daily News* blamed the governor for not closing the woods to everyone, including lumbermen, instead of just to hunters and campers. An editorial in the *Portland Press Herald* criticized the state for its "tardiness" in mobilizing to combat the fires. Other editorials and articles criticized the public for its failure to exercise greater care with fire. Maine State Senator Robert Cleaves, Jr., a lumberman himself, blamed the lack of a slash law for the disaster. "Once a fire gets into slash it can't be stopped," said Cleaves, who had tried unsuccessfully to get the legislature to enact a law that made it mandatory for lumbermen to remove all slash.[4]

But the most severe and sweeping criticism came from out of state. Daniel Tierney, fire chief of Arlington, Massachusetts, came into Maine at the request of the president of the International Association of Fire Chiefs to help in any way he could. Tierney arrived on October 22 and stayed for four days. Later, in a *Maine Townsman* article, he discussed the negative aspects of the firefighting effort in York County and concluded, "Maine has almost a total inadequacy of forest fire prevention."[5]

Others were more charitable. Bill Cunningham of the *Boston Herald* said, "Maine did a great job under the circumstances, but nobody had foreseen the circumstances."[6]

In his final report on the disaster, Austin Wilkins wrote: "It is frankly admitted that there was no fire action plan to meet such a disaster."[7] It had been the scope of the fires that had made the state's firefighting system ineffective, a system that had given Maine a good record until that autumn.

Men who had fought the forest fires called the circumstances unusual. "We'd seen woods fires, but nothing like this," said one. Another, when asked if the Maine Forest Service and the local companies had been at fault for not being ready for such a blowup, said, "You couldn't prepare for something you'd never had before."

Such men had endlessly analyzed the way the fires had been fought. They had recognized errors in judgment and timing, and they believed that if more people had stayed with their houses, more would have been saved. "People in general were unduly scared of being trapped by the flames. There is usually some place near dwellings open enough to allow a person to cross the fire line into the burned area and safety, but many failed to believe this. The livestock, however, proved it," said one town warden.

But such men also believed that, given the circumstances and the way people had reacted, it was a miracle more homes, villages, and lives had not been lost. And they knew that they had done their best. They, and Maine in general—even those who had lost homes and valuable timber—believed that everyone had done his best. They were not looking for a scapegoat.

On December 4 the Maine Forest Service received a National Forest Service report on the disaster. In a covering letter, Regional Forester R. M. Evans wrote: "Maine has suffered a fire season such as has never been recorded before. A system of fire control that has been fairly successful in holding down fire losses, whatever its basic weaknesses may have been, was not sufficient to cope with the extraordinary situation this fall. The U.S. Forest Service, as a co-operator with the state, must fairly accept a part of the blame for not having foreseen the danger of such a calamity."

H. J. Eberley, who directed the control center in Wells, wrote in his report, "If any attempt is made to fix responsibility for what happened, then it should be directed at the system which prevails rather than at some individual."[8] In the final analysis everyone who was looking for villains agreed that blame could be placed on the unusual weather conditions and Maine's firefighting system.

"I just hope in what remaining years I've got I never see it again," said Earl Bibber, who fought the fire in Kennebunkport.

"I wouldn't want to see it repeat," echoed Arnold Stinson of Cape Porpoise.

Even before the fires were officially declared out, newspaper editors all over the state were calling for an analysis of Maine's firefighting system and changes in it. An October 27 editorial in the *Portland Press Herald* pointed out, "Fire on this giant scale can be fought effectively only by one central authority. In Maine Commissioner Ray E. Rendall is referred to as the State Forestry Commissioner. . . , but as he has frequently and with truth pointed out, . . . of the sixteen million acres of forest land in Maine, Rendall has only ten million under his control—the unorganized lands. The other six million are dealt with under the authority of the various towns and cities. [Fire] knows no boundaries. It knows nothing of our distinction between organized and unorganized lands. Once it is loosed, it may carry its own red passport across any and every doorsill.

"If it was never clear before, it should be clear now that fighting forest fires wherever they occur should be the state's business. It should be the constant pre-occupation of one central authority."[9]

Three days later another *Press Herald* editorial urged that the new system be worked out immediately while lessons learned by firefighters were still fresh in their minds.

Now and not later is the time to work out such a plan in detail. For it is now that the experience of Maine's great army of firefighters is really hot. They have been in there lashing at it. They know the tricks that fire plays, and a good many of the human makeshifts that balk fire and stop it in its tracks. They have seen the effect of every conceivable kind of attack, good, bad, and indifferent; and there on the ground with the fire all but in their lungs, they have sifted these things out, and come to certain practical conclusions.[10]

Commissioner Rendall and Supervisor Austin Wilkins did not need to be told changes were needed in Maine's firefighting organization or that valuable lessons could be learned from the men who had fought the fires. As soon as he caught his breath, Wilkins wrote to his state wardens, town wardens, selectmen, fire chiefs, and other experienced firefighters, asking for "a straight forward account from you in your own way of writing in pen, pencil, or typewriter, of what took place when the fire was burning in your town." On January 5, 1948, at a meeting of the Maine Forest Forum at the Tarratine Club in Bangor he discussed in detail proposals for change.

Wilkins called the need for centralized control the "greatest object lesson of 1947."[11] A control center with full authority should be formed through legislative action. "Such a bold step might bring opposition from towns which already have some form of organized protection," said Wilkins, "yet it is apparent most towns can't cope with major fires. It is believed public opinion wants this change."

During the fires men and equipment had been wastefully dispatched, and supply bottlenecks had developed. Town fire departments had jealously guarded their jurisdictional prerogatives. There was a failure to anticipate, because anticipation was no one's major job. There was a shortage of trained fire bosses and proper communication centers. Towns had failed to maintain patrols once fires were under control. "In my opinion," said Wilkins, "this was the most costly mistake. It is possible to speculate that had sufficient patrols been maintained on these fires in their early stages, we never would have had a major disaster."

Wilkins called for a complete study of existing forest fire laws and for new legislation. A revision of the slash law was needed. State wardens should be on the job all year, not laid off during winter months because of insufficient funds. This would make it possible for the state to attract, and keep, experienced men. Towns should be required to purchase a minimum amount of firefighting equipment, and the commissioner should select or have a say in the appointment of town fire wardens.

Wilkins urged that the Maine Forest Service lead the way in educating the public to forest fire danger, sending speakers to schools and clubs, reaching the public through the movies, the radio, with signs, slogans, and literature.

Better fire detection was needed. The state's network of lookout towers should be doubled in the organized territory, and towers should have more effective radio communication.

The state needed a master plan for forest fire control, which would cover small fires as well as major conflagrations. State officials needed to know the location of all firefighting equipment, including that owned by each town. A rigid training program was needed to prepare a staff to train local firefighters or to help during major fires. Each town should have its own plan, developed from an awareness of available manpower, and should maintain fire hazard maps identifying cut-over areas, sawdust piles, uncut hay fields, and dumps. Purchase of new and better equipment should be encouraged. The nature of fire—how it travels and the effects weather and topography have on it—should be understood by firefighters on all levels.

Maine's disaster had exposed the weaknesses of the state's system, but it had also "brought a realization that no single state could afford to employ and equip a forest fire fighting organization adequate to cope with such a catastrophe."[12] Officials saw the need for a regional, perhaps even an international, plan or agency, assuring that any state facing a fire of major proportions could call on neighboring states and Canadian provinces for aid. In November 1947, the governors of the New England states and New England's forestry officials conferred to explore the practicalities of creating just such a cooperative agency.

The people of Maine did not wait for legislative action. During the winter of 1948 the Forest Service and individual towns took steps to deal with some of the immediate problems of forest fire control. On the state level, $125,000 was appropriated by Governor Hildreth and

his council to build new lookout towers and to provide equipment—
pickup trucks, pumpers, hose, Indian pumps, and hand tools—for use
in the District *and* the organized towns. A "Keep Maine Green" cam-
paign was launched to educate the public to the dangers of carelessly
handled fire. In March two training schools for Forest Service personnel were conducted by experts from the National Forest Service,
and in April three-fourths of the organized towns' fire wardens attended a special state-sponsored training school. During the winter
the Forest Service held three hundred public meetings on all levels to
determine what the people wanted for a fire control system and what
was needed. From these meetings came five major bills to be presented to the legislature when it convened in 1949.

In the fall of 1948, before the beginning of the forest fire season,
Governor Hildreth announced an emergency chain of command for
firefighters, pointing out to local fire chiefs that the system was not
law and could not be until the legislature met, but asking them to accept it as such.

Local officials struggled with the question of how to pay the firefighting bills incurred during the disaster and how to replace and supplement their firefighting equipment. Small towns like Bowdoin,
whose costs had equaled its complete annual operating budget, were
hard-pressed to pay all of their firefighting bills, even with help from
the state.

Some towns borrowed money to meet their debts. But many fire
departments, businesses, and individuals who had helped fight the
fires did not expect to be paid, and bills were never presented. Alfred's
municipal officers sent a letter of gratitude to every town that had sent
men and equipment to help them. "Alfred thanks you," they wrote.
"But for your timely assistance our village would have been consumed." Such remuneration was acceptable. A sincere thank-you and
the shared knowledge that the fires had finally been defeated were
enough.

Ways were found to get new and better equipment. The state provided some. Hose and pumps were made available by the War Assets
Administration. Special town meetings authorized selectmen to buy
new trucks and pumpers. On January 21 at town meeting in Hollis,
which had three small volunteer fire companies, the voters were asked
to allow the selectmen to borrow money to buy a firetruck to replace
the old Larrabee truck at the West Buxton station. Fire Chief Carleton
Hill filed a special report for the warrant. "Should the citizens not vote

to buy a new truck," he explained, "the old one will need extensive repairs. It has two wheel brakes, the tires are old, the front end is bad, and the booster tank leaks. It is really dangerous to drive. We have no forestry pump at West Buxton [which] is considered a necessity by any fire department today."

The Hollis Center Fire Department asked for 1,500 feet of hose, another 500 feet of hose "for a trailer unit, 250 feet of booster hose and a new roof ladder. Six new Indian tanks would also be useful."

The voters of Hollis were also asked to raise $5,250 to pay for services rendered the town by various companies and individuals in October. And finally, they were asked to authorize the building of "water holes for use of the fire companies."[13]

Some of Maine's small towns had never had their own fire departments because they just didn't have the money to buy trucks. Recognizing this, the Forest Service sent District 1 Warden Clayton Weymouth from York County to Fort Kent with a makeshift tank truck that had been put together by one of the department's mechanics to show what could be done with very little money. The "tank truck" was an old Ford truck, which the state owned, with the body taken off and replaced with a 650-gallon tank equipped with a pump from an old portable pump. "It worked good," Weymouth remembers.

Few fire departments were turned down that year when they asked for money for equipment. If the town treasuries could not be stretched, special fund drives were held. In Kennebunkport the old 1850 Arundel 2 hand tub and hose, still hung with leather fire buckets, was put on display in Dock Square to call attention to a drive to raise $15,000 for new equipment. The Kittredge family of Cape Porpoise took a special interest in the town's fire departments, and thanks to their leadership and personal generosity new trucks were acquired.

In 1949 the legislature enacted a rash of fire bills. At long last the forest commissioner was given ultimate authority at forest fires within the organized territory. Responsibility for fire suppression rested first with a municipality's fire warden, appointed by the forest commissioner with the approval of local officials, but the state's wardens, acting as the commissioner's deputies, had the authority to take over when in their judgment it was necessary. This meant every forest fire had to be reported to a state warden as well as the local warden as soon as it was discovered. Other bills dealt with problems of financing forest fire suppression, slash disposal, and the legalization of backfiring by wardens.

The legislature also authorized the governor to enter into compacts with other states for mutual fire protection. During 1948 and 1949 a conference of foresters from the New England states and New York, under the auspices of the Massachusetts Commission on Interstate Cooperation and the Council of State Governments, drafted a proposal for an interstate forest fire control agency. The powers, immunities, rights, and liabilities of the cooperating states were discussed, as was the matter of expanding membership to include the bordering Canadian provinces.

On June 25, 1949, the U.S. Congress enacted Public Law 129 establishing the Northeastern Forest Fire Protection Compact. Within four months, six of the seven specified states (the New England states and New York) had joined. Rhode Island joined the following year when its legislature convened.

Funds were assessed from all member states to finance the uniform training of personnel who would move where needed and would fit smoothly into whatever firefighting organization they found. The Compact also made it possible for the member states to share the cost and use of expensive equipment.

At the Compact's first annual meeting, in July 1950, a technical committee of state foresters was established "to supervise a coordinated training program and to formulate procedures in all technical fire control problems. Uniform closure laws, regional and state fire plans were discussed."[14] Representatives of the provinces of New Brunswick and Quebec attended. On May 13, 1952, the U.S. Congress authorized Canadian participation in the Compact, but not until 1969 were forestry officials in Quebec able to convince their legislators. On September 23, 1969, "an historic day in the annals of forest fire protection,"[15] the Province of Quebec joined the Compact to share fire protection duties along the five hundred miles of common border shared with Maine, New Hampshire, Vermont, and New York. In 1970 New Brunswick joined, bringing five million more acres of forest under the jurisdiction of the Compact.

On June 8, 1972, twenty-five years after the disastrous fires that had made officials aware of the need for an agency like the Compact, Senator Edmund Muskie of Maine read the story of Maine's forest fire disaster and the development of the Compact into the *Congressional Record*. He called the Compact "one of the most unique and significant pieces of forest fire protection legislation ever enacted in the history of our country."[16]

The Compact has worked. It was invoked for the first time in August 1952 when extremely dry conditions and stubborn fires were affecting Maine, New Hampshire, Massachusetts, and Rhode Island. Maine officials asked for help and received pumps and hose from New York in less than five hours. In 1963 Rhode Island, Connecticut, and Maine sent hand tools, pumps, and hose to New York. In 1965 when a large, uncontrolled fire was burning at Centerville in Washington County, five member states rushed help to Maine. Although more than twelve thousand acres of forest land burned, Maine officials credited the Compact with preventing another disaster like 1947's.

Austin Wilkins became Maine's Forest Commissioner in 1958. He was instrumental in the creation of the Compact, and attended the 1969 and 1970 ceremonies when Quebec and New Brunswick joined. He speaks today with pride of this organization which became a national model, but he is quick to point out, "I've always said, and I still believe, that the volunteer fire department is the first line of defense." The local firefighter, well equipped by his neighbors' tax dollars, trained through programs provided by the state, ready to leave his job to fight a fire in his town, or in a neighboring town under the system of mutual aid practiced by most small companies today, is vital. He will always be the first line of defense against wildfire.

Advances have been made in firefighting technology since 1947. Mechanization, meaning the use of bulldozers and other heavy equipment, which really began in 1947 when men were desperate, has been refined. Today it is recognized that one bulldozer does the work of eighty men. Light planes are used for aerial surveillance to spot and track fires and for "water bombing," a technique where water is flown over a fire in a plane with a specially equipped tank and released through bomb-bay-type doors. Two-way radios permit instant communication and more efficient deployment of men. Equipment has been standardized.

Everything considered, could what happened in 1947 happen again? It did not happen in 1965 following three years of drought when conditions were worse than they had been in 1947. Subsoil was dryer and water tables were substantially lower than in 1947. Seventy-five fires were smoldering the week the Centerville fire blew up. Forest Service officials viewed that fire as the first real test of the improvements they had made in the state's firefighting organization since 1947 and the Compact. Both systems passed the test, but the pubic raised the question, "Could what happened in 1947 happen again?" Forest Commissioner Wilkins's answer was: the chances are much slimmer, but it could happen again.

There would be differences, but, yes, it could happen again. One York County man points out that a forest fire today does not have the same vegetation to feed on. "Then it was junipers and evergreen trees, old moss, big pine trees with dead limbs. All of that burned off in '47. Now it's mostly hardwood trees—maple, birch, oak." But he adds, "There are more houses now. Take a town like Goodwin's Mills. Look at the houses there, most of 'em built in the woods. You've got a much greater potential for loss, valuable loss, than you had then. Don't forget, in '47 most of the houses were old farmhouses. A lot of 'em didn't have inside plumbing. A lot of 'em didn't even have electricity."

It could happen again because 90 percent of all forest fires are caused by people,[17] and the risk of human behavior is always with us. Although Maine's well-equipped, well-trained firefighting forces now function "like a military command with responsibility carefully fixed from the top to the warden at the town level,"[18] it could happen again. As Lloyd Davis says, "You take any time that Nature goes on a rampage—I don't care whether it's a flood, an earthquake, fire, a cyclone, or tornado—until Nature herself quiets it down a mite, a human being is almost a useless thing. There's just nothin' you can do. It's too big."

NOTES

1. "Forest Interpreter's Primer."
2. Edward Allen Brotak, "A Synoptic Study of the Meteorological Conditions Associated with Major Wildland Fires," Ph.D. Dissertation, Yale Graduate School, 1977.
3. Senator Edmund Muskie, "The Northeastern Forest Fire Protection Compact," Congressional Record—Senate, Vol. 118, June 8, 1972.
4. Edward D. Talberth, "Lack of Slash Law Termed Fire Cause," *Portland Press Herald*, October 28, 1947.
5. Daniel B. Tierney, "New England's Indian Summer Fire Disaster," *The Maine Townsman*, June 1948.
6. "Master Fire Plan," *Portland Press Herald*, October 30, 1947.
7. Wilkins, "The 1947 Forest Fire Disaster," p. 81.
8. H. J. Eberley, "The Maine Forest Fire Disaster," U.S. Department of Agriculture, Forest Service, Eastern Division, Division of Cooperative Forest Protection, November 19, 1947.
9. "Forest Control," *Portland Press Herald*, October 27, 1947.

10. "Master Fire Plan."

11. Austin Wilkins, "What Shall Be the Forest Fire Organization for The State of Maine?" a paper presented to the Maine Forest Forum, Tarratine Club, Bangor, January 5, 1948.

12. Muskie, "The Northeastern Forest Fire Protection Compact."

13. Annual Report, Town of Hollis, Maine, For Fiscal Year Ending January 21, 1948.

14. Muskie, "The Northeastern Forest Fire Protection Compact."

15. *Ibid.*

16. *Ibid.*

17. "Forest Interpreter's Primer."

18. Waldo E. Pray, "Maine Not Likely to Face 1947 Fire Tragedy Repeat," *Portland Press Herald,* August 15, 1965.

Epilogue:
The '47 Fire

In Maine they call what happened in October of 1947 "The '47 Fire." Some use the phrase in a general sense, others are referring specifically to the fire that burned in their town, took their home, or the '47 fire they fought.

Actually people don't talk much about the '47 fire any more; after all, it has been fifty years. But a lot of people remember vividly that week in autumn when it seemed that all of Maine was burning. It is a milestone in their lives. It is not uncommon to hear someone say, "Before the fire . . ." or "But that was after the fire went through."

A lot of things in Maine begin and end with the '47 fire. A lot of things are different because of it. In Kennebunkport, where houses are labeled with dates from the eighteenth and nineteenth centuries when they were built, for many years there was a house on top of Crow Hill with "1947" over its front door. The community of Cape Porpoise, whose houses cluster around the foot of the hill and spread out to the coves and inlets of the ocean, hasn't changed much since 1947. Thirty-two houses burned in Cape Porpoise, but they were on the outskirts of the village, and their loss did not affect the flavor of the community as a whole.

Such was not the case in nearby Goose Rocks Beach. Although only about half the settlement burned, Goose Rocks is a different community today from what it was fifty years ago. The houses that quickly replaced burned cottages were of a better quality, many built for year-round occupancy. Goose Rocks Beach today is not only a summer colony, but a thriving year-round community too.

Even thirty years ago it was not easy to find a Goose Rocks Beach resident who was there in 1947 when the fire came through, who was forced to retreat into the ocean, who saw Timber Island burn. But many Kennebunkport people still remember Goose Rocks before the fire, when the eastern end of the beach, where the cottages are modern with simple lines, looked like the western end where the trees are taller and more prolific and shade Victorian cottages.

Bar Harbor too was changed by the fire. The year-round residents rebuilt, but few of the summer residents rebuilt their burned cottages or even came back. Millionaires' Row along Frenchman Bay is lined now with motels, and most of Bar Harbor's summer visitors are transients with two or three weeks vacation, or weekenders. Bar Harbor's economy, once tied to its cottage owners, now depends on its tourists.

This was a change that had been coming even before the Great Fire. As Cleveland Amory wrote in *The Last Resorts,* "Bar Harbor cottage life was on the way out long before the fire [which] was merely the *coup de grâce.* This cottage life had started in the 1880s and had boomed from the 1890s; then it had begun to collapse. Although it had a brief renaissance in the 1920s and staggered through the depression, it virtually disappeared when World War II gave marching orders to taxes, servants, and the Old Way of Life."[1]

Many of the cottages that burned had long been unoccupied, and their owners had already planned to have them torn down. Some survived the fire only to be torn down a few years later. Kenarden Lodge, once home of John Stewart Kennedy, the railroad king, had been built in the 1890s at a cost of more than $200,000. It had its own electric power plant and "at night when its hundreds of incandescents [were] lit it looked like a fairy palace from Frenchman Bay."[2] It was torn down in 1960. This was also the fate of Wingwood House and the Oakes estate on Frenchman Bay, where a motel and the terminal for the Bluenose Ferry are now. One of the grand houses on Frenchman Bay that survived is now the home of the College of the Atlantic.

Christine Rowell never rebuilt Barberry Ledge. She returned to Mount Desert Island once or twice, staying with friends at Seal Harbor or Northeast Harbor. She never considered rebuilding, and a few years after the fire she donated her Bar Harbor property to Acadia National Park. Today it is not possible to locate the site of Barberry Ledge on official maps of the town. That well-loved place has passed into history.

The loss of the mansions and their occupants changed the social life of Bar Harbor. Organizations like the old Kebo Valley Golf Club, whose members had been exclusively cottagers, opened their doors after the fire to local residents too. For the Kebo Club this was a boon. By 1942 its membership had shrunk to only thirty-two, and while the list was "studded with some of the wealthiest names in the country," they could not seem to keep the club in solvent figures."[3] By 1963 when Sargent Collier wrote the history of the club, it had 250 members, many of them year-round residents, and Collier was calling Kebo representative of the "so-called new Bar Harbor spirit."

But there is nostalgia in Bar Harbor for the days when the town seemed to exist because of the wealthy cottage owners. Natives who remember that they were not allowed to play golf at Kebo or swim in the pool at the Bar Harbor Club, also remember wealthy dowagers being driven into the village by chauffeurs in uniforms the colors of their cars. Their own lives were touched by such elegance: Bar Harbor was "dignified" then—graceful, peaceful—not the busy tourist town it is today.

As Bar Harbor was able to survive economically because of vacationers, so too was Lyman. Lyman has a vital life during the winter months, but once summer comes its population expands. Its four largest ponds—Wadley, Swan, Bunganut, and Kennebunk—are ringed with summer camps and cottages. It was this "resource" of pretty ponds that helped Lyman back on its feet after the fire.

Dayton, Waterboro, Newfield, and Brownfield are relatively unchanged. All look different because they lost so many colonial and Victorian houses and the trees that shaded them. All lost a measure of prosperity through the destruction of valuable timber, but basically they are the same towns; "not different," as Esther Boynton said, "only changed as everything has changed."

But the woodlands and forests that were swept by the '47 fire are different. In fifty years they have had time only to begin the process of rejuvenation. The blackened wastes are gone, there is new growth, but tracts that should be dense pine woods are now airy groves of narrow birch.

A map of Maine prepared by the Forest Service in 1972 to show commercial stands of white pine illustrates the absence of this species in southwestern Maine. A white swath, indicating an absence of pine trees, extends on the map from the New Hampshire border through Oxford and York Counties to the sea. This swath corresponds with the path of the '47 fire.

Because of the scope of the burn in southwestern Maine, the cost of artificial reforestation was prohibitive. Most areas were left to rejuvenate themselves naturally. A forest of primarily softwood trees—pine, spruce, fir, hemlock—once swept by fire, will grow back to hardwood. The black ashes hold the heat of the sun and are inhospitable to the seed of softwood species. And whereas the root systems of softwood trees burn, those of hardwood trees, from which new trees will sprout, survive.

But although hardwoods like poplar and white birch will spring up, they do not flourish in the fire damaged soil and will stay small. Foresters call them "junk" trees. Eventually they will die and be replaced by better quality birch trees and sugar maple. Eventually even the softwood trees will come back, but it takes years for that to happen. There are people living in southwestern Maine who will not see again the pine forests they remember from before the '47 fire.

Even forests that have rejuvenated themselves quickly because they were swept by fast-moving crown fires that left lower growth and root growth systems intact, look different from forests that were not burned. Even in Acadia National Park, which surprised foresters with the variety of growth that quickly sprouted within the burn, there are differences. The drive up the Loop Road in Acadia is beautiful. It takes a practiced eye to see the effects of the fire, to know when you have passed beyond the limits of the burn. But the careful observer is aware suddenly that the trees growing in the parklands beside the road are taller. The birch trees are big and tall; the pine trees are lush. They crowd right up to the road, growing in clumps, in varying heights, smaller trees growing out of every crack and crevice of the rocks. The careful observer realizes that he has passed through parklands where there was too much bare rock, where the trees were too small, where there was too much light from the wide sky that should have been obscured by tall, dark pines.

But it is in southwestern Maine that the effects of the fire are most noticeable. Driving through York County one often has the sense that something is wrong, that the countryside doesn't look as it should. People who know about the '47 fire know why and look in among the groves of birch trees and see the gray stumps of the trees that were killed by the fire, scattered like a pox among the birches.

Arthur Moulton of Newfield remembered the woman from Massachusetts who said to him, "What happened to your trees up here? Did you have some kind of a blight?"

"Yes," he told her wryly. "We had a blight all right."

Newcomers to Maine discover that a lot of people in Maine speak with authority about forest fire. They talk about crown fires and of fire burning underground in the root systems of trees. They say, "A forest fire makes its own wind, you know." They know that a forest fire dies down at night when the sun and the wind go down, and they know that a fire that is big enough and moving fast enough will jump a river as easily as a child steps over a crack in the sidewalk. This knowledge, unexpected in housewives, businessmen, grandmothers, and fishermen, is a legacy from 1947.

The newcomer who builds his house at the edge of the woods probably won't know that his Maine neighbors are shaking their heads and thinking him foolhardy not to have left an open space—a firebreak—between his house and the forest.

Visitors driving through southwestern Maine in the summertime probably think it is nice that so many farms have ponds and so many houses have swimming pools. They don't know that those which were installed by thoughtful owners are there as a source of water if a forest fire comes.

Young men who buy wood lots in certain parts of Oxford and York Counties will, sooner or later, cut down a tree whose heart is scarred by fire. "Looks like this one's been through a fire," they might say to the old farmer who is helping them clear the lot, and then they will hear about the '47 fire.

Sooner or later people who weren't around in '47 will hear stories about the fires from people who were. In Waterboro someone will tell them how Mike Ferguson fled the tower on Ossipee Hill and about Myron Huff whose shoestrings got burned off while he was saving houses in South Waterboro village. They will be told how Charlie Lynfield moved everything out of his house, even taking the doors from their hinges; moved everything that could be moved out of the path of the fire to a safer place where it all burned, while his house survived. Someone might remember how the hands of the clock on the Baptist Church at South Waterboro stopped at 5:34 the afternoon the fire came through, and how the next morning coal was still burning in the cellar holes of the houses on Main Street.

In Newfield someone will tell them that the fire was so hot it literally melted the bell that hung in the steeple of the church at Lower Village, and that when some of the metal was dug out of the ruins of the church it still "tinkled like a bell" when it was tapped.

Arthur Moulton used to tell about the mowing machine that stood about twenty feet from a barn full of hay that burned. The cutter bar of the machine was raised, and the heat from the fire twenty feet away was so intense it melted the metal bar so that it "drooped like a soft candle."

Thirty years after the fire Warren Walker of Clark's Mills would tell how he stood so long directing traffic on the corner in front of his house that his feet swelled and he had to cut his shoes away. When he finally could stop to sleep, his house was so full of soldiers he had to bed down in his children's playhouse. After the fire he and others found that bulldozers, clearing firebreaks around the village, had displaced stone markers that had been set out to mark lot lines. Finding the bounds of some lots has been a problem ever since.

Marjorie Walker remembers her anxious wait and admits that even today, "When I hear the wind, I tense up."

In Brownfield those who are interested in the earliest history of the town tell how the fire exposed the rock foundations of an old settler's cabin that had been hidden from view by thick underbrush. Others remember how a colony of beavers moved into a stand of scorched poplar near Ten Mile Brook and began their own salvage operation even before the men of the town could set up their portable sawmills.

For years when asked if a house that was obviously not very old sat on the site of one of the houses that burned in '47, Esther Boynton would answer, "No. They had a private fire later."

In Kennebunkport people who remember the fire still speculate about houses like George Seavey's that didn't burn while everything around them did. People in Wildes Town chuckle about the man who, with the fire coming fast, got so excited he loaded his goats into his truck and took off for Kennebunk, leaving his wife and children behind. In the village one or two remember that Mrs. Ivory Ross set fire to her kitchen while frying up doughnuts for the firefighters. In the woods off the Wildes District Road vestiges of "Doherty's Boulevard" are still visible, but not many people know that.

In Bar Harbor people are still speculating about who called the boats for the evacuation from the pier, and when someone says that the fire started in Bill Dolliver's dump, someone who is better informed will quickly correct that bit of misinformation, adding that it was upsetting to Mrs. Dolliver to have people say that the fire started in "Bill's dump."

Near Whitneyville someone talking about the fire will tell how it was traveling so fast that it burned a house and barn but jumped right over a load of hay sitting in the barnyard.

People who experienced the '47 fire don't talk about it much . . . unless they are asked to. Then the stories come flooding out. Only a few would agree with the woman who, when asked about it, said, "There's some things you like to forget." Most people like a good story, and there are a lot of good stories to be told about the '47 fire.

At least one story quickly made the transition from fact to folklore. To travel around Maine and bring up the subject of the fire was to hear more than once the story about the man and the barrel of cider. In Dayton, where it happened, you would get the facts: Lesley Meserve saved his house by dousing encroaching flames with a barrel of cider that had just been delivered a day or two before from the cider press. In Kennebunk the story came out, "One guy saved himself from the fire by jumping into a barrel of new cider and bobbing up and down for air." Farther afield, in Camden perhaps, someone would laugh and say, "Did you hear about the guy who saved himself by jumping into a barrel of hard cider. . .?"

But most of the anecdotes told about the '47 fire are not humorous. People who were burned out dealt with their loss and personal tragedies with dignity and courage, and this is what most choose to remember. The story of the Abbott family in Dayton is typical.

Two days after the fire went through Dayton, a picture appeared in the *Portland Press Herald* showing the burned ruin of a farmhouse. On a flagpole in the dooryard hung an American flag. The photographer who had stopped to take the picture had found the place deserted and could not even supply the name of the owner of the property. The newspaper captioned the photo, "A homeless farmer returned to his fire-ravaged hillside at Dayton to raise Old Glory above the ashes of his buildings. What prompted the action no one knew." Three years later when the editor of the paper learned the story he published it under the heading, "Our Flag Is Still There."[4] It was one family's very personal story, but universal in what it said about courage and faithfulness.

Roger Abbott was a veteran of the Spanish American War. At the beginning of World War II on the day his son and daughter joined the Army Air Force and the Women's Army Corps, Abbott began a daily ritual of raising the flag. Accompanied by his dog, Toby, at sunrise every morning he would carry the flag into the yard. He would take off his hat and lay it on the ground. The dog would stand at attention, his paws on his master's arm while the flag went up. Mrs. Abbott would watch at the kitchen window. Her husband never missed a day.

Mr. Abbott died in 1946, but his son, who had returned from the war, continued the ritual, raising the flag for his father who had raised it for him.

On the day the fire swept Dayton the flag was one of the things Mrs. Abbott and her son saved. Her son took it down, folded it, and laid it on the seat of the truck between them. They were almost trapped by the fire because they stayed too long trying to coax Toby into the truck. He would not leave and died in the burning barn.

After the fire had passed they returned to their farm and, finding the flagpole still standing, raised the flag. Three years later when their story was finally told, the same flag was still being flown every day from the same flagpole in front of a new house.

It was the loss of things—possessions—that kept the fire fresh in people's minds in the years that followed. Those who had lost everything furnished their new houses. Life went on, and the fire was forgotten until the day when, frustrated in a search for some well-remembered object, the searcher would say, "Well, I guess that went in the fire."

Florence Salisbury remembered how for quite a few years after the Bar Harbor fire people would stop by the house or call her saying, "Allen said we could borrow your crib . . ." or high chair, or some tool. "I'd just tell 'em to go back and tell Allen there was a fire in 1947!" said Florence.

It took a while for people to realize how much they had lost to the fire—great-grandmother's rocking chair; the marriage license that had been put away in the trunk in the attic; the dates of births, marriages, and deaths that were in the church or town records; even the spirit of the old people. "The older people never really got over it," Bessie Ricker said. "Not the way the young ones did."

Anything that survived the fires took on symbolic importance, even though its beauty or usefulness was gone. Most burned-out families kept a fire object: a distorted spoon, a badly burned piece of china, a fragment of screen imbedded in melted window glass picked out of the rubble of their home. From the ruins of her cottage at Goose Rocks Beach, Eleanor Nickerson salvaged a pair of owl-shaped fireplace andirons whose glass eyes had melted and flowed like tears down their breasts.

On a high shelf in her kitchen cupboard Esther Boynton kept a small china mug. It was given to her when she was a baby. On it was a transfer print of the old church on the hill in Thomaston where she was born and grew up. Survivor of two fires, it was discolored, but it was whole. For many years, after 1947, Esther picked up in her dooryard old, hand-forged nails from the house that burned. They were still working their way up through the earth that covered what was left of the old place. They too were kept.

And then there were the three maple trees that stood in her dooryard. They were badly burned by the fire, but not killed. Every year her son said, "We ought to cut down those trees. They'll be comin' down on the roof."

"All right," said Esther. "Give the order." But the order was not given: the trees still stood.

Only the wise will understand the man who said, "I hope before I die I have one more good fire to fight." He remembers the spirit of the people in '47—the way everyone worked together toward a common goal. He remembers particular men, a particular breed of men. "There was Alva Werren, Tom Scott, Ray Burbank, Carroll Stevens, the Kittredges down to the Kennebunks, Charlie Nedeau . . . fellas like that. They were damn good men."

Many look back almost with a sense of nostalgia to the '47 fire because it marked the end of coming to the family cottage in Maine or of cutting a Christmas tree in a particular wood. For some it serves as a way to mark the end of their own youth, not because they suffered personal loss, but because they remember the '47 fire so vividly, and they were young then. Some, looking around them now and seeing the changes in people's lives and values—even in Maine—look back to 1947 as a time when everyone knew everyone else in their town, and people were, it seems to them, different—more honest, more trusting, more generous.

Maine people are writing down what they remember of the '47 fire. During the Bicentennial in 1976, Newfield and Hollis published town histories and both contain accounts of the fire. Students at Massabesic High School in Waterboro wrote about it for their publication, *Country Roads*. High-school students all over Maine choose the '47 fire as a topic for term papers. They have looked at the Pictorial Review published by the Gannett newspapers or have discovered in the attic a scrapbook of clippings that their mother put together when she was a teenager, or a copy of a letter some family member wrote about the fire to someone who lived away. They remember how, when they were younger, they loved to hear their grandparents tell how "for days you couldn't see the sun and when the fire came it sounded just like an express train."

It is important that all the stories be written down, for a hundred years from now, when the forests have rejuvenated themselves, and the people are gone who remember when the wind carried fire, there will be people in Maine who will want to know what happened in October 1947. It is history.

NOTES

1. Cleveland Amory, *The Last Resorts* (New York: Harper and Brothers, 1948).
2. Sargent F. Collier, *Green Grows Bar Harbor: Reflections from Kebo Valley,* 1964.
3. *Ibid.*
4. "Our Flag Is Still There: Schoolgirl's Story Recalls Forest Fires," *Portland Sunday Telegram,* November 19, 1950.

Appendix A

Glossary of Firefighting Terms

(Most of these definitions are taken from the *Manual for Forest Fire Control: Fire Fighting Methods and Techniques*, Northeastern Forest Fire Protection Commission, Region 7, U.S. Forest Service, 1958.)

Backfire: 1. Fire set along the inner edge of a fire control line to stop a spreading wildfire. 2. A prescribed fire set to burn against the wind. 3. To set a backfire.

Blowup: Sudden increase in fire intensity or rate of spread sufficient to preclude direct control or to upset existing control plans.

Burn: An area that has been burned over.

Crown fire: A fire that burns through the tops of trees.

Crowning: Fire advancing from crown to crown of trees or shrubs.

Duff: The partly decomposed organic material of the forest floor beneath the litter of freshly fallen twigs, needles, and leaves.

Fire line: The part of a control line that is scraped or dug to mineral soil.

Firebreak: 1. A strip of cleared or plowed land used to stop the spread of a fire. 2. A natural or constructed barrier utilized to stop or check fires that may occur or to provide a control line from which to work. (Also called a fire line.)

Ground fire: Fire that burns surface litter, other loose debris on the forest floor, and small vegetation. (Foresters call this a surface fire.)

Hot spot: 1. A particularly active part of a fire. 2. An unseen, smoldering fire that can flare up.

Knock down: To reduce the flame or heat on the more vigorously burning parts of a fire edge.

Mineral soil: A soil derived from minerals or rocks and containing little humus or organic matter.

Mop-up: The act of making a fire safe after it is controlled, such as extinguishing or removing burning material along or near the control line.

Patrol: 1. To travel a given route to prevent, detect, and suppress fires. 2. To go back and forth watchfully over a length of control line, during or after its construction, to prevent breakovers, control spot fires, or extinguish overlooked hot spots.

Slash: Debris left after logging, pruning, thinning, or brush cutting. It includes logs, chunks, bark, branches, stumps, and broken trees or brush.

Smoldering: Behavior of a fire burning without flame and barely spreading.

Snag: A standing dead tree or part of a dead tree from which the leaves and smaller branches have fallen.

Spot fire: Fire set outside the perimeter of the main fire by flying embers or sparks.

Wildfire: 1. An unplanned fire requiring suppression, as contrasted with a prescribed fire burning within prepared lines. 2. A free-burning fire unaffected by fire suppression measures. 3. A raging fire that travels and spreads rapidly.

APPENDIX B

1947 Fires of 100+ Acres (October 16 to October 25)
Organized Towns

Town	Land Acres in Town	Acres Burned	% of Town Burned	1996 Damages*	1947 Damages
Durham	24,640	130	.528	$642,048	$1,400
Livermore Falls	13,056	1,200	3.809	16,883,830	22,000
Fayette	18,451				
Brunswick	30,404	307	1.010	9,592,475	2,025
Fryeburg	37,350				
Brownfield	28,877				
Hiram	24,006	20,120	13.568	65,730,176	744,000
Porter	20,595				
Denmark	22,976				
Cornish	14,483				
Richmond	19,245	2,650	13.770	13,907,700	14,000
Shapleigh	25,280				
Waterboro	34,976				
Wells	40,160				
Lyman	25,491				
Saco	25,280				
Hollis	21,715	109,110	35.251	1,232,145,829	3,532,000
Kennebunk	22,048				
Dayton	11,840				
Alfred	18,438				
Newfield	18,688				
Limerick	27,721				
Parsonsfield	37,888				
Biddeford	19,680	21,910	45.194	681,728,893	1,372,000
Kennebunkport	28,800				
Bar Harbor	27,213	17,188	63.161	326,226,565	5,812,000
Centerville	26,208				
Jonesboro	24,160				
Machias	9,734	19,970	26.279	45,186,741	327,000
Roque Bluffs	6,560				
Whitneyville	9,331				
Carmel	23,974	900	3.754	2,408,191	2,000
Anson	32,109	410	1.277	913,694	5,225
Madison	34,157	2,496	3.783	13,964,945	37,875
Norridgewock	31,814				
TOTALS		196,391		2,409,331,087	11,871,525

*Estimate of damages if same percentage of town acreage had been destroyed in 1996 as was burned in 1947. Numbers based on 1996 total town property valuations.

If 1947 costs are simply adjusted for inflation, total 1947 damages converted to 1996 dollars equals $81,131,369. (6.834 is factor to convert consumer purchasing power from 1947 dollars to 1996 dollars.)

These figures have been provided by the Maine Forest Service, Department of Conservation, and are reproduced with their permission.

Bibliography

Explanatory notes: This selective bibliography is intended to direct students who wish to write their own accounts of the 1947 forest fires to articles of a brief, general nature, as well as to sources which give information on a particular aspect of the disaster. I have included material that I found particularly helpful and reliable and have purposely omitted articles that I found sensationalized and inaccurate.

I urge the researcher to consult the newspapers listed. The Bangor, Biddeford, and Portland papers are all available on microfilm. Many of the articles I used, some of which appear in the footnotes, although not in this bibliography, are from these papers.

Many of the reports listed here can be found in the 1947 files of the forest commissioner, which can be found at the University of Maine in Augusta.

It is my intention that my own collection of material concerning the fires, which includes copies of all the reports listed, maps, and a chronological card file of events in October 1947, as well as transcripts of the tape-recorded interviews, correspondence with people who experienced the fires, and notes on conversations with people who were involved, will eventually be placed with the Maine Historical Society in Portland where it will be available for research purposes. The tapes of my interviews and copies of the transcripts have been placed with the Northeast Archives of Folklore and Oral History at the University of Maine, for preservation, and in order that they will be accessible for future generations.

Books

Amory, Cleveland, *The Last Resorts.* New York: Harper and Brothers, 1948.

Chadbourne, Ava Harriet, *Maine Place Names and the Peopling of Its Towns,* Illustrated County Edition, York, Freeport, Me.: Bond Wheelwright Company, 1975.

Collier, Sargent F., *Green Grows Bar Harbor: Reflections From Kebo Valley,* Introduction by Cleveland Amory, including profiles of the town that refused to die, 1964.

Coolidge, Philip T., *History of the Maine Woods.* Bangor, Me.: Furbish-Roberts Printing Company, Inc., 1963.

Freeman, Melville C., *History of Cape Porpoise.* Cape Porpoise, Me.: Privately Printed, 1955.

Hale, Richard Walden, Jr., *The Story of Bar Harbor: An Informal History Recording 150 Years in the Life of a Community.* New York: Ives Washburn, Inc., 1949.

Jewett, Martin H. and Olive W. Hannaford, *A History of Hollis, Maine: 1660–1976.* Farmington, Me.: Knowlton and McLeary Co., 1976.

Libby, Steve, *Newfield, Maine: The First 200 Years.* Town of Newfield, Me., 1976.

MacKenzie, Gertrude with Ruth Goode, *My Love Affair with the State of Maine.* Camden, Me.: Down East Books, 1997. Reprint.

Manual for Forest Fire Control: Fire Fighting Methods and Techniques, Northeastern Forest Fire Protection Commission, Region 7, U.S. Forest Service, 1958.

Manual for Forest Fire Control: Fire Organization, Northeastern Forest Fire Protection Commission, Region 7, U.S. Forest Service, 1954.

Morison, Samuel Eliot, *The Story of Mount Desert Island, Maine.* Boston, Mass.: Atlantic Monthly Press, 1960.

Roberts, Kenneth, *Henry Gross and His Dowsing Rod.* New York: Doubleday and Company, 1951.

Teg, William, *History of Brownfield, Maine.* Cornish, Me.: Carbook Press, 1966.

Pamphlets

Forest Interpreter's Primer on Fire Management, U.S. Department of Agriculture, Forest Service, 1976.

Maine Fire Disaster of October and November, 1947, Pictorial Review, Published by Guy P. Gannett, Publisher, 1947.

Telephone Topics, Special Edition. "The Maine Fire Story," New England Telephone and Telegraph Company, n.d.

Articles

Barter, J. Malcolm, "800 Homeless As Fire Sears Kennebunkport," *Boston Globe,* October 22, 1947.

——, "Inferno in Maine," *Boston Globe,* October 24, 1947.

——, "Maine Towns Beginning to Rebuild," *Boston Globe,* October 26, 1947.

——, "York County Men Return to Survey Ruins of Homes," *Boston Globe,* October 24, 1947.

Boyle, Hal, "The Way It Was. 1947: The Great Fires," *Maine Sunday Telegram,* June 12, 1977.

Caldwell, Bill, "30 Years Ago Today Maine Burned . . . Bar Harbor Remembers," *Maine Sunday Telegram,* October 23, 1977.

Charles, Dick, "That's the Way It Was: State Nearly Went up in Smoke," *Journal-Tribune,* October 25, 1977.

"Company's Fire Losses Comparatively Slight As Some Areas of Maine Suffer Severe Setbacks," *The Exciter,* Vol. 29, No. 10, Central Maine Power Company, Augusta, Maine, November 1947.

Cook, Julia Anna, "Maine's Forest Fires of Twenty Years Ago," *Down East,* October 1967.

Cook, L. F., "The 1947 Forest Fire Record: One-Third Acadia Burned," *National Parks Magazine,* January-March 1948.

"Disaster: A Lovely Time of Year," *Time,* November 3, 1947.

Dyer, Ted, "Rebuilding York County Resorts," A Picture Story, *Portland Sunday Telegram,* May 2, 1948.

Ferriss, Lloyd, "Here and There, a Miracle," *Maine Sunday Telegram,* October 23, 1977.

Fobes, Charles B., "Historic Forest Fire in Maine," *Economic Geography,* Vol. 24, No. 4, October 1948.

Ford, Corey, "Brownfield's Still Here," *Collier's,* February 21, 1948.

——, "The Statue," *Collier's,* February 14, 1948.

Gooley, Walter R., Jr., "In Quest of Smoke: Maine's Forest Fire Aerial Patrol," *Down East,* October, 1971.

——, "Time Fails to Erase Scars of 1947," *Maine Sunday Telegram,* October 22, 1972.

"Great Fire of 1825 Burned 832,000 Acres of Maine Woods," *The Moosehead Gazette,* June 13, 1975. Reprinted from *The Northern,* 1927.

"The Great Forest Fire of 1825," *Down East,* November 1975.

Hall, A. G., "Four Flaming Days," *American Forests,* December 1947.

Hendrick, Peg, "The Peg Board," *York County Coast Star,* September 3, 1975.

——, "25 Years Ago: The World Was Aflame," *York County Coast Star,* October 18, 1972.

Hendrickson, Dyke, "Fire and Courage in York and Oxford Counties," *Maine Sunday Telegram,* October 23, 1977.

Howe, Amasa, "What Four Men Went Thru at Bar Harbor," *Boston Sunday Globe,* October 26, 1947.

Johnson, Ethel M., "Brownfield Two Years After: People Show Courage but Problems Face Town," *Portland Sunday Telegram,* October 23, 1949.

Kelley, Mary Carpenter, "Maine Looks Back: Gift of Old Maryland Ridge Meeting House Cheers Newfield Folk," *Portland Sunday Telegram,* October 24, 1948.

"La Ville De Bar-Harbor est à demi détruite par un incendie que l'on croit criminel," *Le Figaro,* Paris, France, October 25, 1947.

Langzettel, Bill, "Maine's Ordeal: Could It Happen Again?" *Kennebec Journal,* October 22, 1977.

——, "Maine's Worst Natural Disaster Hit 30 Years Ago," *Kennebec Journal,* October 21, 1977.

"Maine Forest Service Fights Woods Fires by Bombing with Water from Special Plane," Down East Enterprise, *Down East,* September 1964.

"Our Flag Was Still There: School Girl's Story Recalls Forest Fires," *Portland Sunday Telegram,* November 19, 1950.

Pert, P. L., Jr., "Largest and Least Remembered: 1825 Forest Fire Covered 832,000 Acres of Maine," *Portland Sunday Telegram,* August 29, 1965.

——, "Lesson of '47 Paid Off at Centerville-Wilkins," *Portland Sunday Telegram,* September 5, 1965.

Pray, Waldo E., "Maine Not Likely to Face 1947 Fire Tragedy Repeat," *Portland Sunday Telegram,* August 15, 1965.

Ring, Elizabeth, "Catastrophe Again Changes the Economy of the Ossipee Towns," *Portland Sunday Telegram,* November 2, 1947.

Smith, Esther L., "The Two Waterboro Fires," *Maine Life,* October 1974.

Snow, Roger V., Jr., "The Reporter: The Man Who Covered the Bar Harbor Fire Also Brought a Ship," *Maine Sunday Telegram,* October 23, 1977.

Spiker, LaRue, "Like a Giant Blowtorch," *Ellsworth American,* October 19, 1972.

"Ten Years Show Bar Harbor's Recovery," *Bar Harbor Times,* September 12, 1957.

Thompson, Huston, "Has Nature Performed a Miracle in Acadia National Park?" *National Parks Magazine,* July-September 1955.

Tierney, Daniel B., "New England's Indian Summer Fire Disaster," *The Maine Townsman,* June 1948.

"Two Destroyer Escorts Come to Maine As Record Drought Lowers Hydro Output," *The Exciter,* Vol. 29, No. 11, Central Maine Power Company, December 1947.

Wallace, Caroline, "Graphic Description of Recent Disastrous Fires in 4 Kennebunks," *Kennebunk Star,* November 1947.

Weir, George, "When Satan's Minions Stalked the Land," *Portland Press Herald,* October 23, 1972.

Wescott, Chester, Letter to the Editor, *Hotel and Restaurant News*, Boston, November 8, 1947.

Wilkins, Austin H., "The Story of the Maine Forest Fire Disaster," *Journal of Forestry*, Vol. 26, No. 8, August 1948.

Williams, Anson R. and Margaret, as told to Mary Wilkes Haley, "The Big Fire," *Down East*, October 1962.

Wright, Franklin, "Maine Looks Back on 1947: Burned-Out Families Living in New Homes Year After Big Fires," *Portland Sunday Telegram*, October 24, 1948.

——, "Man's Generosity to Man Helped Him Back Along the Fire-Blackened Road," *Portland Sunday Telegram*, November 13, 1949.

Reports

American National Red Cross, Eastern Area. "Expenditures in Connection with the Maine Forest Fires, 1947," January 25, 1950.

Bar Harbor Fire Department. "The Bar Harbor Fire," by Chief David A. Sleeper and Lieut. John Heath, n.d.

Bar Harbor Police Department. "The Bar Harbor Fire: Record of Law Enforcement, October 21–27, 1947," Prepared for the Record by Members of the Bar Harbor Police Department.

Central Maine Power Company. Annual Report, 1947.

Jackson Laboratory. 19th Annual Report of the Roscoe B. Jackson Memorial Laboratory, 1947–48.

Maine, "Report on Forest Fires in Maine, Fall of 1947," by Crosby A. Hoar and Edward Ritter, U.S. Department of Agriculture, Forest Service, Eastern Division, December 1947.

Maine, southwestern. "Maine Fire Damage Survey. Report on the Survey of Timber Damage by Forest Fires in Southwestern Maine, October 1947," Northeast Forest Experiment Station, Philadelphia, Pa., January 30, 1948.

Maine, southwestern. "Rehabilitation of Fire-Damaged Forest Lands in Southwestern Maine," by A. D. Nutting, James C. Rettie, and Wayne C. Banks, Northeastern Forest Experiment Station, Upper Darby, Pa., Station Paper No. 33, February 1949.

Maine, southwestern. "The Southwestern Maine Fire Area—Four Years Later," by Wayne C. Banks and Myron D. Ostrander, Northeastern Research Notes, No. 18, Northeastern Forest Experiment Station, Upper Darby, Pa., December 1952.

Maine, State of. 27th Biennial Report of the Forest Commissioner, A. D. Nutting, 1947–48. Including "The 1947 Forest Fire Disaster," by Austin H. Wilkins, Deputy Commissioner, January 1, 1949.

Maine, Washington County. Maine Fire Damage Survey. Centerville-Jonesboro Fire Area, Northeastern Forest Experiment Station, Philadelphia, Pa., January 30, 1948.

Maine, York County. "The Maine Forest Fire Disaster," by H. J. Eberley, U.S. Department of Agriculture, Forest Service, Eastern Division, Division of Cooperative Forest Protection, November 1947.

Maine, York County. "Status of the York County Burn: Analysis of Deer Kill and Woody Plant Regeneration and Growth," Project W-37-R-6 and 16-R, Department of Inland Fisheries and Game, State of Maine, October 1947 to December 1956.

Maine, York County. "York County Fires, 1947," submitted by Colonel Laurence C. Upton, Chief, Maine State Police, Department of State Police, Augusta, Maine, December 1947.

Maine Extension Service. "Maine Extension Service Reviews a Busy Year. for the Year Ending June 30, 1948," Maine Extension Bulletin No. 383, August 1948.

New England. "Climatological Data: New England Section," by W. H. Tracy, Weather Bureau, U.S. Department of Commerce, Vol. LIX, No. 10, Boston, Mass., October 1947.

New England. "Climatological Data: New England Section," by W. H. Tracy, Weather Bureau, U.S. Department of Commerce, Vol. LIX, No. 13, Boston, Mass., Annual 1947.

New England. "Monthly Average of Temperature and Precipitation for State Climatic Divisions 1941–70," U.S. Department of Commerce, National Oceanic and Atmospheric Administration, Environmental Data Service, National Climatic Center, Ashville, N.C., July 1973.

New England Council. Forest Fire Loss Figures, 1947, for New England, January 12, 1949.

New England Forest Emergency Fire Hazard Reduction Project. Final Report on Cleanup After the 1938 Hurricane, n.d.

The Northwestern Forest Fire Protection Compact, Presented by Senator Edmund Muskie, *Congressional Record,* Vol. 118, p. 6, June 8, 1972.

Newspapers

Bangor Daily Commercial
Bangor Daily News
Bar Harbor Times
Biddeford Daily Journal
Kennebunk Star
Portland Press Herald and *Portland Sunday Telegram*

Unpublished Manuscripts

Brotak, Edward Allen, "A Synoptic Study of the Meteorological Conditions Associated with Major Wildlands Fires," Ph.D. dissertation, Yale Graduate School, 1977.

Marston, Merwin A., "Game and Fire," a paper dealing with the Maine forest fires of October 1947, and their immediate effect on game, and game problems arising from them, Department of Inland Fisheries and Game, State of Maine, n.d.

Rowell, Christine, An account of her experiences in 1947 during the fire at Bar Harbor. Collection of the Bar Harbor Historical Society.

Smith, Esther L., "The 1947 Fire," a paper read to the Waterboro Historical Society in 1976.

Stanley, Dorothy, A letter written on October 26, 1947, about her experiences during the Bar Harbor fire. Collection of the Bar Harbor Historical Society.

Wilkins, Austin H., "What Shall Be the Forest Fire Organization for the State of Maine?" a paper presented at the Maine Forest Forum in Bangor, Maine, January 5, 1948. Archives of the Maine Forest Service.

Collections and Archives

Archives Maine Forest Service. These papers include thirty-three reports filed during the winter of 1948 by state wardens, town wardens, town managers, selectmen, fire chiefs, etc.

Collection Bar Harbor Historical Society

Collection Kennebunkport Historical Society

Oral History

(Tape-recorded interviews conducted by Joyce Butler, 1976–78.)

Barter, J. Malcolm
Beard, Althea C.
Bibber, Earl V.
Boynton, Esther W.
Burrows, Thelma A.
Butler, G. Robert
Craig, Carolyn F.
Davis, Lloyd W.
Day, Kenneth C.
Dolby, Lawrence T.
Emery, Mabel
Gobeil, Ruth Emery
Gould, Champ C.
Gould, Elizabeth L.
Handlen, Frank
Hawkes, Bernard
Higgins, Josephine
Ireland, Lawrence

Kelley, Dr. John W.
Littlefield, Elizabeth D.
Littlefield, Emery S.
Meserve, Coyle R.
Moulton, Arthur C.
Moulton, Dr. Marion K.
O'Hara, Desmond
Ricker, Bessie H.
Roberts, Arthur L.
Russell, Louise
Russell, Raymond P.
Salisbury, Allen
Salisbury, Florence
Schmaltz, Carl N., Jr.
Smith, Charles W.
Smith, Dorothea F.
Smith, Esther L.
Spofford, Juanita D.

Stinson, Arnold
Stuart, Charlotte C.
Walker, Marjorie C.
Walker, Warren L.
Wallace, Linwood

Wallace, Violetta
Weymouth, L. Clayton
Wildes, Martin V. B.
Wilkins, Austin H.

(Unrecorded interviews)

Coleman, Harrison   Perkins, Anne Louise B.   Seavey, Clifford

Index

Abbott, George, 75
Abbott, Roger, 132, 247, 248
Acadia National Park (*See* Mount
    Desert Island)
Acme News Service, 175
ALFRED (*See also* North Alfred),
    12, 39, 44, 90, 91, 93, 95–98,
    147–149, 157, 161, 181, 188,
    189, 199, 235; Back Road, 147,
    148; Notre Dame Institute, 148,
    157; Shaker Pond, 148;
    Whitcher's Mills, 192; York
    County jail, 149, 181
Alfred Fire Department, 43
American Cancer Society, Maine
    Chapter, 221
American Institute of Architects,
    Maine Chapter, 214
American Legion, 117, 151, 156, 168,
    169, 183, 206, 226; Andrews
    Post, 168; Caldwell Post, 45
American Red Cross, 14, 22, 26,
    74, 79, 96, 116, 117, 140, 151,
    153, 164–173, 197, 198, 205,
    211, 213, 215–217, 219, 221,
    224–226
American Sardine Company, 157
Amory, Cleveland, 176, 242

Andrews, Dana, 5
ANDROSCOGGIN COUNTY, 36
Annis, "Mike," 22
ANSON, 150
Army-Navy Day, 197
AROOSTOOK COUNTY, 4, 36,
    209
ARUNDEL (*See also* North Kenne-
    bunkport), 15n
Associated Press, 175, 209
AUBURN, 43, 44, 199, 227
Audie, Joe, 169
AUGUSTA, 13, 33, 150, 174, 196,
    197; State House, 151, 210;
    Augusta Airport, 206, 224

backfiring, 40, 195, 201, 236
Baker, Arthur, 86–88, 196
Baker, Henry, 171
BALDWIN (*See also* West Bald-
    win), 84, 150
BANGOR, 1, 5, 56, 57, 74, 156,
    170, 181, 190, 227; Dow Field,
    51, 56, 63, 65, 69, 74, 75, 154,
    177, 181; Tarratine Club, 233;
    WJOR, 156
Bangor Daily Commercial, 71, 74,
    175

Bangor Daily News, x, 57, 220, 231
Bangor Humane Society, 190
Bangor Hydro-Electric Company, 54
Bangor Theological Seminary, 157,
    169, 220
BAR HARBOR (*See* Mount Desert
    Island)
BAR MILLS, 6, 179, 180, 204
Barter, J. Malcolm, xi, 89, 90, 92,
    97–99, 163, 181, 193
Barton, Philip, 7
Bates College, 157, 199
BATH, 217
Bath Iron Works, 157
Bean, Daniel, 78, 84
Beard, Althea, 27, 31
Beard, Frank, 27, 31
Berry, Captain William, xi, 70
BERWICK (*See also* North
    Berwick), 199
Bibb, 70
Bibber, Earl, 232
BIDDEFORD, 12–14, 29, 39, 48,
    57, 90, 98, 115, 119, 124–126,
    139–144, 146, 153, 157, 166,
    168, 169, 174, 177, 181, 182,
    194, 198–201, 210, 211, 217;
    Bates Mill, 141, 157; BIDDE-
    FORD POOL, 19, 25, 124,
    142, 143; Birch Street, 140;
    Chapman's Clothing Store,
    217; Christ Church, 140, 141,
    166; Clifford Park, 139, 141;
    Elm Street, 141; Emery School,
    140; Five Points, 12, 48, 139,
    141, 149; FORTUNES ROCKS,
    12, 15, 19, 124, 139, 142–144,
    174; Fortunes Rocks Road, 21;
    Granite Point Road, 142, 143;
    Guinea Road, 14, 17, 21, 48;
    May Street, 139, 141, 142;
    Mountain Road, 139; Newtown
    Road, 48, 139, 141, 142; Oak

Ridge, 17; Pepperell Hall, 115,
    170; Pepperell Mill, 141, 157;
    Pool Road, 126, 139–141, 200;
    Proctor Road, 14, 18; Saco-
    Lowell Shops, 17, 141, 156,
    157; South Street, 139, 141,
    142; St. Joseph's Hall, 14, 18,
    140, 169; St. Louis High
    School, 157; Tea Kettle Corner,
    21; Trull Hospital, 139, 141;
    Webber Hospital, 139, 141,
    142; West Street, 12, 14, 17, 18,
    139, 153; Western Union office,
    169; White Church, 141, 169
Biddeford Daily Journal, x, 23, 227
BINGHAM, 150
Blaine, James G., 53
Blanchfield, Margaret, 62, 75
BLUE HILL, 52
Bodycott, William, 181
Boothby, Harry, 195
BOSTON (*See* Massachusetts)
Boston and Maine Railroad, 12, 139
Boston Evening American, 18
Boston Globe, 75, 89, 163, 181
Boston Sunday Herald, 176, 231
Bousfield, Reverend, 64
Bowden, Ada, 178
BOWDOIN, 6, 9, 57, 157, 235;
    Bowdoin Center, 8, 10
Bowdoin College, 7, 9, 198
Boy Scouts of America, 169, 211
Boynton, Esther, x, xix, 78–82,
    223–226, 228, 243, 246, 248,
    249
Boynton, Guy, xix, 80–82, 224–226
Bradley General Omar, 214
Bradshaw, Dr. Marion, 220
Brassua Pond, 4
BREWER, 56, 67, 74
Brewster, Senator Owen, 184
Brookhaven National Laboratory,
    221

Brooklyn Dodgers, 1
Brooks, Leon, 224
Brown, Allan, 162
Brown, Sewall, 75
BROWNFIELD (*See also* Brownfield Center, East Brownfield, West Brownfield), xv, xix, 38, 76–84, 87, 130, 150, 170, 172, 174, 188, 191, 192, 199, 204, 214, 217, 223–226, 243, 246; Birches, The, 77, 83; Burnt Meadow Mountains, 77, 83; Congregational Church, 84; Dugway Road, 83; Icabod Merrill house, 77; Intervale, The, 80; Pequawket Trail, 77; Shepard's River, 77, 83, 226; Stickney mansion, 77, 83; Sundial House, 78, 83; Ten Mile Brook, 246
BROWNFIELD CENTER, 77, 78, 80–83
BRUNSWICK, 37, 38, 157, 182, 205, 211
Brunswick Fire Department, 37
Brunswick Naval Air Station, 38
Brunswick-Topsham Water District, 37
BUCKSPORT, 67, 182
Burbank, Ray, 90, 91, 249
Burns, Howell, 57–59
Burrows, Joe, 11
Burrows, Thelma, 11, 14, 25, 32, 153, 164–166
Butler, Dorothy, xi, 140
Butler, George, 141
Butler, Martina, 14, 140, 141
Butler, Robert, 141
BUXTON (*See also* West Buxton), 179

C. H. Sprague Company, 218
Callahan, James, 89, 90, 92, 97–99

CAMDEN, 67, 182, 247
Campbell, Donald, 19
CANADA, 237; New Brunswick, Province of, xxi, 237, 238; Quebec, Province of, 237, 238
Cantara, Frank, 119, 139
CANTON, 38
CAPE ELIZABETH, 25, 42, 44, 183
Cape Elizabeth Fire Department, 199
CAPE PORPOISE (*See* Kennebunkport)
Cape Porpoise Fire Company, 12
CARIBOU, 4, 36
Carter, Fritz, xi
CENTERVILLE, 36, 40, 47, 128, 150, 157, 182, 189, 205, 238
Central Maine Power Company, 180, 183, 192, 210, 223
Chapin, Bill, 70
CHERRYFIELD, 40
CHINA, 182
Civilian Conservation Corps, 154, 156, 229
Church, Letitia M., xv
Civil Air Patrol, Maine Wing, 9
Civilian Defense, 151, 197, 206
Clark, Cecil, 194
Clark, Frank, 222
CLARK'S MILLS (*See* Hollis)
Cleaves, Senator Robert, J., Jr., 231
Clough, Eleanor, 164
Coates, Walter, 74
Cohen, Rabbi, 201
Colby College, 157
Collier, Sargent, 243
Collier's Magazine, 192
CONNECTICUT, 238; Hartford, 175
Coombs, Curt, 193
Cormier, Edward, 67
Cormier, Helen, xv, 67, 69, 73, 74

Cormier, Jane, 67–69, 73, 74
Cormier, Mary H., 67–69, 73, 74
Cormier, Robert, 68
CORNISH, 81, 84
Cote, Aurele, 157
Cote, Maud, xv
Country Roads, 249
Craig, Allen, 24
Craig, Carolyn, 23–27, 32
Craig, Frank, 23–27
CRAWFORD, 205
Crocker, Robert, 83
CUMBERLAND COUNTY, 6, 169
Cunningham, Bill, 231

Damon Runyan Fund, 221
Damrosch, Margaret Blaine, 220
Damrosch, Walter, 53, 76, 220
Daniels, Edmund, 38
Daughty, Irving, 4
Davis, Dick, 31
Davis, Elizabeth, 54, 55. 59, 61
Davis, Hazel, 31
Davis, Lloyd, 92, 93, 98, 147, 148, 155, 239
Davis, Orison, 17, 18
Day, Adelaide, 164
Day, Harold, 146
Day, Holman, 82
Day, Kenneth, 154, 194, 195
Day, Percy, 146, 193
Daylight Saving Time, 209
DAYTON, 90, 123, 127, 132, 147, 179, 189, 192, 199–205, 209, 243, 247; Clough's Corner, 201, 202; Freetown, 201
Deep Water, 5
DENMARK, xx, 77, 79, 80, 84, 175, 189
DENNYSVILLE, 157
Depression, The, 156, 214, 242
Deyo, Admiral, 70
Dineen, Robert, 216

Doherty, John, 145
Dolby, Lawrence, x, 3, 140, 181
Dolliver, Bill, 50, 246
Donnell, Ruth, 178
Dow Field (*See* Bangor)
Drummond, A. H., Jr., xv, 198
Dubois, Donald, 169
Dunnell family, 89
Durgin, Mrs. Harry, 224
DURHAM, 182
Durrell, Oliver, xi
Durrell, Zoe, xi

Eagles, Fraternal Order of, Casco Aerie, 168
EAST BROWNFIELD, 77, 78, 80–83, 192, 224
EAST HIRAM, 175
EAST LIVERMORE, xx, 36, 37, 85
EAST MADISON, 182
EAST PARSONSFIELD, 194
EAST WATERBORO, 41, 89, 98, 114, 149, 201
Eberly, H. J., 196, 206, 210, 232
Eldridge, John, 12, 32, 153
Elks Lodge, 217
Ellis, Marjorie (*See also* Marjorie Mosser), xi
ELLSWORTH, 56, 63, 69, 73, 74, 169, 170, 175
Elwell, Fred, 183
Emery, Mabel, x, 17, 18, 21, 22, 48, 141
Emery, Richard, 17
Emery, Ruth, 17, 21, 22
Emery, Sid, 92
Emmons, Buck, 3
Emmons, Claude, 91, 218
Emmons, Roy, 19, 143
Evans, R. M., 232

FALMOUTH (*See also* West Falmouth), 3, 7, 198

Farm Home Association, 214
FARMINGTON, 37
Farnsworth, Dan, 142
Farnsworth, Dr. Philo, 78, 79, 83
Farrand, Mrs. Max, 55, 57
FAYETTE, 37
Federal Reserve Bank of Boston, 214
Fekete, Elizabeth, 60
Ferguson, Donald "Mike," 6, 12,
    38, 39, 45, 245
Fire Prevention Week, 5
Fish and Game Associations, 212
Fitzpatrick, Father Edward, 71
FLORIDA, 75, 153
Foley, Dale, 60, 61
Foote, Harry, 29, 192, 193
Forbis, Isabelle, xi, 54, 63
Forbis, Judith Ann, 72
Forbis, Welch, 72
FORT FAIRFIELD, 150, 174
FORT KENT, 236
FORTUNES ROCKS (See Bidde-
    ford)
Foster, Theresa, xv
Foye, Robert, xi
Freedom Train, 1, 197
FRYEBURG (See also North Frye-
    burg), 38, 39, 47, 77–80, 84,
    150, 162, 170, 189, 195, 225;
    Brownfield Road, 79, 80; Frost
    Mountain, 77; Lovewell's Pond,
    80; Oak Hill section, 38, 78
Fryeburg Fire Department, 38, 79
Furfey, Dr. J. Austin, 220

Gagnon, Alphonse, 38
Gannett, Guy, 189; Publishing
    Company, 227
General Electric Company, 210
GEORGIA, 153
Gibbs, Arthur, 144
Gifford, George, 31
Gilbert, Mrs., 50

Gile, Leland H., Jr., xv
Gilley, Morris, 220
Gillies Lumber Company, 91, 140,
    174
Glovinsky, Monty, xi
Goldthwaite, Sheldon, 219
Goodwin, Marshall, 143
Goodwin, Thoady, 24
Goodwin, Walter, 25
GOODWIN'S MILLS, 90, 91, 123,
    147, 183, 199, 201, 239
Googins, Hugh, 183
GOOSE ROCKS BEACH (See
    Kennebunkport)
Goose Rocks Beach Fire Company,
    12, 18
GORHAM, 44, 140, 182
Gould, Champ, 41, 47, 92, 93
Gould, Liz, xx, 41, 47, 92, 93, 160
GOULDSBORO, 70
Graham, Gertrude, 143
GRAND ISLE, 36
Graves, Mr., 61
GRAY, 7, 44
Great Northern Paper Company, 180
GREENVILLE, 210
Gregory, Captain Hanson, 227
Greyhound Bus Lines, 156
Gross, Henry, 11
GROVEVILLE, 179
Grumman amphibian, 30

Hale, Richard, 176
Halloween, 197
Ham, Josephine, xiii
Hamlin, Cyrus, xv
HANCOCK, 70
Handlen, Frank, x, 19, 20, 142
Handlen, Fritzie, 143
Hannaford, Doris, 88
Hansen, Carl, 92. 93
Harland Bartholomew Associates,
    221

Harmon, Charlie, 81, 172, 224
Harmon, Frank, 78
Harriman, Charles, 4
HARRISON, 79
Harrison Fire Department, 83
Hawkes, Bernard, 62, 71–73, 219
Heath, John, 176
Henchey, John, 17, 18, 21
Henchey, Laura, 21, 22
Herlihy, Edward, 57, 198
HERMON, 150
Higgins, Josephine, 63, 72
Higgins, Robert, 63
Higgins Classical Institute, 217
HIGHLAND LAKE, xviii, 37
Hildreth, Governor Horace, 4, 6–8,
    13, 25, 35, 47, 89, 151, 187,
    188, 196, 206, 209, 210, 212,
    213, 215, 218, 227, 234, 235
Hill, Carleton, 235
HIRAM (See also East Hiram and
    South Hiram), 77, 79, 81, 83,
    84, 175, 189
HIROSHIMA, xvii
Hobbs, William, 218
Holbrook, Mrs. Frank, 169
HOLLIS, xii, 6, 41, 179, 189, 193,
    194, 199, 201, 210, 235, 236,
    249; Clark's Mills, 167, 168,
    179, 183, 189, 194, 199, 201,
    204, 216, 246; Hollis Center,
    199, 204; Union Falls, 199,
    201, 204
Hollis Center Fire Department, 236
Home Builders Association of
    Maine, 215
Hubbard, Reverend Russell, 177
Huff, Myron, 98, 245
Hurricane, 1938, xix, 229

IOOF, Windham Lake Shore Lodge,
    217
Indian Joe, 5

Ingalls, Lillian, 75, 178
International Association of Fire
    Chiefs, 231
International News Pictures, 175
Ireland, Lawrence, xv, 18, 19, 161,
    213

JACKMAN, 150, 174
Jackson Laboratory (See Mount
    Desert Island, Bar Harbor)
JAY, 37
Johnson, Hallet, 75
Johnson, Herschel, 227
Johnson, Paul, 202
Jones, Earlan, 225
Jones, Orel, 92, 93
JONESBORO, 36, 47, 128, 157,
    162, 187, 189, 198, 205
Junior Chamber of Commerce,
    Bangor, 157

Karst, Raymond, 71
Karvonides, Constantine, 198
Keating, Major General Frank, 197
"Keep Maine Green," 235
Kelley, John, x, 45, 162, 163
Kelley, Hugh, 51
Kennebec Limited, 13
Kennebec River, 4
KENNEBUNK (See also West
    Kennebunk), 14, 144, 146, 147,
    153, 163, 167, 175, 177, 189,
    193, 199, 200, 212, 247;
    Alewife Pond,146, 193;
    Alewive, 175, 199; Alewive
    Grange Hall, 146; Cole Road,
    146; Cooper's Corner, 27, 31;
    Day's Mills, 146, 147, 193;
    Green Leaf Inn, 14; Kennebunk
    Inn, 31, 90; Kennebunk Land-
    ing, 25; Main Street, 90; Maple
    Top Farm, 146, 193; Mousam
    River, 147; Narragansett Hotel,

165, 169; Rogers Fibre Company, 26, 194; Sea Side House, 165; Thompson Road, 199, 200; Ward Brook, 199; Water Street, 194
Kennebunk Fire Department, 12, 14, 146, 147
Kennebunk River, 25
Kennebunk Star, 218
KENNEBUNKPORT, xv, xx, 11–15, 18, 37, 41, 47, 57, 89, 131, 141, 142, 144–146, 150, 153, 154, 156, 157, 164–166, 170, 177, 199, 217, 232, 236, 241, 242, 246; Arundel Engine Company, 12, 164; Arundel Grange Hall, 32, 169; Breakwater Court, 165; Buttonwood, 29, 166; Buttonwood Road, 145; Cape Arundel, 28; CAPE PORPOISE, 11, 23–33, 241; Allen Road, 31; Batson's River, 24; Crow Hill, 26–29, 31, 32, 241; Fisher's Lane, 28, 31; Langsford Road, 26; Main Street, 26; Mills Road, 26; Paddy's Creek, 29; Pier Road, 26, 31; Pinkham Island, 26; Stone Haven Hill, 31; Ward Road, 28 Clock Farm, 24; Dock Square, 27, 131, 236; "Doherty's Boulevard," 145, 246; Fire, 1930, 25; Fox Farm Road, 19; Goose Fare Farm, 24; GOOSE ROCKS BEACH, xv, xx, 15, 18, 20–24, 26, 32, 33, 47, 89, 102–104, 134, 135, 142, 161, 173, 213, 241, 248; Eliot O'Hara School of Watercolor, xx, 20, 23, 47, 48; Little River, 21, 23, 103, 142; Timber Island, 23, 48, 242 Green Heron, The, 169; Land's End,

28, 29, 32; Maine Street, 27; Miller's Drug Store, 12; Nessler's Point, 26; Nonantum, The, 26; Old Fort Inn, The, 26; Rocky Pasture, 11, 32, 144; School Street, 27, 28, 31, 166; Spring Street, 27; Turbat's Creek, 28, 145; Walker's Point, 28; WILDES DISTRICT, 29, 31, 144; Wildes District Road, 11, 28, 144, 145, 246; Wildes Town, 12, 32, 144, 145, 246
Kennedy, John Stewart, 242
Kent, A. Atwater, 53, 176
KENTUCKY, 153
Kerr, John, 142
Kerr, Mrs. John, 142
KEZAR FALLS, 84, 164, 167, 199, 205
Kezar Falls–Cornish Road, 12
KITTERY, 44
Kittredge brothers, 26, 236, 249
Kiwanis Club, Biddeford, 217
Kliemann, Ernest, 189
Knight, Kenneth, 37
Knight, Sheriff, 181
KNOX COUNTY, 182

Lafferty, Mrs., 14
LAMOINE, 70
Landry, Francis, 26
Lane Construction Company, 13, 140, 145, 156
Larrabee, Dr., 63
Last Resorts, The, 242
Laurel, 25, 70
Lausier, Louis, 181
Lavoie, Armand, 38
Le Figaro, 176
Leavitt, Fred, 195
LEE, 216
LeGallee, Bud, 19, 20
Lewis, Marjorie Kenney, xv

LEWISTON, 7, 197
Life Magazine, 67, 175
LIMERICK, 84, 87
Limerick Fire Department, 89
LIMINGTON, xiii, 39
LINCOLNVILLE, 36, 182
LISBON FALLS, 6, 7
Little, Dr. Clarence, 191, 221, 222
Little Rock, 197, 210
Little Sugarloaf Mountain, 205
Littlefield, Betty, 96, 97
Littlefield, John, 99
Littlefield, Peggy, 169
Littlefield, Emery "Stan," 43
LIVERMORE FALLS, 37
Long Pond, 4
Lord, Robert, 155
LOVELL, 38, 79
LYMAN, 90, 91, 94, 98, 99, 122,
   123, 129, 146, 147, 149, 154,
   161, 170, 179, 181, 183, 192,
   193, 199, 212, 218, 243; An-
   drews farm, 91; Bunganut
   Pond, 148, 243; Clough's Cor-
   ner, 183; Day's Road, 90, 91;
   Grant's Hill, 147; Kennebunk
   Pond, 98, 99, 243; Kennebunk
   Pond Road, 91; Massabesic Ex-
   perimental Forest, 148, 154;
   Meetinghouse Road, 170;
   Roberts Pond, 90; Swan Pond,
   243; Swan Pond Creek, 147;
   Wadley Pond, 243
Lymburner, Mr., 59
Lynfield, Charlie, 245

MACHIAS, 150, 189, 210
Machiasport Canning Company, 157
Mack Truck Company, 217
MADAWASKA, 36
MADISON (*See also* East Madi-
   son), 36, 48
MAINE: central, xviii, 35; eastern,

xviii; northern, xviii, 4,6, 36,
   205, 209; southern, xviii, xx, 4,
   12, 35, 210; southwestern, 180,
   206, 223, 243–245; western, 6
Maine, state of: Bank Association,
   215; Banking Commissioner,
   215; Congressional Delegation,
   196; Education, Dept. of, 224;
   Emergency Municipal Finance
   Board, 218; Fire Emergency
   and Information Office, 151,
   218; Fire Inspector, x, 3, 140,
   181; Forest Service, xiv, xviii,
   4, 6, 13, 151, 187, 211, 216,
   229, 231, 232, 234–236, 238,
   243; Commissioner (*See also*
   Rendall, Raymond), xviii, 168,
   232, 238; Conservation, Dept.
   of, xiv; District One, 12, 236;
   District Two, 38; Forestry District, xviii, xx, 151, 198, 235;
   Supervisor Forest Fire Control,
   4; Supervisor, Organized Territory, 87; Governor (*See* Horace
   Hildreth); Inland Fisheries and
   Game, Dept. of, 4, 9, 212; Land
   and Forest Preservation Commission, xviii; Legislature, 218,
   219; organized territory, xvii n,
   232, 234, 236; unorganized territory, xvii n, 218, 232
Maine, University of, 157;
   Brunswick Annex, 9, 38, 57,
   68; Forestry Department, 6,
   157
Maine Central Institute, 217
Maine Central Railroad, 130, 150,
   156, 188, 192
Maine Extension Service, 168, 197,
   215, 216
Maine Forest Forum, 233
Maine Life, 45
Maine National Guard, 25, 47, 75,

89, 119, 147, 148, 154, 174,
180, 183, 190, 191, 194, 196,
201, 206, 211
Maine State Police, 155, 156,
182–184, 206
Maine State Society, 217
Maine Townsman, The, 231
Maine Turnpike, xx, 13, 139, 140,
156
Maine Unemployment Commission,
214
Maling, Cliff, 24, 32
Marshall Plan, 227
Masons, Free and Accepted, 168
MASSACHUSETTS, 154, 238;
Amesbury, 25; Arlington, 231;
Boston, 13, 70, 154, 169, 175,
196, 197, 209, 210; Marble-
head, 142; Somerville, 188
Massachusetts Commission on In-
terstate Cooperation, 237
Massachusetts Envelope and Drink-
ing Cup Company, 218
Mavrakos, Andrew, 154, 155
McCormick, Mildred, 190
McCulloch, 70
McLean, Mary, 47
Merrill, Carleton, 38, 39, 79
Merrill, Eva, 91
Merrill, Rob, 91, 92, 99
Merrill Transportation Company
(*See* Portland)
Merrymen, The, xv
Meserve, Clement, 201, 203
Meserve, Coyle, 147
Meserve, Lesley, 202, 247
Meserve, Roy, 127, 201–204
Methodist Church Conference of
Maine, campground, 37
Mignault, Dot, 21–23, 103
Miramichi Fire, xviii, xxi
MISSOURI, 169
Mitchell, Jacqueline, 36, 37

Moore, Ruth, 5
Moosehead Lake, 4, 198, 205, 210
Montgomery, Frank, 169
Morrill, John, 89
Morris, Paul, 181
Mosser, Marjorie, 144
Moulton, Arthur, 39, 40, 85–88,
196, 244, 246
Moulton, Everett, 195
Moulton, Dr. Marion, 86, 87, 168
Mount Ararat, 151
MOUNT DESERT ISLAND, 36,
48, 49–76, 106–110, 113, 150,
153–156, 174–178, 189, 198,
205, 216; Acadia National
Park, 50, 52, 56, 76, 150, 153,
222, 242, 244; ASTICOU, 64;
Aunt Betty Pond, 56; BAR
HARBOR, 9, 36, 48–76,
106–110, 150, 154, 156, 157,
169, 170, 174–178, 180–182,
188–190, 210, 217, 219–223,
242, 246; Alpheus Hardy Cottage, 221; Athletic Field,
62–64, 67–69, 189, 219; Bar,
The, 63, 71; Bar Harbor Club,
243; Bar Harbor Banking and
Trust Company, 219; Bar Harbor Motor Inn, 228; Bar Island,
63; Barberry Ledge, xix, 49,
52, 54, 55, 57–59, 61, 62, 242;
Bay Drive, 53, 67, 75, 189,
190, 220; Bluenose Ferry Ter-
minal, 242; Bluffs, The, 73;
Clark Coal Company, 71; Cleftstone Road, 54; College of the
Atlantic, 242; Cottage Street,
61; Crooked Road, 50; DeGregoire Hotel, 61,71–73; Doll
House, The, 53; Dolliver's
Dump, 50, 246; Duck Brook,
53, 65; Duck Brook Bridge, 65;
Eagle Lake Road, 52, 54, 55,

58, 59, 61, 67; Eden Street, 67, 72, 178; Express office, 57, 60, 61; Farm, The, 53; Fresh Meadow, 8, 50; Geranium Cottage, 53; Havre Forest, 220; Holy Redeemer Church, 71; How's Park, 71; Jackson Laboratory, 5, 59, 60, 65, 66, 75, 110, 175, 191, 221, 222; Jessup Memorial Library, 177; Kebo Street, 68; Kebo Valley Golf Club, 242, 243; Kenarden Lodge, 242; Loop Road, 244; Main Street, 62, 63, 67–69; Maine Sea Coast Missionary Society, 55, 64, 70; Malvern Hotel, 68, 109, 219; "Millionaire's Row," 67, 242; Mount Desert Hospital, 54, 63, 176; Mount Desert Street, 67, 72; Mountain Road, 52; Municipal Pier, 68, 106, 175, 176; North Atlantic Packing Company, 62; Norway Drive, 51; Odd Fellows Hall, 65; Pleasant Street, 55; Rodick Street, 67; Shea farm, 50, 51; Shore Club, 69, 219, 222; Spring Street, 72; St. Edward's Convent, 72; St. Savior's Church, 177; Strawberry Hill House, 53; Tripp's Restaurant, 63; Turrets, The, 53; West Street, 62, 67, 72; Wingwood House, 53, 190, 242 Bar Harbor Airport (*See* Trenton); Bar Harbor Citizens' Committee, 220; Bar Harbor Fire Department, 50, 56, 176; Bar Harbor Land Company, 221; Bar Harbor Police Department, 170; *Bar Harbor Times*, 58, 177; Cadillac Mountain, 49, 52, 55, 60, 67, 156, 190; Champlain Mountain, 67; Eagle Lake, 52; Eagle Lake Road, 52, 54, 55, 58, 59, 61, 67; Frenchman Bay, 49, 53, 68, 70, 190, 242; Great Hill, 52, 55, 60, 61, 67; HULLS COVE, 50, 52, 53, 58–60, 63, 65, 67, 72, 73, 174, 205; Farnsworth Boat Yard, 52; Hamor House, 52, 60 Jordan Pond House, 52, 58; Kebo Mountain, 67; McFarland's Hill, 52, 58; NORTHEAST HARBOR, 52, 75, 174, 190, 198, 242; OTTER CREEK, 64, 75, 160, 190, 198; SALISBURY COVE, 191; Hamilton Station, 191; Schooner Head, 176 SEAL HARBOR, 52, 64, 66, 75, 176, 178, 190, 198, 242; Seal Harbor Road, 67; Rockefeller estate, 176 Sieur de Monts Spring, 60; Somes Sound, 190; SOMESVILLE, 57, 58, 64; SOUTHWEST HARBOR, 54, 69–72, 178; TOWN HILL, 64, 190; Trenton Bridge, 190, 191

Mount Megunticook, 36

Moxie Pond, 4

Mullet, Harry, 183

Muskie, Senator Edmund, 237

Mutual Insurance Company of New York, 214

National Forest Service, 153, 184, 188, 196, 229, 235

National Park Service, 50, 56, 153, 160, 177, 222

Native Americans, 5, 157

Nedeau, Charlie, 24, 145, 249

NEW ENGLAND, 189, 197, 234, 237; Council of State Governments, 237

New England Telephone and Telegraph Company, 180
NEW GLOUCESTER, 7, 197
NEW HAMPSHIRE, 7, 25, 81, 84, 188, 237, 238; Governor Dole, 188; Pease Air Force Base, 199; Portsmouth, 29, 43, 44, 160; Province Lake, 98, 195; Rochester, 96, 149, 199, 205; University of, 157; Wakefield, 38; White Mountains National Forest, 154
NEW YORK, 153, 154, 197, 211, 237, 238; Lake Success, 227; Mitchell Field, 154; New York City, 175, 221; Schenectady, 210; Utica, 188 *New York Herald Tribune,* 175
New York Stock Exchange, 180
New York Times, 175
New York Yankees, 1, 5
NEWFIELD (*See also* West Newfield), xix, 39–41, 47, 85–89, 98, 120, 121, 154, 168, 174, 184, 194–196, 199, 214, 229, 243, 245, 249; Adams Pond, 87, 88, 100n; Boozer's Store, 196; Drew Pond, 39, 40; Dunnell's Mountain, 87; Ethan Stone School, 89; Gertrude Hall Road, 87; Long Bridge, 87; Lost Mile Road, 195; Lower Village, 86, 87, 89, 120, 196, 245; Maplewood, 86, 87, 195; Maplewood Road, 86, 87; Mee's Corner, 39, 40; Methodist Church, 89; Moulton's Mill, 88; Old Parsonsfield Road, 85, 86; Poor Farm Flats, 89; Rock Haven Lake, 100n; Sanborn Road, 40; Stevens Corner, 39, 40, 87
Nickerson, Eleanor, 248

Nolan, Mr. and Mrs., 54, 55, 60–62
NORRIDGEWOCK, 36, 48, 128, 150, 157
NORTH ALFRED, 147
NORTH BERWICK, 44
NORTH FRYEBURG, 224
NORTH KENNEBUNKPORT, 8, 10–13, 24, 30, 39, 85, 101, 139, 142, 150, 157, 162, 163, 206, 212
NORTH NEW PORTLAND, 227
NORTH WATERBORO, xiii, 41, 43, 45–47, 89, 98, 137, 138, 149
Northeastern Forest Fire Protection Compact, xiv, 237, 238
Norwalk Shoe Company, 157
NORWAY, 3, 4
Norway Fish and Game Association, 3
Nuremburg Trials, xviii

Oakes, Lady Harry, 170, 242
Obermeyer, Jane (*See also* Jane Cormier), xv
Ogden, Harriet, 57
OGUNQUIT, 44, 199
O'Hara, Desmond, 20
O'Hara, Eliot, 20, 47, 48
O'Hara, Shirley, 20, 47
OHIO, 197
OLD ORCHARD BEACH, 140
OREGON, 154
Ouelette, Willie, 18
OXFORD COUNTY, 38, 130, 154, 215, 243, 245
PALERMO, 182
Palestine, xvii, 5, 227
Palmer, Mrs. Potter, 220
Paramount Pictures, 13, 18
Parent, Tom, xiv
Parks, Deborah, xv
PARSONFIELD (*See also* East Par-

sonfield, South Parsonfield), 85, 154, 184, 194, 195
Paul, Roy, 129, 192, 193
PENNSYLVANIA, 153
Penobscot Bay, 67
PENOBSCOT COUNTY, 4
Perkins, Anne Louise, 29
Perry, 70, 177
Peters, Jean, 5
Philco Dealers of Maine, 217
PHIPPSBURG CENTER, 4
PISCATEQUIS COUNTY, 4
Piscatequis River valley, xviii
Pleasant Mountain, xx, 38, 79, 81, 84
Pleasant Point Reservation, 157
PORTER, 77, 79, 81, 83, 189, 195, 205; Porter High School, 195
PORTLAND, ix, xxi, 5, 6, 10, 41, 42, 44, 70, 116, 140, 153, 154, 156, 168, 170, 184, 185, 189, 198, 210, 217, 227; A. H. Benoit Company, 157; Clark Memorial Church, 168; Cole's Express, 225; Deering High School, 45; Falmouth Hotel, 215; Fort Williams, 25; General Ice Cream Corp., 189; Hood's Dairy, 165; Maine General Hospital, 14, 154; Maine State Pier, ix, 90, 150, 174; Merrill Transportation Company, 26, 162, 165, 188; Milliken-Tomlinson Company, 225; Portland Coach Company, 156; Randall and McAllister Company, 188; State Street, 116; Union Station, 13; Western Promenade, 184, 185; Woodford's Corner, 45
Portland Airport, 189
Portland Fire Department, 26, 90, 153

Portland Independent Retail Grocers Association, 217
Portland Press Herald, x, 1, 5, 29, 35, 70, 132, 166, 170, 173–175, 184, 192, 203, 223, 226, 231–233, 247
Portland School Committee, 217
Portland Sunday Telegram, 84
Portland Water District, 3
Portland Weather Bureau, 85, 189
Pottle, Miriam, 71, 75, 175
Powell, 70, 154, 177
Pritchard, Mrs., 54, 55, 61
Project Cirrus, 210
Province Mountain, 38, 39
Pulitzer, Joseph, 53, 220

radio, "ham," 197
Randall, Irene, xi, 36, 37
Rattlesnake Mountain, 84
READFIELD, 37
Red Cross (*See* American Red Cross)
Red Thursday, 85, 195
Rendall, Raymond, xviii, 4, 6–8, 35, 150, 154, 195, 197, 206, 232, 233
Revere, Anne, 5
RHODE ISLAND, 237, 238; Newport, 53, 205
RICHMOND, 118, 150, 166, 174, 197, 198
Ricker, Bessie, x, 93–96, 148–150, 248
Ricker, Colby, 92, 93
Ricker, Harold, 94, 95
Ricker, Mame, 94, 95
Ricker, Ruel, 93–96, 148–150
Rinehart, Mary Roberts, 53, 76, 222
Roberts, Arthur, x, 90–92, 99, 183, 201, 216
Roberts, Jim, 41
Roberts, Kenneth, xi, 11, 15, 32, 144

Roberts, Lorraine, 91, 218
Robinson, Jackie, xx
ROCKLAND, 70
ROCKPORT, 227
Rod and Gun Clubs, 212
Roll, Warren, 175
Romero, Caesar, 5
Ross, Mrs. Ivory, 246
Rotary Club, 217
Route #1, 6, 12, 14, 27, 101, 139,
    140, 149
Route #1-A, 12, 13
Route #3, 174
Route #5, 140, 201–203
Route #9, 19, 24, 26, 145
Route #11, 86, 89
Route #35, 91, 98, 99, 122, 146,
    183, 193, 194, 199–201
Route #111, 90, 91, 98, 99, 122,
    139, 147, 149, 212
Route #112, 140
Route #113, 79
Route #201, 128
Route #202, 90, 97, 147, 148
Rowell, Christine, x, xix, 49–55,
    57–62, 242
Rowell, Donald, xi
Russell, Carl, 193, 194
Russell, Louise, 193, 194, 200
Russell, Raymond, 194, 200

SACO, 12, 48, 93, 94, 96, 139, 140,
    148, 149, 154, 168, 177, 194,
    205; Beach Street, 140; Camp
    Ellis, 48, 200, 201; Ferry
    Beach, 140; Ferry Road, 140;
    Goose Fare Brook, 140; Kin-
    ney Shores, 140; Ocean Park
    Road, 140; Sandy Brook, 205;
    Smutty Lane Road, 140;
    Sweetser School, 3, 93
Saco River, 48, 77, 79, 139, 140,
    156, 200, 202, 203, 205, 226;

Skelton Dam, 156, 183, 199
Salisbury, Allen, x, 58–65, 159,
    160, 164, 191, 222, 248
Salisbury, Florence, 59, 248
Salisbury, Nancy, 59
Salmon Falls River, 199, 205
Salvation Army, 117, 151, 164,
    166–168, 217
Sanborn, Oliver, 90, 153
SANFORD (See also South San-
    ford), 2, 44, 92, 148, 149, 154,
    168; Coca Cola Company, 168;
    Goodale-Sanford Mills, 157
Sanford Tribune, 156
Sanford Water District, 43
Sanford-Springvale Hairdressers
    Association, 217
Savage, Myron, 205
SCARBOROUGH, 3, 140, 174, 182
Scott, Tom, 249
Scripps-Howard papers, 175
SEARSPORT, 218
Seavey, Cliff, x, 24, 28, 29, 145,
    146
Seavey, George, 246
SEBAGO, 84
Sebago Lake, 3
Seidel, Beatrice, 22
SHAPLEIGH, 12, 89, 98, 163;
    Poverty Pond, 8, 39–41, 98;
    Shapleigh Plains, 6, 8, 9, 39,
    94, 105; Shy Beaver Pond, 39
Shapleigh Fire Department, 8
Shields, Hamilton, 215
SKOWHEGAN, 25, 48, 182
Sleeper, David, 50–52, 56, 61, 67,
    72
Smith, Albert, 87, 121
Smith, Dot, xxi, 20–22
Smith, Esther, 45, 94–96
Smith, Everett, 94–96, 149, 150
Smith, Fred, xxi, 20, 22
Smith, Hap, 28

Smith, Ivory, 94–96, 149, 150
Smith, John, xiii
Smith, Midgie, 94–96, 149
Smith, Milton, 29, 189
Smith, Mimi, 20, 23
Smith, Nancy, 94–96, 149
Smith, Roy, 3
Smith, Ruth, 94–96, 149
Snohomish, 70
Snow, Roger, 70, 75
Song of the South, xx
SORRENTO, 70
SOUTH GARDINER, 151
SOUTH HIRAM, 81
SOUTH PARIS, 3, 9
SOUTH PARSONSFIELD, 195
SOUTH PORTLAND, 25, 44, 188;
    New England Shipbuilding
    Company, 44, 156
South Portland Fire Department, 26
SOUTH SANFORD, 12
SOUTH WATERBORO, xix,
    41–43, 47, 89, 92–98, 133, 147,
    150, 155, 156, 212, 245; Bap-
    tist Church, 41, 245; Federal
    Street, 133; Fire 1911, 41;
    Gillies Lumber Company, 97;
    Grange hall, 41, 97; Lindsey
    Road, 95, 98, 149; Lower Main
    Street, 97, 198; Main Street,
    245; Massabesic High School,
    249; Old Corner, 95, 98; Os-
    sipee Hill, 6, 12, 38, 41, 45, 92,
    94, 155, 156, 245; Ossipee Hill
    Road, 41, 92, 98; Ricker Hill,
    94–96; 150; West Avenue, 133;
    West Road, 47, 94, 96–98
SOUTH WINDHAM, 44, 182, 194
Spencer Lake, 4
Spofford, Franklin, 142, 143
Spofford, Juanita, 12, 142, 143
Spoonhandle, 5
Sprague, Fred, 87, 174
Sprague, Mr., 57
SPRINGVALE, 3, 44, 148 Carpen-
    ter's Dairy, 168
Springvale Fire Department, 92, 98
ST. GEORGE, 183
St. Regis Paper Company, 157
STANDISH, 182
Stanley, Dorothy, x, 51, 57–59, 63,
    71
Stanley, George "Stan," 57–59
Staples, Linwood, 85
Stark, Douglas, xi
Stevens, Carroll, 249
Stevens, George, 44
Stevens, Paul, 176
Stickney, Richard, 205
Stinson, Arnold, 12, 24, 161, 232
Stobie, George, 4, 212
Stockwell, Dean, 5
Stone, Mabel, 83
Story of Bar Harbor, The, 176
Stotesbury, A. T., 53
Stuart, Charlotte, 63, 68, 70, 75,
    178
Studley, Bill, 145, 146
SULLIVAN, 70
Sunbeam, xi, 70
SURRY, 67
Swain, Louise, 164
Sylvester, Howard, 37

Tarr, J. D., 151
Taylor, Lillian, 146
Taylor, Ray, 171
Taylor, Roy, 146
Tetreault, Maxie, 217
THOMASTON, 80, 249
Thompson, Evelyn, 42
Thompson, Frank, 24
Thompson, Gib, 42
Thompson, Leona, 25
Thompson, Lewis, 42
Tierney, Daniel, 231

Time Magazine, xxi
TOGUS, 217
TOPSHAM, 6–8, 10, 205
Townsend, George, 8, 121
TOWNSHIP #19, 205, 210
Tracey, Alton, 2, 40
Tremblay, Aurele, 14
TRENTON, 59, 64, 73; Bar Harbor
    Airport, 59
Truman, President Harry, 5, 196,
    214, 227
TURNER, 227
turnpike (*See* Maine Turnpike)
Twentieth Century Fox, 5

UNION, 5
UNIONVILLE, 2
United Nations General Assembly,
    227
United Press, 220
United States: Army, 73, 188, 226;
    Engineers, 154; First Service
    Command, 197; Master Plan
    for Disaster Relief, 197; Army
    Air Force, 247; 14th Fighter
    Wing, 51; Atomic Energy
    Commission, 221; Coast
    Guard, 25, 67, 70, 142, 154,
    175, 197, 200, 211; Congress,
    222, 227, 237; *Congressional
    Record,* 237; House Committee
    on Un-American Activities,
    227; Federal Bureau of Investi-
    gation, 184; Federal Housing
    Administration, 215; Federal
    Reserve Bank of Boston, 214;
    Federal Works Agency, 196;
    Forest Service (*See* National
    Forest Service); Marines, 18th
    Engineers, 154; Navy, 25, 70,
    154, 176, 177, 188, 197, 199,
    205, 209, 210, 226; Recon-
    struction Finance Agency, 214;

Veterans Administration, 214,
    217; War Assets Administra-
    tion, 188, 214, 235; Women's
    Army Corps, 247
Up In Maine, 82

VAN BUREN, 157
VERMONT, 6, 237; Rutland, 197
Verrill, Joan, xi
VINALHAVEN, 5
VIRGINIA, 20, 78, 153, 197, 211

Walker, Marjorie, xx, 168, 194, 204,
    246
Walker, Perley, 83, 224
Walker, Warren, xx, 167, 194, 246
Wallace, Linwood, 180
Wallace, Violetta, 6, 179, 180, 204
Waller, Abbie, 170
Waller, Herbert, 170
War, Cold, 1
War, World II, xvii, 78, 93, 154,
    176, 178, 227, 242, 247
WASHINGTON, 154, 188
WASHINGTON, D.C., 171, 175,
    217
WASHINGTON COUNTY, 36,
    205, 216, 238
WATERBORO (*See also* East,
    North, South Waterboro and
    Waterboro Center), 8, 39–41,
    43–47, 79, 87, 89, 90, 93–99,
    105, 115, 136, 140, 146–150,
    154, 155, 157, 160, 161, 163,
    173, 177, 179, 182, 195, 199,
    209, 216, 217, 143, 245; Ross
    Corner, xv, 39, 41, 98, 147
WATERBORO CENTER, 41, 42,
    45, 46, 89, 98; Little Ossipee
    Pond, 43, 45, 98
WATERVILLE, 197
WAYNE, 37, 48, 150
Welch, Arthur, 3, 18, 26

WELCHVILLE, 38
WELLS, 91, 147, 149, 155, 156,
    189, 193, 199, 206, 210, 232;
    Wells Corner, 91; Wells-Sanford
    Road, 6
Wells, Julia, 192, 224
Werren, Alva, 42, 249
Wescott, Chester, 68, 73, 219, 220
WESLEY, 205
West, Reverend Paul, 9
WEST BALDWIN, 188
WEST BROWNFIELD, 188; Shep-
    herd's River Farm, 224
WEST BUXTON, 235, 236
WEST FALMOUTH, 182; Baptist
    Church, 9
WEST KENNEBUNK, 42, 146,
    147
WEST NEWFIELD, 85–88, 195;
    Masonic Hall, 88; town hall,
    85–88
WEST PARIS, 224
WESTBROOK, 36
Weymouth, Clayton, 12, 38, 39, 86,
    88, 89, 164, 236
White, Albert, 182
WHITNEYVILLE, 36, 150, 157,
    205, 210, 246; Crane Lumber
    Company, 36, 157

Wholean, Colonel Joseph, 75
Wilby, Mitch, 143
Wildes, Martin, 11, 24, 30
Wilkins, Austin, x, 4, 6, 33, 150,
    187–189, 197, 209, 211, 231,
    233, 234, 238, 239
Williams, Margaret, 55, 56, 64, 65
Williams, Reverend Anson, 55, 56,
    65
WINDHAM (*See* also South Wind-
    ham), 157
WINTERPORT, 182
WISCASSET, 36
World Series, xx, 1, 5
Wright, Franklin, 84, 89, 203, 223
Wyman, James, 198
Wyman, Warren, 212

YARMOUTH, 2, 4–6, 143
Yellowstone Park, 50
YORK, 165
YORK COUNTY, xix, 6, 38, 84,
    89, 111, 115, 140, 147, 150,
    153, 154, 157, 160, 166, 175,
    181, 189, 197, 199, 209–212,
    215, 216, 227, 229, 231, 236,
    239, 243–245
Young, Irving, 62, 63
Young, William, 4

About the Author

Stephanie Butler

Author of six books and a contributor to eight others, Joyce Butler has also written numerous articles for newspapers, magazines, and scholarly publications such as the *Maine Historical Society Quarterly,* Boston University's Dublin Seminar for New England Folklife *Annual Proceedings,* and *The Log of Mystic Seaport.* From 1980 to 1995 she was Curator of Manuscripts and Exhibitions at The Brick Store Museum, Kennebunk, where she narrated "The '47 Fire," a video published by the Museum. Currently she is Curator of Museum Collections at Maine Historical Society's Center for Maine History, Portland. A founding member of the Society of Maine Archivists, she has been an advisor and lecturer for many of Maine's historical and educational organizations and is a recipient of a Certificate of Commendation from the American Association for State and Local History.

A Maine native, Mrs. Butler lives in Kennebunk, where she has served as Town Historian since 1990. She was named Citizen of the Year by the Kennebunk/Kennebunkport Chamber of Commerce in 1993. Each year, a graduating senior at Kennebunk High School is selected to receive The Brick Store Museum's Joyce Butler History Award for excellence in history.